WISED UP

BOOK YOUR PLACE ON OUR WEBSITE AND MAKE THE READING CONNECTION!

We've created a customized website just for our very special readers, where you can get the inside scoop on everything that's going on with Zebra, Pinnacle and Kensington books.

When you come online, you'll have the exciting opportunity to:

- View covers of upcoming books
- Read sample chapters
- Learn about our future publishing schedule (listed by publication month *and author*)
- Find out when your favorite authors will be visiting a city near you
- Search for and order backlist books from our online catalog
- Check out author bios and background information
- Send e-mail to your favorite authors
- Meet the Kensington staff online
- Join us in weekly chats with authors, readers and other guests
- Get writing guidelines
- AND MUCH MORE!

**Visit our website at
http://www.kensingtonbooks.com**

WISED UP

Charlie Wilhelm
with Joan Jacobson

PINNACLE BOOKS
Kensington Publishing Corp.
http://kensingtonbooks.com

PINNACLE BOOKS are published by

Kensington Publishing Corp.
850 Third Avenue
New York, NY 10022

All Kensington Titles, Imprints and Distributed Lines are available at special quantity discounts for bulk purchases for sales promotions, premiums, fund-raising, educational or institutional use. Special book excerpts or customized printings can also be created to fit specific needs. For details, write or phone the office of the Kensington special sales manager: Kensington Publishing Corp., 850 Third Avenue, New York, NY 10022, attn: Special Sales Department, Phone: 1-800-221-2647.

Pinnacle and the P logo Reg. U.S. Pat. & TM Off.

First Pinnacle Printing: October 2004

10 9 8 7 6 5 4 3 2 1

Printed in the United States of America

In Memory
Stephen D. Clary, FBI Special Agent

To our families
Gina, Charlie Jr., Mandy, Jason and Justin
Bill, Willie and Alex

Preface

This memoir was written largely in Charlie Wilhelm's voice, and the conversations he quotes directly are reconstructed from his memory, except when the authors were able to use transcripts of recordings made by the FBI or court testimony.

There are also smaller sections of this book written in italics by coauthor Joan Jacobson, in the third person. These are scenes in which Charlie had no firsthand knowledge, such as the setting of a murder or a courtroom scene where he was not present. All direct quotes from these sections come from court transcripts, police reports or conversations heard by Jacobson.

Charlie Wilhelm's story first appeared in the *Baltimore Sun* in a series of four articles written by Joan Jacobson in November 2001. The facts in this memoir, like those in the newspaper stories, were verified through hundreds of documents and many interviews.

Prologue

One August morning in 2002 I met up with Special Agent Thomas J. McNamara at a parking lot near the regional FBI headquarters, just west of Baltimore. Tommy and I had met in plenty of parking lots for our clandestine operations seven years before. But on this day there was nothing secret about our meeting. For me, it marked the moment in my life when I could finally reveal myself as a changed man and prove I would never return to my old ways. I was wearing a freshly pressed tan suit for the occasion. As I waited for my old handler, I was overwhelmed with a feeling of excitement and accomplishment.

We were an unlikely duo, Tommy and I. He was a dead serious, by-the-book FBI agent who had gone to law school. I was a backslapping dropout who had learned countless ways to break the law. As usual, I arrived early for our meeting. As I looked out the window for Tommy's unmarked FBI car, I thought, *Charlie, you sure have come a long way.*

Here I was, about to make the presentation of a lifetime. Just a decade ago, I could never have imagined in my wildest dreams that I would be going on this trip with Tommy today. I admit I was also a little nervous. I had only written a page and a half for my presentation and I thought I wasn't ready, as far as paper and pen went. My past life certainly had never prepared me to give a lecture like this one. I was in a little over my head.

Tommy arrived a few minutes later. I locked my car and grabbed my so-called presentation, then slipped into his passenger side. I smiled at him. He shook my hand. I had known this man for seven years, had hundreds of conversations with him. He'd protected my life, my family's lives. He'd seen me at the lowest point in my life when I thought suicide was the only way to solve my problems. I felt almost as close to Tommy as I did to my own family. But Tommy never let down his guard with me. That morning he still had on his FBI face. Other agents I worked with would relax once in a while, but not Tommy. He really does look like one of those poker-faced actors who play FBI agents on TV.

Maybe that's why my old wiseguy buddies in Baltimore once insinuated that Tommy was an FBI agent the day he came to visit me, posing as a businessman. That was just one of the many close calls we weathered together. Despite our opposite personalities, Tommy and I always got along. There was a special chemistry between us. Maybe it was just mutual respect.

Tommy drove south toward Washington, DC. It was a rare, perfect day for a Baltimore summer, with one of the worst droughts on record. Even though the trees were almost gray from thirst, the air was clear and the sky was bright blue, with beautiful white clouds. We talked about our kids, how they were doing in school and in sports. We reminisced about our old days working undercover together. Then Tommy turned to one of our old, sore subjects—my safety. There was one wiseguy we both feared more than the others. He was in prison, but could be on the streets in about five years, Tommy figured. We both knew he was a vengeful guy. I told Tommy that my wife and I were thinking about buying a house.

Bad idea, said Tommy. The wiseguy could easily hire a private detective to track us down through property tax records.

As we drove over the Woodrow Wilson Bridge into Virginia, I started to get nervous about our destination. I tried to put my thoughts together as Tommy pulled off a main road to a security checkpoint. There were a dozen marines armed with what looked like automatic rifles. The marines stopped Tommy's car and checked his FBI credentials. As we drove a little farther, we heard the cackling of gunfire, then watched as about seventy more marines trotted across the road toward a shooting range.

A little way farther, Tommy pulled into a parking lot. At the end stood an ordinary building surrounded by trees. There was nothing special about it. Nobody was around anywhere. It looked like a ghost town to me. We entered the unlocked lobby, where Tommy signed in with the receptionist. After looking around for a few seconds, I got really excited.

I said to Tommy, "Stop right here. I know where we are at." Tommy said, "Charlie, you've never been here before." I said, " Tommy, this is where Jodie Foster was filmed in the movie *Silence of the Lambs*." Finally Tommy began to crack a smile and laugh a little. As we walked up a flight of stairs, I couldn't believe I had finally arrived in Quantico at the FBI National Academy, where FBI agents are trained. And on this spectacular day I was going to train them.

Chapter 1

How I Became A Taxpaying Carpenter

I was forty-three before I got a job I could tell my kids about. I'd just returned to Baltimore, my hometown, to find work after hiding out for three years. I was willing to do any kind of honest job, as long as I could feed my family, feel safe and get back a little sanity. It was 1998, the year I became a taxpaying carpenter. I worked for a slumlord on filthy old rowhouses in some of Baltimore's roughest neighborhoods, where working poor people struggled to make ends meet. I was struggling just like them. I worked seven days a week and got $9 an hour with no paid sick leave, no vacation and no health insurance. But I figured I had to start somewhere.

Here I was in my forties, a man without a pension. I put up drywall, hung doors and fixed old windows. I was good at it—and fast—even when my back ached from bulging disks. I was lucky to know carpentry, the one skill I'd learned in my reckless youth that wasn't a felony. Now it came in handy as I tried to make an honest living for myself and my family. I went to work every day before dawn with my carpenter's tools, my work boots and jeans, just like normal working men.

Then one muggy, dark August morning I added a new layer to my wardrobe. I rolled out of bed and put on a white bulletproof vest under my denim shirt. I slipped it on over my head and fastened it with Velcro. I was surprised at how heavy it felt. It was quite a fashion statement for a man who used to wear $200 shirts and a $20 gold medallion decked with forty-eight diamonds around it on a solid gold chain.

The vest came from a friend who worked in private security. He was one of the few people I could trust when I returned to Maryland. He drove over to my house one night and handed me the bulky Kevlar vest. "If I was you, I'd wear this," he said.

He'd heard the latest news. There was yet another contract out to whack me. It wasn't the first time my life had been threatened. In the three years since I'd decided to change my life, there had been several contracts out on me and many ugly threats to my family. But this was the first time my life was in danger since moving back to Maryland from where I'd been hiding in Alabama.

Now I was a lot closer to my enemies than I'd been in a long time. I was really nervous and self-conscious, but I put on the vest. It bulked out so bad, I worried people would notice. It showed at the top of my neck no matter what kind of shirt I wore. And it got real dirty. When I bent over to pick up a saw, it rubbed my neck and under my arms and gave me a terrible rash in the blistering Baltimore heat. I wore pants a size too big, just so I could tuck it in.

For every minute I worked, the damn vest reminded me of who I used to be. I'm not proud of who I once was and I don't blame anybody but myself for wasting twenty years of my life as a loan shark, a bookmaker, a drug dealer and an arsonist. I laundered dirty money through a bar where I paid off city liquor inspectors and robbed the video poker machines that the state was supposed to regulate. I ran a crime syndicate with two hundred wiseguys, as we called ourselves.

I was a workaholic and a rich man. On a good week I made $10,000, tax free. And I can honestly say it was an exciting life. By the time I turned forty, I was at the top of my game. My wife and kids got everything they wanted—which was a lot more than I had as a kid. At Halloween I gave the poor neighborhood kids toys stolen off the docks of Baltimore that I'd bought at half price. Fresh Maryland crabmeat and cigarettes came directly to my doorstep, brought by boosters passing by after a shoplifting spree. My wife only stopped her Christmas shopping when she couldn't fit any more packages into our new Dodge Caravan.

When the kids got sick, we didn't worry about having no health insurance. We just paid cash. I kept it in a green fruit bowl in the kitchen, carefully wrapped by denomination. I refilled that bowl almost every night when I came in from a hard day of hustling, collecting fees on our illegal lottery or "juice"—what we called interest—on illegal loans made out to seemingly upstanding businessmen.

But I lived in a warped world where grown men went by the nicknames of kids—Mousy, Fat Ricky, Country, Augie, Gussie, Joey, Charlie and Billy—and made up our own rules. If you always followed the rules, you could become rich and powerful. But if you broke the rules, you could get whacked.

My friends and I were greedy men who were addicted to the adrenaline rush of breaking the law without getting caught. We hurt a lot of people. And we knew it was a matter of time before we would be taken from our families and sent to prison.

That was the downside to the life we led.

Don't get me wrong. I won't exaggerate my story. We were no Mafia and I was no John Gotti. We weren't like the New York or Philadelphia mob, gunning down rival gangs as they ate their spaghetti dinners. Though some of my guys bragged about having ties to the Mafia, we were mostly a band of middle-aged thugs from "Balmer" as we say, "Baltimore." And the Mafia didn't control us, like they dominate crime organizations in other cities. We made our bad decisions all by ourselves. We never got an education but were smart enough to run our own lotteries, drug empires and illegal loan banks on the streets. I bet every midsize city in America has an underworld like ours. And even though we weren't officially part of the Mafia, we still loved calling ourselves wiseguys.

The year I turned forty I had a change of heart. It wasn't like I woke up one morning and said, "I'm going to change my life today." And I didn't all of a sudden find God and become a born-again Christian, though I later met an amazing Catholic priest who kept me from losing my mind. The feeling grew on me and festered for a long time. At first I knew something was missing in my life. And something was wrong with it. My wife noticed I had horrendous nightmares. I worried every car door that slammed outside my little rowhouse might be a Baltimore cop or the FBI.

I wondered if I was getting too old for the business. And I didn't like myself as a father or a husband. I looked in the mirror and said, "What a piece of shit you've become." I knew it would only get worse if I didn't change. In the life we led, you never had peace of mind. You never even had a day off.

But my biggest problem wasn't my conscience. It was my best friend. He was a murderer. And I'd been covering up for him for almost twenty years.

Then one day in 1995 he asked me to help him whack

two people. We never used the word "kill." He just asked me to "do" two guys he thought were stealing from him. I had never "done" anybody before. But I wondered if I said no, would I get "done" instead? I had never killed anybody and I was pretty sure I didn't want to start now. I knew from being on the streets that the hard part isn't killing. The hard part is *not* killing. Once you cross the line, it becomes easy, especially if you get away with your first one.

My friend's name was Billy Isaacs. He was the meanest and most charming guy you could ever meet. He was a very large man, 6'4", with a huge head and neck, a very brawny guy who knew karate—and used it on people he didn't like. My wife, Gina, will never forget the night she watched him knock a man out cold with one punch to the jaw. Billy was smart in a streetwise kind of way, a wiseguy who held a permanent grudge against anybody who crossed him. He never learned to read or write very well. When he wasn't beating people up to get them to repay their debts, he was watching soap operas. I always knew where to find him on weekday afternoons. He'd be at one of his girlfriends' houses watching *Days of Our Lives*.

I was closer to Billy than I was to my own family. Gina would say that when Billy snapped his fingers, I would drop everything and run to him. It made her crazy. I loved Billy so much, you could say I gave up my family for him, especially Johnny, my brother. See, Billy didn't trust Johnny because Johnny's best friend was an FBI agent named Bruce Hall. Bruce is a really smart guy we grew up with in North Point Village, a little neighborhood east of Baltimore City near Bethlehem Steel's Sparrows Point plant. Bruce's friendship with Johnny rubbed Billy the wrong way, to say the least. By 1995 I hadn't seen Bruce in a long time. And I hadn't talked to my own brother for five years. That year I started thinking about changing my life. I wondered if I just moved Gina and the kids away, maybe I could I get away from the wiseguys and start a new life. I even drove out to Carroll County, an hour away from the inner city where I lived, and looked at farmland for sale. But as tired of the life as I was, I knew I also was too addicted to the excitement of the hustle and the daily score. Something or someone would pull me back. If Billy didn't come looking for me, I would probably go back on my own.

Slowly I hatched a plan for getting out. Gina knew I was involved in an illegal lottery, that I sold drugs and that I ran a sleazy bar. But she didn't really know how deep I was in, or about the secrets I kept for Billy. When I told Gina I wanted to get out, she agreed we needed to change our lives if we were going to save our rocky marriage. We were fighting all the time. She would get furious when I went off with Billy and didn't come back for three days. Like me, Gina didn't feel the material things were so important anymore. With all the money we had, she still shopped at Kmart. But she was terrified of my escape plan. It was just too dangerous, she insisted. "Just get out," she said. "Why can't you just walk away?"

I had finally decided there was only one way to get out and make sure I would never turn back. With help from Johnny and Bruce, I went to the FBI and turned in many of my friends. It was the hardest decision I ever made, but the most important one of my life. I became a rat, a big one. I joined a small and infamous fraternity of informants who put their personal safety on the line to help the government solve a lot of crimes.

Of course, not everybody sees us this way. They think we're disloyal for double-crossing our friends, even when our friends are drug dealers and murderers. They think we snitch for the money the government pays us or to beat a long prison rap. In my case, though, I wasn't facing prison when I went to the FBI. As a matter of fact, the Baltimore FBI agents had never heard of me. The Baltimore police had heard of me, of course, and they were tailing me in my trademark white Lincoln Continental with the red roof, wiretapping my phone and raiding my house for illegal gambling. But the Baltimore police had yet to arrest me when I went to the FBI in August 1995.

As for the money, I admit I accepted payment from the FBI, though I never asked for the money. The FBI supported me for two years while I worked undercover for them, lived in hiding and testified in several trials. I got $2,500 a month, plus another lump sum of $55,000. I'm not proud that they paid me. I knew defense attorneys representing my old wiseguys in court would use it against me—and believe me, they did. But I needed to support my family. Whether or not we get paid, nobody likes a snitch. But without us, the government wouldn't have a prayer to bust up organized crime.

I confess I also had an ulterior motive in coming clean. I was saving my own skin from Billy. I was worried he might kill me if I didn't agree to whack two guys. I may have saved my own life, but I also believe I saved the lives of two others.

Though the FBI didn't know me, they knew all about Billy, as well as some other Baltimore wiseguys who had connections to the Mafia in other cities.

Because of my work, some of the Baltimore wiseguys with the kids' nicknames went off to federal and state prison. I helped the government put away almost two dozen people for cocaine dealing, illegal gambling, bribery, conspiracy and murder.

Though I put a lot of crooks in prison, I don't want anybody to think I helped the FBI shut down organized crime in Baltimore. Every job left open by a wiseguy in prison is filled by some up-and-comer who grabs the opportunity to make a dishonest buck. We always knew there were wars in other countries, but it was the wars in our backyards we worried about. The guys were always fighting over who gets the bookmaking, who gets the juice, or interest payments on loans, who controls the bars we ran as illegal gambling casinos, or how to retaliate against somebody who ripped us off for money we didn't earn honestly in the first place. By the time I turned forty, I'd probably known forty friends who died from stabbings, ride-by shootings and drownings.

I don't regret stopping my old friends from committing more crimes. But I do regret splitting up their families. I feel especially bad for their kids. A day doesn't go by when I don't think about them. Losers or not, they were once my family.

I worked undercover for the FBI for nearly five months, back in late 1995 and early 1996. Then, just before my friends were arrested, the FBI moved my family eight hundred miles away from Baltimore for our safety. The long distance didn't stop me from panicking. I had horrible nightmares about the guys murdering me in front of my family. I had flashbacks and anxiety attacks and terrible insomnia. With no legitimate job references, I had trouble finding work. The idle time made me crazy. I didn't know then that I suffered from an acute case of post-traumatic stress disorder. I was too afraid to seek professional help. I just couldn't imagine a counselor believing my wild story. I searched desperately for a way to keep my sanity.

Then on March 29, 1996, I began to write a journal. I thought if I wrote down my deepest feelings, I could keep from falling apart. I didn't know that this is a therapy psychologists recommend; it is "journaling." I wrote my first entry the day the FBI called to say they'd heard there was a contract out to whack me. On those pages I relived my love-hate relationship with the FBI, whose agents had replaced my old wiseguys as my new extended family. I wrote about some of them, especially my handler, Agent Thomas J. McNamara, who kept me going straight from the first day I met him in a safe house in Baltimore, and Agent Stephen Clary, a master investigator who became a father figure to me.

I also wrote about the unique relationship I had with another agent, Bruce Hall, my childhood friend. I can't say enough about Bruce's role in my ordeal. He was the first law enforcement officer to whom I confessed my life of crime. And I sometimes wonder whether I would have had the courage to go straight if Bruce hadn't been there for me. Even though he was not assigned officially to my case, he stuck with me through my wild days working undercover and my suicidal days down in Alabama. He always believed in my resolve to change. Today he is one of my closest friends, and a person I look to as a role model.

My journal also described everyday life for someone like me. My arguments with my wife read like a bad soap opera. The pressures I put my family through were enormous. On our worst days Gina concluded that the only way to make a safe life for herself and the kids was to leave me. Despite our differences, I always believed Gina's insights into our dilemma were dead on. And it wasn't easy for her to watch our two children go through the trauma of being taken from their school and neighborhood without being able to say good-bye to a single friend.

I also used my journal to recount my old life, writing down the rules of running illegal lottery and loan scams, and telling how easy it was to gyp the state and the IRS out of the taxes we owed on state-regulated video poker machines. We also used the poker machines to make illegal payouts to gamblers. I wrote about "dirty" Baltimore cops who tipped off my crime ring about pending raids on our houses. I wrote about the good cops, too, including an amazing detective, "Spanky," who dogged us relentlessly. I described what it felt like to testify against my old friends.

And I wrote about the death threats. There were many, but none worse than the night my brother, Johnny, nearly got whacked on his way to work. I wrote for more than two years, filling 960 pages. That journal forms the basis for this book.

Now do you see why I needed a bulletproof vest? It made me wonder if I would ever be normal. To tell you the truth, I'm still wondering. After all, it's hard to work an honest job when you're a wanted man. How many carpenters do you know who go to work dressed in Kevlar?

That summer I started working as a carpenter back in 1998 I wore the vest for only two months, then took it off when I couldn't stand it anymore. I knew I was taking a chance. But I had survived plenty of chances already. Those were the consequences of becoming an honest man. After twenty years of living the wiseguy life, I realized there really was no honor or loyalty in being a bad guy. I have no regrets about my decision to come clean and work undercover for the FBI. But I have cast a permanent shadow that lurks over me. I know for the rest of my life, people will have their doubts about me. I can almost read their minds: *Has he really changed?* They will always wonder if I am a bad guy or a good guy.

Chapter 2

The Mark Of A Thief

My parents didn't give me much of a childhood. Both had trouble with alcohol. They never took us on a vacation, and they showed little interest in my sports or my schooling. I don't remember them ever helping me with my homework, so eventually I stopped doing it. But my father wanted me and my brother, Johnny, to be the toughest kids in the neighborhood, so he taught us how to fight. It was just the kind of thing that everybody did in our neighborhood. If boys argued, their parents would say, "Let them fight it out." I remember one kid who ended up with two broken hands.

Whenever my older brother and I argued, my father would put twenty-ounce boxing gloves on our hands and make us duke it out right on the front lawn. Sometimes, though, we had to fight with the gloves off. And my father would make fun of the loser. Even worse than having to fight Johnny was having to fight boys who were older and heavier than we were. When we were twelve and thirteen, our dad had us fighting kids who were fifteen, maybe sixteen, years old. What I hated the most was getting punched in the head all the time. I can still remember how hard those big boys used to hit me.

If I cried when I got my ass kicked, I knew my father would kick my ass again. And if I got hurt, I knew better than to cry. I can still see him standing on our concrete porch, gripping onto the black iron railing and looking down on us as if he had the best seat in the arena. I hated that. Sometimes it seemed like the entire neighborhood turned out to watch a fight. The police ignored us, except when the parents started fighting with each other when one of their kids lost.

I guess it could be a pretty violent place, though I didn't think about it at the time. It seemed like everybody had a gun. I remember one boy I knew who accidentally shot his brother in the foot. Another neighbor blew his brains out while cleaning his gun. He was only about thirteen. During the Baltimore race riots of 1968, following the assassination of Martin Luther King, everybody worried that the blacks would leave the city and come terrorize our white community. So they sat on their front steps with loaded rifles, waiting. Of course, nobody came. Our neighborhood was miles from the riots.

We lived in a two-story brick rowhouse in a tiny community called North Point Village. It was part of a bigger working-class suburb called Dundalk, just east of Baltimore. North Point Village sits on the edge of Bear Creek, which feeds into the Chesapeake Bay. We weren't far from the cold sheet mill and the coke ovens of Bethlehem Steel at Sparrows Point, where many of the fathers in the neighborhood worked. We lived so close to "The Point" that you could never hang your clothes on the line. They'd just get covered in rusty soot falling from the sky. The Sparrows Point Country Club sits just to the south, but only the foremen from our neighborhood who worked at Bethlehem Steel were allowed in as members there. I couldn't even get a job washing dishes there because my father didn't work at The Point.

The rank-and-file steelworkers probably spent more

time down at their union hall on Dundalk Avenue. In those days, when union membership was over twenty thousand, the hulking steelworkers halls were jammed with union members. But today, as the American steel industry dies, they are mostly empty, sitting just up the street from a sleazy bar I would one day operate as a cover for many illegal operations.

Our neighborhood had only twelve short streets that were paved when the houses were built in 1955. The builder must have been Catholic because he named almost every street after a saint. There's a St. Claire Lane, St. Bridget Lane, St. Gregory Lane, St. Fabian Lane, St. Patricia Lane and St. Boniface Lane. And there were plenty of Catholic families living on those streets—mine included. I grew up on St. Monica Drive, just down the street from Battle Grove Elementary School. The school, which is still there today, was named for Battle Acre, a monument nearby that marked the spot where the Baltimore forces beat off the British during the War of 1812.

History aside, Battle Grove Elementary School marks the spot for me of happy childhood memories. Despite neglect at home, I don't think my early childhood was all bad. It was the 1960s—the baby-booming years—and there were fifteen or twenty kids hanging out on every corner. I absolutely loved it down there. We'd slip into the North Point Drive-In, jumping the fence to watch the movies for free. Sometimes, though, the management would grease the fence with fat from french fries so it was harder to climb over. When we played tackle football, my friends and I usually met at the corner of St. Patricia and St. Monica by the school. Back then, the roads were made of gravel, so when we'd get tackled, we'd end up with gravel in our legs.

One day when I was a teenager, a new boy moved into the neighborhood. His name was Bruce Hall. He was fifteen and had lived in so many places already, he'd gone to almost ten schools. He was born in Baltimore, but his family moved to Kansas for a few years, then moved back east when they got homesick. He was the oldest of three children when his family moved into another little row-house down the street from ours.

I could tell he was different from the rest of us. For one thing, he always did his homework and he seemed to like school. He got hooked on science when he got a science kit in the third grade. Teachers at Sparrows Point High School must have seen some talent in him because they encouraged him to study. He was so independent, he never seemed pressured to be like the rest of us. If we decided to climb up onto the elementary-school roof to throw eggs at police cars, Bruce would conveniently have something else to do and disappear.

I remember my first encounter with him. We were setting up a tackle football game, choosing captains and picking teams. I didn't know Bruce, but I'd seen him in the hallways of Sparrows Point High School. Bruce and Johnny were on the same team. I was on the other. The streets were full of gravel, which came right to the ends of the boundary line of our football field. Somebody threw me a pass from my quarterback. I ran toward the imaginary goal. Bruce came running out of nowhere across the field and hit me at the knees from the rear or the side. He hit me so hard that he knocked me into the street. I landed in the gravel, cutting up my elbows and knees. I was mad at him, not for knocking me into the gravel, but for hitting me so hard from behind. I was embarrassed that he was somewhat smaller and not as heavy as I was. I was so furious that I started to run after him to punch him out. A group of boys got in between us. My brother, Johnny, stuck up for Bruce. Maybe that's how Johnny and Bruce got to be best friends. They still are.

When we moved into the neighborhood, there were no organized sports leagues for kids. That was before my parents began drinking too much and we still felt like a family. My dad got together with two other men in the neighborhood and started a teen center in our tiny base-ment. It grew too large for our little rowhouse, so they moved it to the elementary school, where we'd have dances on weekends. We'd have local disc jockeys, like Johnny Dark and Buddy Dean, the man whose television show was the basis for the John Waters movie and Broad-way show *Hairspray*. My dad and his friends also started a recreation league so we could play organized sports.

Those early years were great and at Christmas we always got new toys, bikes and clothes. My mother was a house-wife like most of the other women in the neighborhood. I remember a lot of love in the house and it was always up-beat. My dad worked as a Baltimore City policeman in the K-9 unit. Sometimes he would bring other policemen to our house to visit. I remember one of them joking around with me and my brother, trying to get us to taste some dry dog food that he said was good for us. My dad would take us fishing and play ball with us.

But when I reached the age of ten or eleven, something happened. After ten years on the police force, my father lost his job. I never knew why, but something must have gone wrong. That's when the trouble began. My parents began to drink heavily and argue. They stopped showing any interest in our school activities or in our sports.

Then we lost our house. First the electricity was turned off; then my dad stopped making the house payments. We lost everything, the furniture, our TV. A neighbor down the street had a house to rent and let my family move in. I guess she took pity on us.

When I was about thirteen, I'd get up Saturday morn-ings while my parents were still sleeping, get myself breakfast and stay out the whole day. At night we'd go to dances at the teen center. Sometimes I didn't have the quarter to get in. That's how bad it was. I'd collect glass milk jugs and return them to the store to collect money to get into the teen center. Other times my friends' parents would give me a quarter to get in the dance.

At Christmas we'd each get two pairs of the cheapest pants from Epstein's Department Store downtown. Otherwise, we got secondhand clothes. My tennis shoes came from the A & P supermarket. I remember getting on the bus to high school and having girls make fun of me for my cheap clothes. I hated that. At Christmas I would lie to my friends about all the big presents I got under the tree, when there were really only a few little ones. I lay in bed crying and vowing that if I had kids someday I would never let them go without anything.

My dad went to work as a union tractor-trailer driver, but he missed a lot of time from work. He would get paid on Thursday, the night that *Rat Patrol* and *Daniel Boone* would come on TV. By then, there would be no food left in the house. I mean, not a piece of bread or even a glass of milk. The biggest treats we ever got were maybe a Tastykake. We never had fruits, cookies or sweetened cereals in the house. It wouldn't have been so bad if we had felt like a family, but there wasn't much love left in the house.

My older sister was an angel, as far as I was concerned. She started being the parent my brother and I needed. Betty was the one who helped us with our homework and made sure we came home on time. She would hug us and talk to us like a parent should, not that we didn't fight or argue with her. I didn't realize how tough she had it until years later.

All three of us tried to spend our weekends with other families in the neighborhood just to avoid my parents. They were always fighting from the drinking. When we were home, Johnny and I did what teenage brothers do— argued and fought. That's when my father would come into the bedroom and beat the mortal shit out of us with a belt and his fist. I'm not talking about just maybe one or two nights a week. I mean every night. My sister would cry because we got beaten so badly. My brother doesn't remember the beatings today. I guess he has what you call a selective memory. I seem to be the one who remembers everything. From the time I was ten or eleven, my parents never hugged us when it was time to go to bed. And they never said those few simple words "I love you" to us.

By the time I was in high school, my parents' drinking consumed our daily lives. I would get off the school bus and go straight home to see if my mother was there. If she wasn't home, my brother, sister and I would head out to the three local bars in search of her. We'd drag her home and try to sober her up before our father showed up. We didn't want to see the fight they'd have if she was drunk. But when my mother stopped drinking, my father would start. Usually it was a Thursday when he got paid. Instead of putting food on the table, he would blow it all on Pabst Blue Ribbon beer.

Trouble

It was about that time when I started to get in trouble. I would jump through somebody's hedges, throw a milk crate onto an awning or steal beer from somebody's back porch in winter. When all the other kids would be running, I'd wait until the last minute when the police were right on top of me before I would try to get away—just for the thrill of the chase.

When I'd get caught, police would bring me home. My father would slap me alongside my head and knock me to the floor, then kick me with his heavy black shoes. After a while the beatings didn't even matter anymore. And they sure didn't stop me from getting in trouble. But for some strange reason my dad also covered for some of my crimes. One time he knew I'd bought a sawed-off shotgun. I hid it in the bushes outside our house so my mother wouldn't know. A neighbor found it and called the police. When they came to our house, my father let the police in and told them he didn't know a thing about it. But my mother always suspected me of that one.

Another time I broke into a Texaco station with about ten other kids. We stole the cigarette machine and dragged it over to my house. My mother was drinking and playing cards with my grandmother. I told a few friends to keep them occupied while the rest of us hid the cigarette machine in the basement, smashing it apart with hammers to get out the cigarettes. My mother and grandmother never noticed—until a few days later when a cop knocked on the door. He said a couple of kids got caught at school selling cigarettes at half price. One of them squealed on all of us. My mother denied I was involved, insisting I was in the basement with friends the entire night of the theft. When she asked me about stealing the machine, I denied it. A few days later she found broken glass in the basement. She concluded I was up to no good, but didn't tell my father. She knew he'd beat the mortal shit out of me.

When I was fourteen, my father got a job through some of his friends in the carpenters union, local 101. He was finally making good money, though he didn't like to work if he didn't have to. But he was well liked and worked his way up the ladder.

With all the turmoil at home, my education was obviously not a priority for anyone, especially me. I went to Sparrows Point High School, but I didn't stay long. I started gambling in school, playing poker for nickels and quarters. By the time I turned sixteen, I had been suspended three or four times and was on probation. I still remember my school probation officer's name—Mr.

Conquest. The principal finally told my parents there was no sense in sending me anymore. My parents said, "The heck with it," and I dropped out. I regret not finishing high school, though I got my GED years later.

When I was a teenager, one of my first crimes was stealing cars. Some boys in the neighborhood showed me how to start a Chevy without a key. If somebody didn't turn the ignition switch all the way to the off position, you could just turn it back on without the key. It was easy with Corvairs and some of the other old Chevys from the '60s. We would steal the cars from our suburb on the east side, then drive them into Baltimore City near Memorial Stadium, where the Orioles and Colts played in North Baltimore. We could sell the cars for $30 or $40. It was easy money and I saw a long, lucrative career ahead of me.

After I dropped out of high school, my father got me into the merchant marines. I was sixteen. I went to New York for a week, then to Leonardtown, Maryland, to the Seafarers Harry Lundenberg School of Seamanship. My father pulled all kinds of strings to get me into the Seafarers International Union. I lasted two weeks. As you can imagine, I wasn't interested in obeying the rules.

After I came home, my dad got me a job with the laborers union. Now here is a place where I can get a first-rate education in organized crime, I thought. They taught me how to steal everything that wasn't nailed down—lumber, large welding tools. Many of the guys were on parole and took me under their wing. I immediately got involved in making money from an attendance scam for workers who got paid when they didn't show up. The timekeepers and the foremen were in on the take, too. I would get the worker's badge—showing he came to work. The worker would get his salary, but only keep half of it. The other half would go to pay off the foreman, the timekeeper and me. I'd get $10 out of it, which wasn't bad money for a teenager. I hardly did any real manual labor in those days when we worked down in Curtis Bay in South Baltimore. Sometimes I'd just go around all day picking up payments and bets for the older guys who ran an illegal lottery and loan business.

That's where I first saw the little tattoo that caught my eye—"the mark of a thief." Some of the older guys had this tiny cross tattooed on their hands. It was only about an inch long. I was just seventeen, but I was eager to brand myself for my chosen profession. I wasn't old enough to go to a tattoo parlor—you had to be eighteen—so I decided to give myself the tattoo. I did it at a friend's house. I wrapped a thread around a needle and dipped it into India ink. I poked the needle into my hand until it started to bleed. Then I poked and poked until the needle marks formed a little cross along the piece of loose skin between my thumb and forefinger on my left hand. I don't remember it hurting. I wanted to be just like the older guys and I guess I wanted to impress people. I never imagined it would become an embarrassment one day. I was still living with my parents then, but they never said a word about it.

Hampden

It was about that time that I started hanging out in Hampden, my newly adopted neighborhood. Hampden is in North Baltimore, just west of the Johns Hopkins University. The two places are divided by a long, narrow park called Wyman Park. The park isn't very big, but it might as well be the Atlantic Ocean. I can't think of two places more different than Hampden and Johns Hopkins University. Hopkins is where the future doctors and scientists of America are educated. Hampden, at the time, was where regular, working-class people lived among thugs like me. For generations the neighborhood had a reputation for having tough white kids who were racists. Black kids walking home from school would know to run through the neighborhood without stopping. It was a crowded neighborhood with hundreds of small, two-story brick rowhouses covered with gray and blue "formstone" tiles sealed over the red bricks during the 1940s and '50s. The houses had little or no grass out front—and plenty of street corners and alleys for people like me to do our dirty business.

Today, though, Hampden is becoming a yuppie neighborhood. On Thirty-sixth Street, which we called "The Avenue," there are art galleries and trendy restaurants. The little houses, their formstone chiseled off to expose the original brick, are selling for more than $100,000, which is a lot for a little rowhouse in Baltimore.

Love At First Sight

One day in 1973, when I was seventeen, I was riding in a stolen car on Keswick Road in Hampden with a friend and we stopped to change a flat tire. My friend began talking to a beautiful girl with long, straight, dark hair. I thought she was pretty enough to have her picture on a billboard. Her name was Melonie. I immediately started to put the moves on her, but she didn't want any part of me. She told me to get away from her.

"Go screw yourself," I told her. I fell in love with her right there. The more she said she didn't want anything to do with me, the more I wanted her. For the next six months I made sure I was in Hampden almost every day, trying to get Melonie to talk to me. I finally succeeded, but I had to hide my illegal activities from her. She didn't want anything to do with me if I was getting into trouble, she said.

She'd always be telling me to stop fighting. "Can't you pick better friends?" she'd ask. Though I wasn't working half the time, I told her I was. She didn't know it, but I already had $10,000 stashed away. To impress her, I stopped stealing cars and made my first legitimate car purchase. I went out and bought a Pontiac LeMans. I really tried to straighten up, but it didn't last long. Like a drunk, I always went back to making scores.

On November 17, 1973, Melonie and I got married. She was sixteen. I was eighteen and officially unemployed. We had a big wedding at St. Luke's Methodist Church in Hampden. The reception was at a Polish hall on the other side of town in East Baltimore. My whole family was there. Even Bruce Hall showed up. Since I was Polish, we had a real Polish wedding reception, with a Polish band that didn't play any modern music. I had to wear the hat with all the little baby dolls around it. My aunt Mill, a heavyset woman, wore an apron to collect the money. When it was time, I threw my wallet into the apron and picked up Melonie and carried her out of the reception hall. The bride and groom weren't allowed to come back into the hall after the groom threw his wallet into the apron. My mother was the one who truly believed in the Polish tradition, which included a three-day reception. And that is exactly what we did. For three days we partied at Melonie's parents' house in Hampden. I really didn't want the Polish wedding and neither did Melonie, but she went along with what my mother wanted.

It was a promising beginning, but I was never a very good husband. When I wasn't hustling, I was cheating on Melonie with other women. I messed up for not loving her enough. All she wanted was an honest husband and a family. It doesn't seem like a lot to ask for now, but it certainly wasn't something I could give any woman back then—or for a very long time afterward.

After the wedding we lived with my parents in North Point Village, but that didn't last long. I would disappear and leave her stranded with my father and mother. She caught on to my act pretty fast and decided to move us in with her parents. We lived there for about six months, then rented a house across the street from them on Keswick Road. Back then, when I wasn't working at the laborers local, I was collecting unemployment and hustling on the side at a couple of nightclubs and pool halls a few blocks from the house. We should have been living pretty well with all the money coming in, but I blew it in the clubs and bars and on other women.

Melonie was seven months pregnant when she developed toxemia in early 1976 . The doctors gave her a fifty-fifty chance of surviving. They said the baby had no chance. But on February 12, 1976, she gave birth to a baby boy, who weighed 3 lb 11 ¼ oz. We named him Charlie Jr. I no longer worried about giving my child the things I didn't have as a kid. I was just glad they were both alive.

You'd think I'd want to spend more time with my family after that, but I was still in my early stages of hustling and was an eager young recruit for the wiseguy life. I also had a legal job for a while. I had picked up carpentry skills by watching other people work over the years. I got a job working for the city as a carpentry foreman, assigned to a drug-counseling center, where I taught basic carpentry skills to recovering addicts. I had a city car and a gas card so I could fill it up with city gas. It was a gravy job. There were no time clocks, so I could come and go as I pleased. Sometimes I didn't see anyone from the city until I picked up my paycheck. I became friends with people who worked at the counseling center; so when my friends got busted for drugs, they got themselves sentenced to do community service at the same drug-counseling center. I would tell them to donate money to the drug center so they wouldn't have to show up for counseling. If they had to take a urine test, I would get someone else to piss in the bottle for them so they could keep taking drugs. But I kept my job as a carpentry foreman separate. I never sold drugs to the recovering addicts who worked for me and I never told them my real business. I drove my city car by day, but at night and on weekends, I drove my Eldorado Cadillac for my real job.

The Perfect Match

In the late 1970s, I met my criminal partner of a lifetime. His name was Billy Isaacs.

I had seen him around Hampden and we knew each other through my brother, Johnny. Both Johnny and Billy were into karate and somebody told them they ought to fight each other. But when they met, they decided to be friends instead.

Billy was born in York, Nebraska, one of the middle children in a family of six. His family moved to Baltimore when Billy was five. His father was a brakeman on the railroad and did side jobs like moving furniture and fixing cars. When Billy was a teenager, he was already a pretty big kid and he helped his father deliver refrigerators and washing machines after school, sometimes working until 9:00 P.M. He went to Baltimore's Northern High School, but dropped out in the tenth grade. I got the impression that he spent most of his time in school fighting with other kids. By the time I met him, he was twenty-four. I had heard he was a pretty good fighter. He was also illiterate. He could hardly write, could barely read a newspaper and couldn't even measure with a ruler. But Billy was no dummy. I could tell he was a really smart guy. He was eager to learn anything he didn't know. He was always asking questions and soaking up the answers. Though he couldn't even sound out unfamiliar words in the newspaper, he would ask me how to say them and what they meant. Not that I am the best-read guy in the world, but I could read a little better than Billy.

Once, when he and I were working the door of a club called Les Gals on Baltimore's North Charles Street, the owner asked us to build an office upstairs for him. It would also be a place for the hookers to take the johns. When we started working, Billy couldn't tell a half inch from a quarter inch. But by the time we were done, he could have built the room by himself. He was a fast learner. Looking back, I now think that if we had become partners, using one-tenth of our brains for some legal enterprise, we could have been rich men—legitimately.

I shake my head now to think that the same young man I met back in the 1970s who couldn't even measure an inch, would build up so much money and power that he could jam a courtroom one day with men willing to put their houses up as collateral to bail him out of jail. This is the same man who would afford one day the best defense lawyers in Baltimore. And he would be cunning enough to hire a private investigator and even a jury consultant like the one O.J. Simpson used to help him pick a jury in his California murder trial.

But back in the old days, we were just a couple of young thugs getting started in the business.

I still remember how we first became friends. It was the spring of 1977.

One Saturday morning I got into a fight in a bar called Jack's at the corner of Thirty-third Street and Keswick Road, just up the street from where I lived. I went there to play a game of nine-ball pool for money. As soon as I got in the game, I started kicking ass. I was really stroking the balls that day. There was an older guy playing. He was in his thirties. I'd seen him around and heard he was a pretty good fighter. I won the game, but he tried to cheat me out of the money he owed me.

He was a big guy with some real size on him and I was

hesitant at first to fight him for my winnings. But I wanted my money and everyone else in the game had already paid me. He kept making fun of me, saying, "What are you going to do about it if I don't pay you?" He was trying to make an idiot out of me, and in those days nobody made an idiot out of me. I started to lose my temper. I hoped I could just knock the heart out of him so he would pay me. Even if I got my ass kicked, he would know I wasn't a punk. I hooked him with a right and caught him above his left eyebrow, splitting it wide open. He was on the floor, blood gushing down his face. I picked up one end of a pinball machine and dragged it over to where he was lying. Everyone was yelling at me to stop, just as I was about to drop it on his head. "Stay out of this," I yelled back. I looked at the guy, passed out on the floor. I was screaming at him: "Are you going to pay me my money now?" All of a sudden I heard a familiar voice. It was Norm, a cop from the neighborhood, telling me, "Charlie, this guy has had enough." So I dropped the machine—but not on the guy's head. Norm told me to get out of there fast, so I did.

At about 8:00 P.M. I headed back to Jack's to face the crowd again. It was a matter of honor to go back there, but I also wanted to collect my money. I thought for sure somebody was going to have something to say to me because all the people who had been there that morning were friends of the guy I knocked out.

I was twenty-two years old and weighed only 140 pounds on my six-foot frame. I was wearing my white tennis shoes and my leather coat. When I walked in, there was Billy. He had his usual blue dungaree jacket with a hole in one of the pockets. He stood 6'4" and weighed 250 pounds. He had a big head, a tremendously thick neck and large hands. And everybody in Hampden knew he was a black belt in karate. We started talking, and once the crowd got a look at Billy, nobody wanted any part of me. That day began the best friendship I ever had. We were inseparable.

I soon discovered that Billy's power wasn't all physical. It was mental, too. He had an amazing talent for manipulating people—especially me. I wasn't afraid of Billy. I respected him. But he had a way of making me feel he was giving 100 percent to our friendship, while I wasn't giving enough on my end. He could be kind and generous to people, but he could be vicious, too.

We owned an after-hours bar together. One night a pretty, long-haired blonde schoolteacher came into the place. Billy tried to put the moves on her, but she just ignored his advances. He started to get ignorant with her. "You're probably just a whore," he told her. Then the girl started to get the best of Billy with words, talking back to him. He told the barmaid to go in the bathroom and piss in a cup. When the barmaid came back, she handed Billy the cup. He poured it over the schoolteacher's head. Then he picked her up and literally threw her out of the place. It wasn't the first time he'd done that. Once before, he did it to two lesbians.

In our early years together I thought his behavior was funny. But as we got older, I found it so damn humiliating to women. When I criticized him, though, he'd make me feel bad for being disloyal. By the end of the day I'd feel sorry for him, like it was the girl's fault for not accepting his advances. Billy had a talent for reversing things on me. For everyone else he placed fear in their hearts.

He wasn't just an ordinary tough guy when he fought. There are other people who can knock somebody out cold with one punch, but Billy could crush the bones in your face or break your ribs when he hit you with a body shot. I knew a couple of guys who had reconstructive surgery after being in a fight with him. He would also divide and conquer our wiseguy friends. He'd get them to argue among themselves. Then each one would confide his problems to Billy. He'd have them thinking he was their only friend.

It wasn't long before he replaced my family. I gave up my relationship with my brother and sister for him. Johnny's friendship with Billy soured when Billy discovered Johnny's friend Bruce Hall had become an FBI agent. And even in my marriage, Billy came first, while Melonie came second. She never liked him. She said she saw a drastic change in me after we became partners. Melonie would not be the last woman in my life who resented my partnership with Billy.

By the time I was in my early twenties, I was already addicted to the life of a hustler. And Billy and I made a great team. I was good with numbers. He was good with his hands—and with intimidation. I was already into small-time loan-sharking by the time I met him. So I showed Billy how we could loan $20, charge 30 cents on the dollar and make $6 profit by the end of the week. Billy was the perfect enforcer when it came time to collect our money. Usually he didn't need to hurt people. One look at him and you'd pay that man anything.

In those days there were lots of older wiseguys in Baltimore we looked up to and worked for. But it wasn't long before we began to swindle the bookmaking business from them. Eventually they began to come to us for money. And very few of the old guys dealt drugs, so that business was wide open for us. It was no different from what John Gotti and Sammy "The Bull" Gravano did to Paul Castellano in the Mafia.

Billy and I sure loved our power. And as our business grew, we started to get more and more violent. In those early years our threat of violence was exciting. Whenever we'd walk into a bar on "The Block," Baltimore's X-rated strip district, heads would turn and people would stop talking. I loved that. Billy used to say, "With your brains and my brawn, we are going a long way together."

We certainly did go a long way together, but not on the path either of us ever imagined as cocky young punks. Events in the next few years would set our partnership on a collision course. One day I would be forced to make decisions that went far beyond our friendship. And these decisions would be just as permanent as the little blue cross that's tattooed on my hand.

Chapter 3

The Murder

On June 10, 1978, I woke up at my house in Hampden. It seemed like any other Saturday morning, until I walked up the street to the bar and restaurant at the corner of Thirty-third street and Keswick Road. It was the kind of place that changed hands a lot. This year it was called Benjamin's Tavern. The year before it was called Jack's, the place where Billy and I had sealed our friendship.

Billy was in the back today with two other guys we hung out with, John Derry and Ronnie Rogers. Ronnie was married to Billy's sister Susan. They all looked tired and strung out, though their clothes looked fresh. They were back there giggling, acting like they had been drunk. Ronnie—we called him Fat Ronnie—looked scared and confused as if he weren't feeling good. And he wasn't carrying on like John and Billy. The two of them acted like they didn't have a care in the world.

When I walked to the back, they stopped talking. That was unusual. Billy and I never kept secrets from each other. I knew they had been up to something.

Billy turned to the others. "Should I tell him?" he asked. Then John answered, "Let's tell him."

They'd been out all night. "That sick John, that sick motherfucker, we killed a guy last night," said Billy.

Billy was all over himself. He acted like he was proud that he made his "bones." John didn't seem nervous, either.

I asked them what happened. Billy told me they took this guy from the Holiday House on Harford Road and drove him out to the Gunpowder Falls. Ronnie stayed in the car while John and Billy dragged the guy down a long railroad track to a bridge. John hit him in the head with a baseball bat. John hit him real hard, said Billy. Then Billy threw the guy over the bridge into the water. Billy had to climb down to the river to see if the guy was still alive. He waded in and stepped on the guy's head to drown him. They never said why they killed him and they never told me his name.

They had already gotten rid of the baseball bat. It was an aluminum one that belonged to Ronnie's son, who was six or seven years old. When they got back to Hampden, they threw it over a bridge near the Boy Scouts of America headquarters into the Jones Falls. They also dumped John's bloody clothes into the stream.

I frankly was excited for them. In our world, doing a murder was the ultimate accomplishment. From this point on, I thought, nothing could stop Billy and me from getting ahead. And the murder itself didn't matter to me one way or the other. But I hated the fact that they told me about it. It wasn't long before we heard police were questioning people at the Holiday House. I knew if the investigation got hot, people would start pointing fingers at anybody who might know about the murder. That made me the weakest link. I told them they should shut up about it. We should keep the killing to ourselves. But Billy and Ronnie told Susan. That was the first bad move they made. I knew she could never keep her mouth shut.

They had been driving Ronnie's blue car that night. I

told them they'd better go down to his house and clean his car, including the carpet. I was afraid there would be hair fiber.

Billy later told me they had cleaned out the car, even hosed it out. He had also taken his clothes and put them in a bag. Billy and I got into my father's old Buick Regal and drove over to Greenmount Avenue and Thirty-third Street. Nearby was a gas station with a storm drain. We weren't nervous, but we looked carefully for police cars. I pulled the Buick up next to the storm drain. We quickly got out of the car with the bags, threw them on top of the drain, then kicked them down through the hole. That was my involvement with the murder. And I would hear no other details about the killing for nearly two decades.

The Scene Of The Crime

The same morning Charlie heard the killers confess, a Baltimore County police officer named James Holthaus was starting his Saturday-morning shift when a dispatcher called his radio from police headquarters with an assignment to locate a dead body. It was just after 7:00 A.M. when he headed up Route 40 to Jones Road, a rural street that crossed the B & O Railroad tracks. Off the heavily traveled Route 40, it was quiet. Nothing but woods and farms and the occasional whistle of a train coming through. It was not unfamiliar territory for Officer Holthaus. He had spent his life on the east side of this Baltimore suburb and had patrolled it now for six years as a cop. He'd grown up several miles away, in North Point Village, the same little neighborhood where Charlie was raised.

He parked his patrol car on Jones Road and started walking southwest along the tracks toward the railroad trestle. It would be a long walk, more than a quarter mile, to get to the bridge. He first noticed a light blue shirt lying near the road. As he walked farther, the officer saw a blood splatter on rocks by the tracks. Soon he entered the boundary of Gunpowder Falls State Park, where he saw more and more blood along the rocks. And as he neared the bridge, the officer looked to the right of the tracks. There was one light brown cowboy boot for a left foot near the trestle, surrounded by more blood. From that spot he followed what looked like drag marks, as if someone or something heavy had been dragged onto the railroad trestle.

The bridge was a high one, resting on mammoth stone pillars at least sixty feet above the Gunpowder Falls. In the bushes Officer Holthaus found a steep path that led to the river, so he climbed down, watching his step along the way. In the early-morning summer light, he saw a man's shirtless body floating face down in the shallow river, where three fishermen had found it. The dead man was white with brown hair. He wore one cowboy boot, on his right foot.

On the riverbank near the body, the officer searched for more traces of blood or signs of struggle, but found none. He scrambled back up the embankment to reexamine the trestle. By the flimsy guardrails he found more blood on the bridge, on both the north and south sides along the steel beams that held the tracks. He radioed in to his supervisors at the Essex District and roped off the area.

Within minutes the others arrived. A corporal and lieutenant from Essex District, two railroad police officers, two detectives from the county's crime lab, a park ranger, a homicide detective, with his lieutenant and captain, and a doctor from the medical examiner's office. Two divers from the Middle River Volunteer Fire Department hauled the body out of the water so the man from Bruzdzinski's Funeral Home could drive the body to the medical examiner's office downtown.

Crime lab detectives took photographs from the railroad bridge. Down by the riverbank they took more close-ups of the body. The detectives noted the dead man's single boot. The body wore blue jeans and gold socks.

The detectives noticed a large cut on the man's left temple, a smaller cut on the right temple, many abrasions on his back, chest and stomach. His upper lip was swollen and discolored.

They searched the dead man's pockets, finding a black comb, a yellow plastic coupon worth 50 cents, and a $10 bill. From the left rear pants pocket, they lifted out a brown leather wallet. From inside, they pulled out identification for Mark Stephen Schwandtner. He was twenty-two years old.

At 9:30 A.M., Dr. K. S. Ahluwalia from the medical examiner's office pronounced Mark Schwandtner dead.

Officer Holthaus and homicide detective William Viands took the address from Schwandtner's driver's license and drove to the house on Parkmont Avenue, arriving just before 11:30 A.M.

Mark's sister Glenda was sunbathing in the backyard when she heard her mother scream out in an awful, painful cry. She ran into the house and found the police there. All she would remember for many years were these words from one officer: "Your brother was beaten, dragged and thrown in the river." She wondered, Why, why, why? She hoped he hadn't suffered much.

Her father turned to her. "Take care of your mother," he said.

Norman Schwandtner asked the officers to step onto the back patio for a private discussion. The father told them he was not surprised to hear his son was dead. He was actually expecting it. His son had been in and out of trouble many times. The father had thrown him out of the house after his son's twenty-first birthday. Once, during an argument, he had shot his son, putting him in the hospital with a collapsed lung, he told the stunned officers. This was certainly not the typical reaction police got when they told someone his child had been murdered. Detective Viands made a note in his report that the father had a "who gives a damn attitude" to the news of his son's murder.

From the Schwandtner house Detective Viands headed downtown to the city's central criminal records office to get old arrest reports involving young Schwandtner. Then he and Officer Holthaus met up at the state medical examiner's office to find Dr. Bert F. Morton, the deputy chief medical examiner.

Mark Schwandtner had drowned, the pathologist told the of-

ficers. The many wounds were not enough to kill the young man, though he would have lost his left eye. His written autopsy report would describe the dead man's respiratory tract as full of watery fluid and sand. It would note the multiple bruises and cuts to the body and hemorrhaging to the head. His left eye was lacerated. His pupil was "obliterated."

Later the dead man's brother-in-law arrived at the morgue and identified the body. Fingerprints were also taken and proved to match the prints from his criminal records. In those days before DNA testing, blood samples were taken from the railroad bridge that proved to be Type A. Mark Schwandtner's blood was also Type A.

The following Monday, the Baltimore Sun *reported the drowning in a brief article that included three other "water accidents" over the weekend. The newspaper allotted four paragraphs to Schwandtner's death. The article quoted Detective Viands as saying the case was being investigated as a homicide because "police did not know how Mr. Schwandtner got into the water."*

In the early days of the investigation, the police got nowhere. Visits to several Northeast Baltimore bars led them to a dead end as people claimed to know nothing about the victim. Some said they might have seen Schwandtner frequent the bars, but nobody recalled seeing him the night he was killed on Friday, June 9.

An interview with one of Mark's coworkers gave a glimpse of his last day alive. He and a friend were working for C.C. & T. Tunneling Company on a construction job in Alexandria, Virginia. After finishing work, they arrived back in Baltimore a little after 5:00 P.M. They went straight to a bank and cashed their checks. Mark should have had more than $100 in his pocket before he went out drinking that night. But when police searched the body the following morning, they found only a $10 bill in the dead man's pocket. Now at least police had a possible motive—robbery.

Within weeks of the murder, the dead man's family began to look for the killers themselves. Though Norman Schwandtner may have had a violent relationship with Mark, it didn't mean he didn't love him as much as he loved his other seven children. He was desperate to find the killers—and to learn the reason for his death. He was too anxious to wait for the police to solve the murder, so he wrote up a flyer offering a $5,000 reward for any information that might lead to an arrest. But when the grief-stricken family went to the Holiday House to post the flyer, they were surprised by the reception they got from people who may have been the last to see Schwandtner alive. The bar employees and patrons treated the family members with hostility and suspicion. They were made to feel as if they were wrong to search for the killers. A young woman walked up to one of Mark's sisters. "You should leave," she said.

Mark's brother Rick tried to ask questions in the neighborhood surrounding the bar. But one neighbor told him, "Leave it alone or you'll wind up like your brother." Another man actually pointed a gun at him.

He didn't know at the time that Billy Isaacs was a suspect, but he could tell somebody powerful was involved in his brother's murder.

With no good leads, the case went cold until the following March when a Baltimore County homicide detective named Henry Wysham got a call at his Towson office from a detective down in Baltimore City named John Kurinij. The city detective had just spoken to an informant who knew about the murder of a white man who was thrown into the Gunpowder Falls the previous June.

The informant, a woman, claimed three men were responsible for the killing. And she had all their names. Detective Kurinij had already made arrangements for Detective Wysham to interview her.

Three days later Detective Wysham arrived at the informant's house in Hampden. In the course of three hours, Patricia Sellers told him she had not witnessed the murder, but had heard about it from Susan Rogers, wife of Ronnie Rogers and sister of Billy Isaacs. She named both men as being involved in the killing. The third man's name was John Derry. She described Billy Isaacs as an expert in martial arts and a former bouncer at a bar on Harford Road in Northeast Baltimore.

Sellers told the detective that she believed the dead man lived in Towson and worked for a construction company in Virginia. He had a reputation for being "mouthy" and had a last name that was hard to pronounce, probably a German or Polish name. Maybe his first name was Dennis. Wysham asked if she'd ever heard the name Mark Schwandtner.

"That's the guy's last name, but I still can't get the name of Dennis out of my mind," she said. She also told him the body was found on or about July or August 1978. Though she wasn't sure of the summer month, she was certain it was a Saturday, the tenth of the month. She also remembered reading about it in the newspaper and hearing it on television.

Sellers worked as a waitress at a bar and restaurant at the corner of Thirty-third Street and Keswick Road that was called Benjamin's Tavern at the time of the murder. On a Friday night, the ninth of the month, she was there with Susan Rogers, Ronnie Rogers, Billy Isaacs and John Derry, she told the detective. Sometime around 10:00 P.M. the three men left the bar in Rogers' 1968 blue Chevrolet Malibu sedan. When they were gone, Susan Rogers told Sellers that the men were driving out to Harford Road to a bar called the Holiday House to beat up a guy whom Billy Isaacs had trouble with about a week before.

The next day was Saturday, the tenth of the month. Sellers arrived at work at 4:00 P.M. to find Rogers, Isaacs and Derry having a secret meeting in the back room of the bar. As soon as Sellers arrived, Susan Rogers pulled the waitress aside. She told Sellers about a man's body being found in the Gunpowder Falls. This was the same man from the Holiday House that Isaacs, Rogers and Derry were talking about the night before. Sellers told the detective she remembered seeing the three acting upset, confused and frightened.

Susan Rogers told Sellers that the men had driven over to the Holiday House on Harford Road. At closing time they took *the victim and beat him to death with an aluminum baseball bat that belonged to Susan Rogers' son, Ronnie Rogers Jr. It had been in their blue Malibu. Isaacs had been in an argument with the victim a few nights before at the Holiday House, his sister told Sellers.*

Susan Rogers heard about the murder from her husband the next day. Ronnie Rogers told his wife that they killed the man and threw him into the Gunpowder River.

They weren't sure he was dead until they read it about it later in the newspaper. Sellers told police that the men brought the baseball bat back to Baltimore City and threw it off the bridge at Twenty-eighth Street, near the Boy Scouts of America office. Sellers remembered seeing little Ronnie's bat in his father's car prior to the murder. She described it as being regulation size, aluminum, light sparkle blue with gray tape around the grip. For a long time after the murder, Ronnie Jr. kept asking, "Where's my bat?"

Susan also told Sellers she cleaned out the car and washed the blood out. Then she threw away the floor mats. Sellers gave Susan new floor mats to cover a hole in the front floorboard.

Sellers asked the detective "Was his shirt missing?" When the detective asked why she wanted to know, she said, "I remember Susan telling me that they tore the boy's shirt off." Sellers assumed that the shirt and other items of clothing were also thrown off the Twenty-eighth Street bridge, along with the bat.

Isaacs' sister also told her, "The cops don't even know that the guy came from the Holiday House."

Detective Wysham then asked Sellers if she knew anyone else who might know about the murder.

Yes, said Sellers. His name is Charlie Wilhelm. But he is "tight" with the killers and would never tell police. Sellers also said that Ronnie Rogers was a nervous wreck after the murder and for a while he and his wife made plans to move out of state. But when things died down, they decided to stay in Baltimore. She also said something that could be a hindrance to proving the case in court someday: she would never testify against these three men for fear they would retaliate against her and her two small sons. She then begged Detective Wysham to keep her identity secret.

Nine months had passed since the killing. But news from Sellers that the murder weapon and the victim's shirt may have been tossed into the Jones Falls in Hampden sent Detective Wysham on a search. He wrote his plans in a report to his captain, hoping "a stroke of luck might produce the bat, the shirt or anything of value in this investigation." A few days after his interview with Patricia Sellers, he began a hunt just before noon under the busy Twenty-eighth Street bridge. It was a messy place to search, a typical city stream, muddied with storm water and garbage. The steep slopes were covered with bushes, weeds, trees and rocks mixed with trash dumped by people and carried by storms from upstream. The mess made his search difficult and time consuming. He searched "every step" of each stream bank. He drew a detailed map of the area to turn in to his captain, but he found no baseball bat and no shirt. Perhaps, he theorized in his report, "the bat is covered by . . . months of foliage and storm debris" or "the swiftness of the current could easily have swept the bat or any article downstream out of sight."

With no hope of finding a weapon, police continued their investigation with more interviews. On May 21 a detective in the county's robbery squad got a tip from an informant that a man named Marshall Steineger might know something about the murder. Steineger had lost an eye in a beating from Billy Isaacs and three other men in February at the Holiday House. When police questioned Steineger, he said he had heard Isaacs was responsible for the Schwandtner murder and that police were going to use the assault on him to strengthen their murder case against Isaacs. Steineger had no fresh information pinning the murder on Isaacs or the other two, but police were still looking for any insight he could give them about Isaacs' violent nature.

Detective Wysham asked him, "After you were beaten and laying on the ground, what, if anything, did you hear Billy say?"

"I'm not sure if Billy said it, but I think he said, 'We have to get rid of him.' Then when he saw me moving, Billy picked my face up and punched me in the teeth. Then my friends came out of the bar and the police came."

On May 23 two detectives drove to the Maryland Correctional Center in Jessup, one of Maryland's main prisons. They were looking for a man who was at the Holiday House on the night Mark Schwandtner was killed. Police were told the inmate had made a statement—prior to the murder—that he knew Mark Schwandtner was "going to get it."

The inmate told the detectives he knew Isaacs from the Holiday House, where Isaacs was a bouncer. But he told them he did not remember ever saying that Schwandtner was going to get it. In fact, he told the police he hadn't even learned of the young man's death until they showed up that day. And he knew of no trouble between Schwandtner and Isaacs. He had never heard of the other two suspects, John Derry and Ronnie Rogers. Police showed him some mug shots. He said he'd seen Rogers' face before, but couldn't remember where. But he did remember the night of June 9, 1978, because that was his last night of freedom before he was sentenced to prison on drug charges. The inmate said he was drunk at the Holiday House and was positive Billy Isaacs was there, too. He offered no other concrete information. Nevertheless, the prisoner offered a chilling afterthought. He told the detectives he had no doubt Billy Isaacs beat Mark Schwandtner. Isaacs, he said, was vicious and violent and had a reputation for beating and maiming people.

A week later a detective went to see a man interviewed in the early days of the investigation. Police had found him to be the best source of information as to who was with Schwandtner at the Holiday House the night he died. Now, a year later, the man seemed to have lost his memory. He looked at photographs of Isaacs, Rogers and Derry. None of them looked familiar, he told the detective. It had been too long. Now he couldn't say for sure if any of them were in the Holiday House that night.

On June 2, 1979, nearly a year after the murder, Patricia

Sellers called one of the detectives in the case. She said she was at the Keswick Inn at nine o'clock in the morning when Ronnie Rogers walked in.

He pointed to a piece of paper hanging on the wall, then left the bar in a huff. When she went over to read the paper, the waitress saw that it was a new flyer offering a reward for information about Mark Schwandtner's death. The victim's father had been posting the flyers around town in hopes of finding his son's killer. Rogers returned three hours later with the other two murder suspects and showed them the flyer. Rogers still appeared to be upset, but the other two remained calm. They left the bar after a few hours. Later that day, the waitress said, she got a call from Susan Rogers. She said she was worried about her brother because he was throwing up blood and acting nervous about the "kid" being murdered. Isaacs had also been drinking more lately and had supposedly told a cop that he was sorry about beating a boy.

Detectives met with a county prosecutor in July to talk about the best way to approach the three suspects. Without any physical evidence to link them to the murder, one of the suspects must testify against the others, the prosecutor told them. They decided to try and get both Ronnie and Susan Rogers to talk. Ronnie could testify against the other suspects, and Susan could corroborate the facts. Again the detectives contacted the Hampden waitress. The time was right, she said, to confront Rogers because he was upset about the recent reward flyers.

On June 28 detectives went to see the couple. Police read them their Miranda rights. Then the couple said they would talk, but the interview went nowhere. They said they knew nothing about the murder. Police told them they would not be charged with a crime if they came forward as state's witnesses. But Ronnie Rogers refused their offers until he could talk to his lawyer.

Detective Wysham got a call the next day, from a Baltimore defense lawyer named Donald Daneman. The lawyer said he represented all three murder suspects. The three men were in his office and denied any involvement in the killing. The lawyer *then warned the detective not to contact his clients again without a warrant.*

When told of Daneman's call, the Baltimore County prosecutor told the detectives the case was now at a standstill unless they developed fresh leads. Until then, the investigation would be suspended. There was no mention in police reports of the name Charlie Wilhelm as somebody to interview about the murder, even though Patricia Sellers had told police months before that he knew of the murder. It would not be the last time Charlie Wilhelm would slip through the fingers of the Baltimore County police.

Off The Hook

Billy told me about the meeting at Mr. Daneman's office. Though the lawyer managed to put up a roadblock in the way of the investigation, we knew it wasn't really over. We all waited for the police to come question me. But they never came. And no one was arrested for the murder of Mark Schwandtner.

At home things were not so quiet. Somehow Melonie had heard about the murder and believed both Billy and I were guilty. "I know you guys are all involved in the murder," she'd say.

"You're crazy, you're full of shit, nobody told you nothing. It's not true," I'd shoot back. She'd keep trying to get me to admit to the murder. I'd just say, "There's nothing to admit."

But my wife was persistent. "I know you helped Billy get rid of stuff," she'd say. Within a few weeks of the murder, her attitude toward Billy changed. I noticed she could barely tolerate him. And her belief that we were involved continued to bug her. She wouldn't let it go. She'd dredge it up every time I was MIA with Billy. That's what we called it when we'd stay out all night—Missing in Action. The next morning Melonie would be belligerent with me.

"What did you do? Go out and kill somebody that night?" she'd ask. I'd just tell her she was crazy. But it started to get to me.

One time when I was MIA, Melonie tracked me down to a neighborhood bar. As soon as she walked in, the cheeks in my ass started to pucker. I knew I was going to hear it from her. She ordered a soda—she never drank alcohol. Billy was drinking his usual Silver Bullet, or Coors Light. I was drinking from a Miller pony bottle. Melonie insisted I come home with her, but Billy said, "You ain't got to go home." Melonie and Billy got into a bad argument. I finally had to defend her to my best friend. I said, "Hey, Billy, that's my wife. You can't talk to her that way."

Shortly after the murder there was some talk by a few of the killers that they might need to bump off one of the others in case he might roll. I started to worry about myself. I didn't kill anybody, but I sure knew too much. Maybe the other guys figured I was the weakest link. I could put them in prison for murder, but practically walk away scot-free—though I could be charged as an accessory after the fact of murder for helping throw away the bloody clothes. I went to tell my father, of all people, in case they were going to whack me. A small part of me hoped my father would tell me to do the right thing. I wanted to hear my ex-cop father say, "Let's go to the police." But instead he told me, "Keep your mouth shut." I was disappointed in my father's advice that day, but a part of me was glad I didn't have to roll.

Looking back, I think I could have changed my life if I'd done the right thing with my father's support. The funny thing is, he used to tell me, "Charlie, one day you're going to get into something you can't get out of." He repeated those words when I told him about the murder. And I would hear them in my head many times, long after he was dead.

As the years went by, the great accomplishment of committing murder was overshadowed by the stress of having to keep it secret. But I managed to keep my conscience under control. I wouldn't start having nightmares about it until years later.

Among ourselves we would only occasionally talk about it. Every six months Billy sent me around to talk to John and Ronnie to remind them to keep their mouths shut. And they did. We all did.

Billy even coined a saying about the murder. And he would repeat it as the years went by: "Nobody talks, everybody walks."

Chapter 4

The High Life

By the time I was thirty, I was a bank president, a lottery director and a freewheeling entrepreneur. I paid a fraction of the taxes I owed and had little overhead. I bought anything I wanted, from lump crabmeat to imported crystal, wholesale—*very* wholesale. In those early years I ran my operation out of my white Eldorado Cadillac with the mint green vinyl roof. The street corners and bars of Baltimore's white, working-class neighborhoods were my satellite offices. Though I snorted cocaine, I was more addicted to the life of hustling than I was to the drugs. I absolutely loved the life. I loved the fast cash. I loved the power to intimidate. I loved the license for violence. I loved the adrenaline rush of staying one step ahead of the police. It gave me a greater high than any drug you can imagine.

One of the best things about organized crime in Baltimore was our independence from the Mafia. For some reason, Baltimore has never been a town the Mafia controlled. From the time I was a teenager, I was told there were just too many rats in Baltimore for the Mafia to trust any of us. Today they don't control the docks, the unions, the horse tracks, the bars or the restaurants. Some people think that means there's no organized crime in Baltimore. But, of course, that couldn't be further from the truth. Sure, some of my Italian wiseguy friends had connections to Mafia bosses in other cities, but I never took my orders from anybody in La Cosa Nostra. I only took my orders from Billy.

In my business I was a kind of traveling salesman, moving around all the time, always on the lookout for action. I'd go to the east side of town hunting for boosters, or professional shoplifters. I'd head to the docks of the massive Dundalk Marine Terminal looking for stolen goods heisted by dockworkers. At night I'd show up at Baltimore's red-light district looking for gamblers eager to bet on professional sports or our illegal lottery. On The Block I'd also sniff out anybody down on his luck needing to borrow money—at any price. And I'd sell cocaine anywhere I thought I couldn't get caught.

You could find boosters almost anywhere, but in my book the capital of shoplifting was an East Baltimore neighborhood called Highlandtown. It's a neighborhood officially known for big 1950s beehive hairdos and rowhouses with white marble steps scrubbed clean every day by little old immigrant ladies. People there talk in heavy Baltimore, or Balmer, accents. They say "water" like "warter" and "ocean" like "ashen." I'd find boosters in bars and on street corners. One of the best boosters around in the 1970s and 1980s lived next door to a longtime city councilman from the First District in Highlandtown who has since passed away. But there was no booster who could match the skill of another Highlandtown master shoplifter. He used to go to stores in Ocean City, Maryland, dressed in disguises so he wouldn't be suspected of shoplifting. He had a U.S. Postal Service carrier uniform he often wore, but sometimes he just dressed as a woman. You'd give him your suit size. Three days later he'd show up with an Oscar de la Renta suit worth $500. You'd generally pay a quarter of what it was worth, sometimes even less. It all depended on how badly he needed the money. If he had four or five things that came to $1,000, you could buy them all for 15 percent of value. While I did plenty of business with the boosters, the fencing racket was even more lucrative on the docks of Baltimore. Dundalk Marine Terminal is the destination for millions of dollars in foreign goods unloaded off ships that come up the Patapsco River from the Chesapeake Bay. And I was well connected to dockworkers who had a side business in fencing everything you can imagine that just happened to fall off the ship. I could get anything from them—imported crystal in the shape of swans, the latest toys, even the hottest athletic shoes. And I'd always get them for less than half the price. The trunk of my car was always filled. We'd unload the hot stuff at bars and businesses around town.

Billy and I put aside our evenings for The Block, Baltimore's red-light district down the street from Baltimore police headquarters and just two blocks from City Hall. On those two little blocks we could find drug dealers, strippers, prostitutes and pimps. It wasn't until years later that I learned you also could find undercover city cops there. There was one bartender I never suspected who turned up at the Gaiety and another bar not far from The Block called the Tic Toc Club. He was a long-haired guy with a mustache who also drove a cab and often took the dancers home at night. The girls called him "Jim the cab-driver."

Word on the street was that he had been a cop, but had an "integrity problem" and had to leave the force. Turns out that was just his cover. He never really left the force. Little did I know how closely he was watching us. Back then, I would have said you were crazy if you told me he was an undercover cop. And I'd say you were even crazier if you told me we would one day be on the same side of a criminal investigation. It would be many years before I learned his full name: James I. Cabezas.

Billy and I spent plenty of quality time in the clubs on The Block as part of our ongoing public relations campaign. In our business we could never be out of sight or out of mind. People needed to see us everywhere so they'd know we were available to do business with them. If they needed to borrow money, we wanted to get into the action as loan sharks, or shylocks. If other bookmakers needed to chase down customers who didn't pay their bets, they'd hire us to track them down.

But Billy and I even found a way to rip off the other bookmakers. We'd make a bookmaker pay us half of what the customer owed, say $500 from a $1,000 bet. When we'd find the deadbeat customer, we'd tell the customer we didn't care if he paid or not. But we'd make him call the bookmaker to prove we'd made our visit. When the customer refused to pay up, the bookmaker would hire us again six months later—for another $500—to find him.

For Billy and me, no hustle or scam was too small. We even collected $20 from drug addicts and alcoholics who were under court order to attend Alcoholics Anonymous and Narcotics Anonymous meetings. The meetings were upstairs from a bar where we often hung out. The bar owner rented the room to NA and AA. Somehow we got hold of an official rubber stamp that proved attendance at the meetings. The addicts would pay us their $20, we'd stamp their court papers and they'd go home without ever attending a meeting.

While no scam was too small for us, we made the bulk of our living from bookmaking and shylocking.

Bookmaking

Before I left the wiseguy life, I thought everybody knew

how bookmaking, or illegal gambling, works. There are so many thousands of people in Baltimore placing illegal bets every day that I just assumed everybody knew the laws of bookmaking as easily as they knew the rules of baseball.

Here's how warped I was: When my family lived in hiding in Alabama, we went to our first Little League baseball game. I looked around me and saw six hundred crazed adults screaming and yelling for the two teams. I turned to my wife and said, "They're betting on these games. I tell you, Gina, these people are too upset over these eight- and nine-year-olds. They must have bet big money on this game."

My wife told me, "Get out of here, Charlie." She didn't believe me. And of course, she was right. Pretty soon I became one of those crazed, screaming parents. And I didn't even have any money riding on the game.

After my first eighteen months of living a straight life, I came to the conclusion that the majority of the population doesn't understand the mechanics of bookmaking. Even law enforcement officers don't understand it. They just know the term, "bookmaker."

Bookmaking is a complicated, five-tiered pyramid scheme that takes in hundreds of thousands of dollars in bets every day in Baltimore. The bets are made on professional and college basketball, football and other sports. There's also a lucrative business on an illegal lottery played by workers at large manufacturing plants like General Motors, Domino Sugar and the Social Security Administration, which is headquartered in Baltimore. In my world everybody played numbers. I even knew a priest who occasionally wagered a few dollars on days he felt lucky.

You may wonder why people would play an illegal lottery when Maryland has had a legal one for thirty years. State officials argued that legalizing numbers would put bookmakers out of business, but it's had the opposite effect. In the old days a customer could never be sure if his bookmaker was truthful when he told the customer his number didn't hit. Today the winning lottery numbers for bookmakers are the same as Maryland's legal lottery. The bookmakers' customers just have to watch TV or check the Maryland Lottery Web site to find out if they won.

So why play the illegal lottery? Customers have a better chance of winning more money with a bookmaker than with the Maryland Lottery. The Maryland Lottery pays $500 for every $1 wagered. The bookmaker pays up to $700 for every $1. And it's tax free!

Here's how it works: At the bottom of the pyramid scheme is the "writer." This is the guy who walks the streets getting customers to place bets. He finds his clients in bars, in offices, in factories. The writer works on a commission. He gets anywhere from $150 to $200 for each $1,000 in action he brings in. He also gets 10 to 15 percent of his customers' winnings. Customers can't just bet once or twice. They have to be committed to bet every week for a year, for example. That way the writer is assured he's got business coming in all the time.

There is also an advantage for the regular customer. Once the writer comes to trust him, the customer doesn't have to put any money up front. There are no lottery machines and no tickets to produce. The customer can bet now and pay a week or even a month later. The writer then calls the bet into a "clerk." The clerk is a person working from home or in the back room of a bar. Sometimes clerks also work out of "safe houses," which are secret locations set up just for the bookmaking business. The clerk uses a phone with a tape recorder attached to it by a suction cup, to record each wager. That way the accuracy of the customer's bet is assured. The tape also lets clerks detect a lying customer who might claim he bet the winning number when he actually picked a loser.

The clerk works six days a week from noon to 2:00 P.M. and from 5:00 to 8:00 P.M. The clerk also works every holiday with no sick days. The clerk can make anywhere from $400 to $1,200 a week—tax free, of course—depending on how many writers call in with wagers.

The bets go from the clerk to the bookmaker. A good bookmaker has several clerks working for him. And each clerk has many writers, who could have hundreds of customers. A good bookmaker can gross $75,000 a week from his writers if his customers don't hit too many winning numbers. When I was a bookmaker, I grossed between $40,000 and $75,000 a week and had between one thousand and two thousand customers coming to my writers and clerks.

But I still had to pay my clerks and writers, any apartment rentals where the clerks worked, as well as their phone bills. And I also had to pay the "layoff guy."

The layoff (LO) guy is the man at the top of the organization. He only handles very big bets, but he also serves as a kind of insurance company to the bookmaker. If the bookmaker is taking in too many bets on one popular number, he "lays off" extra bets to the guy at the top, paying him money as an insurance policy. You don't want to take too many bets on the same number. If that number hits, you could lose your shirt. This is known as "busting out." So you lay off extra bets to the layoff guy. He'll then pay 5 percent of the bets laid off back to the bookmaker, so he can pay off his customers and not starve himself.

I used to work for a layoff guy who was a big money man. He was one of the richest wiseguys I knew. I swear the guy sometimes had more money than God. One time I owed him $70,000 to pay off on bets. When I started counting out the money I owed him, I tried to give him all the small bills I'd collected on the streets. No wiseguy wants to give up his hundred-dollar bills. You always try to pay money out in small bills like twenties, tens, fives and even ones. It's hard enough to hide the hundreds, but just try carrying around bags full of small bills. I counted the money several times before putting it all in a brown paper shopping bag and heading up to an old Howard Johnson's in a northwest suburb of Baltimore. I handed him the bag and headed back to the city. By the time I got back home, the LO guy had paged me.

I called him back right away.

"You're one dollar short," he said.

"I can't believe you're calling me over one dollar," I said.

A week later I owed him another $50,000. I called him to arrange a meeting.

"You still owe me that dollar," he reminded me. "This is business, Charlie. I just want to keep the records straight," he said.

He was a funny guy. You'd think he'd be glued to the TV every day waiting for the lottery number to come out. He had thousands of dollars in bets from customers riding on that number. But one time I met him when he owed me about $50,000 and he handed me the money in large bills. I got in my car and was beginning to drive away when he came running over to the driver's side.

"Charlie, what was the winning number today?" he said. I just laughed. You'd think he'd check the winning number before paying out so much money.

When you play numbers as much as I did, you had a sixth sense that a certain number was about to hit. We just knew the odds. One time there was a particular number that was hot on the streets. I was loaded up with it on my book. My clerk had a hunch about the number, so I decided to play it myself. But no other bookmaker would take my bet. They were all worried they'd get wiped out if the number hit. My only option was to make my bet legal. I bought about $130 in tickets from the Maryland State

Lottery. I hit for $64,000. Two weeks later I played the Maryland Lottery again and won $45,000.

A smart bookmaker will stash money away for bad times. If you have a few good weeks, you can make a fortune. But if you have a few bad weeks, it will put you right out of business. You could lose $25,000 to $30,000 a day if too many of your customers' numbers hit.

The bookmaking organization is a secretive business. Customers rarely meet their bookmakers. The clerks never meet the LO guy. The clerks recruit the writers, who in turn are checked out on the streets by the bookmakers to make sure they're legit—actually to make sure they're *not* legit—so the bookmakers can trust them. Even though the clerks and writers may work together for years, they may never learn one another's real names. Everybody uses code names or numbers, like R6, Triple X, Zero or just any phony first names. Sometimes writers have two nicknames—one as a wiseguy and one as a writer. There was a guy we called Baldy in the underworld. But when he wrote numbers, his code name was Zero. His real name was Melvin.

Here's a diagram of a bookmaking organization:

Layoff Guy

bookmaker	bookmaker	bookmaker	bookmaker
clerks	clerks	clerks	clerks
writers	writers	writers	writers

thousands of customers

Shakespeare's Juice Man

If you repay me not on such a day
In such a place, such sum or sums as are
Expressed in the condition, let the forfeit

> *Be nominated for an equal pound*
> *Of your fair flesh, to be cut and taken*
> *In what part of your body pleaseth me.*
> —Shylock setting loan terms, in
> *The Merchant of Venice*

I was a shylock on the streets of Baltimore for decades. But not having paid much attention in school, I had no clue it was a name from a Shakespeare play. If you told the shylocks of today that they are named after a character in a play William Shakespeare wrote more than four hundred years ago, they'd probably say you were out of your mind.

Let me explain modern-day shylocking, since you won't find the rules in any textbook or instruction manual. In fact, there is never anything in writing to back up an illegal loan. There are no papers to sign, no coupon booklet to make your payments easy. No paper trail at all. And for good reason.

You also will find that today's shylocks are much slicker than the one in *The Merchant of Venice.* They'll never tell you up front what will happen to you if you don't make your payments. But, frankly, today's shylocks are just as coldhearted as Shakespeare's original "juice man."

A loan shark is also called a juice man because "juice" is the word we use for "interest." The people who borrow money illegally are often just regular people. Some are business owners, ordinary working people, housewives or even drug dealers hard up for cash.

Often they are gamblers in debt, big time. They bet on professional sports—baseball, basketball, football—or they play the illegal lottery, sometimes stealing thousands from their own legitimate businesses to support their habit. Then they come to the loan shark to bail them out. Now they're in even more debt than they were to begin with.

First, there is the small shylock who works in some le-

gitimate company or construction trade. Most small shylocks will lend no more than $500 to one person. He
charges 25 or 30 percent interest per week. And he may
ask for collateral such as a couple of TVs, stereos or
tools. This way if you don't make your weekly interest
payments, at least the loan shark doesn't lose his money.

Here's how the interest works on a small loan: Say you
borrow $200. You've agreed to pay him back in four
weeks. You have to pay him $25 weekly interest on each
one hundred dollars you borrowed. At the end of the
fourth week, you would have paid $200 just in juice, or in-
terest, alone. At the end of the four weeks, you also have
to pay the $200 principal. That doesn't seem like much
money if you're in a bind and you need quick cash. Once
you figure the loan was easy to repay, you go out and find
a bigger shylock, this time borrowing $2,000. The larger
shylock lends money by the "point" system. And most of
the time he doesn't want collateral. He just wants your
word that you agree to pay each week. When you discuss
your payment arrangements with him, he is nice and
humble to you. You think about all the bad rumors you've
heard and stories you've seen on TV dramas where the
shylocks are mean and break your head if you miss a payment. You feel sorry for the guy that his profession has
gotten such a bum rap. After leaving the meeting you are
under the impression the shylock is one of the best-
dressed, nicest and classiest people you'd ever want to
meet. But looks and first impressions can be deceiving, especially in this business.

You walk away with $2,000. You've borrowed it at three
points for ten weeks. Each point is worth $10 for every
$1,000 you borrow. In this case one point equals $20. That
makes your payments at $260 per week with $200 going toward the principal and $60 goes toward the juice. If you
make all your payments on time, you'll end up paying
$600 in interest alone. But say you're low on cash one

week and you can't make your entire payment. Your friendly loan shark makes you fork over an extra $100 in juice for that week, with nothing toward the principal. So, you're already falling behind. The next week you go back to your original payment schedule.

Here's another payment plan: You borrow the $1,000, but you only have to pay $50 in juice each week and no principal. Here's the catch: you have to pay $50 a week until the day you die, unless you come up with the principal in one shot. The shylock will only accept the full $1,000. You can't give him $300 this week and $700 the next week. It doesn't work that way. The system works similarly with large loans. If you borrow $100,000, you can choose the ten-week plan, at $13,000 a week. Or you can pay $5,000 a week for life—or until you come up with the $100,000 (though loan sharks are more willing to accept partial principal payments when you owe in the six figures).

This system is designed especially to prey on the kind of client who can never hold on to money long enough to repay his loan. Since many are compulsive gamblers or drug dealers—or just regular people with bad credit— they rarely save enough cash to come up with the principal they owe you. They just keep on owing.

I once loaned $1,000 to a woman who worked in an office of a big insurance company. She was just a regular, hardworking person with kids. I never knew what she needed the money for, but she met me at a Laundromat every week and paid me $50 in juice. It took her four years to come up with the original $1,000 loan. By then, she had paid me $10,400 in interest.

Here are examples of four loan payment plans:

Three points for ten weeks

loan	payment	from juice
$1,000	$130	$30

total after ten weeks = $1,300

Four points for ten weeks

loan	payment	from juice
$25,000	$3,500	$1,000

total after ten weeks = $35,000

If you miss a week on the ten-week plan, you pay a penalty. Your juice goes up to $1,250 from $1,000. And your payments extend to an eleventh week.

One point loan for life

loan	principal	juice
$1,000	0	$50

Two point loan for life

loan	principal	juice
$25,000	0	$2,500

If you can pay the principal at the end of ten weeks, your total payment for the last scenerio would be $50,000. Otherwise, the juice just adds up. In one year alone, your juice payments would total $130,000.

If you don't make your payments on time, you'll get a visit from your shylock. And the first time or two he will be nice, but firm. But after that, he will take drastic measures and you won't think he's such a swell guy anymore. "Sell your wife's ass if you have to," he'll tell you. You can tell him about all the hard times you're having, but he will simply say, "That's not my problem."

At this point the juice man doesn't even have to tell you what will happen if you don't make your payments. You just know you'll get busted up, if not killed. You think about going to the police, but you realize you have nothing in writing to prove you borrowed money. It's not like you're dealing with a loan company or bank. And you figure the shylock might have the police in his pocket, anyway, so you're in deep shit.

Shylocks are careful and cunning when it comes to the police. They warn you once or twice. Then one night someone you don't know will sneak up on you. You won't have any proof of who busted you up. If you report it to the police, the shylock will deny even lending you money, let alone having you busted up.

I can tell you from firsthand experience, it's not worth borrowing from a juice man. And it's even worse being one. I spent countless nights chasing people down for their juice payments. I even sat out in front of a bookmaker's house on Christmas Eve one year for half the night trying to catch a guy to get his payments The guy owed us $150,000 and Billy had already slapped the guy around once after hunting him down at a suburban restaurant.

The guy ended up leaving his family three days before Christmas because he knew Billy and I were after him. He took off for San Diego. We had a guy in California track him down. Arrangements were made for him to send us a few payments. We got stiffed for the rest.

One time I was summoned by Billy, who was stuck in Allenwood Federal Prison in Pennsylvania, where he was doing time for loansharking and witness tampering. But being in prison didn't stop him from conducting business. He just used me and his girlfriend to take care of things. Back in those days we tagged his girlfriend as "The Queen."

One day she called and told me Billy needed to see me. It was urgent. I never liked The Queen and I hated going to see Billy with her. Everything I told her she blew out of proportion. I thought she was jealous over how tight I was with Billy. And besides, every wiseguy on the street knew never to let a woman know your business. They can't keep their mouths shut—especially when they're mad at you. Billy was adamant about that until he went to federal prison. Now he was starting to trust her more than he trusted me. Still, I knew if The Queen said it was urgent, something must be up.

I thought maybe Billy found out that we were going to be indicted or that the FBI was investigating Joe's Tavern, where we gypped the state out of taxes for the video poker machines, bribed the liquor inspectors and laundered our drug money.

Billy called me several times to make sure I was coming. The Queen and I drove up to Pennsylvania in my Lincoln. Well, it was urgent, all right. A Baltimore businessman who owned a small manufacturing company wasn't making his juice payments on $200,000 he owed Billy. He was supposed to be paying The Queen $5,000 a week. Instead, he was paying $2,000, but sometimes he didn't pay anything. The guy was a heavy gambler. He liked to bet on football and basketball games and play our illegal lottery. The businessman started borrowing $50,000 from us, making weekly juice payments of $5,000 for seventeen weeks. After he'd made $85,000 in interest payments, he still owed Billy the original $50,000. But then he'd need more money to make his weekly payments—and to gamble with. So he borrowed another $50,000. Eventually he came to owe Billy $200,000.

In the visiting room in the newly built Allenwood Federal Prison, there are no glass partitions between prisoner and visitors. Visitors are searched first, but they can meet freely with prisoners. When The Queen and I arrived, there were a few guards nearby, but if we talked low enough, they couldn't hear us. If one walked near us while we were talking, we'd just change the subject. Billy also cupped his hand over his mouth in case somebody watching the security cameras could read lips.

When the guard was out of hearing range, Billy told me he found out the businessman had just bought airtime on the local TV stations to advertise his business. Billy also heard the guy made some wise investments buying Home Depot stock.

"This guy is screwing me out of money," he said.

Then Billy sent me on a mission. He ordered me to accompany The Queen to the gambler's office. "Once he sees you, he'll know we mean business." He didn't need to say any more. This was routine for us.

A few days after we got back to Baltimore, The Queen and I went to the businessman's office unannounced and told the secretary we had an appointment. She asked our names. The Queen gave hers, but I said I was just a friend. The secretary made us wait. After a while the owner came out and ushered us into his plush office.

As soon as he saw me, he knew why we had come. The Queen did all the talking at first. I didn't say a word. I just kept staring at him like I was going to rip his head off. His face was pale and he looked uncomfortable. The Queen was beating around the bush and I got impatient. I stood up, pointed my finger at him. I was blunt, arrogant and to the point.

"You owe Billy all this money and he wants it. He told me to do whatever I have to do to make you start paying it," I said. "I don't have time for this bullshit." I had to be at the Dundalk Marine Terminal to pick up some other money and I was late. The guy tried to explain that he was having hard times.

I said, "Don't jerk me off. If I want to get jerked off, I'll call Mousy the pimp and get one of his girls to jerk me off." The Queen's mouth almost dropped to her knees. After all, she had gone to Catholic school. I then told him that Billy was strongly advising him to sell his stocks that he just made a ton of money on. The guy looked totally surprised that we knew about the stocks. I told him not to make me come back and do something that I didn't want to do.

I actually liked the guy, but this was business. Sometime later, he paid us all the money he owed. He lost his business, sold his house and moved to Philadelphia.

Love, Divorce, and Marriage

While business boomed for me, my personal life was starting to bottom out. I was rarely home to see my son and totally unfaithful to my wife. It didn't help matters that she believed I was involved in a murder.

Melonie was a good girl and she put up with my shit for nine years until she filed for divorce in the summer of 1982. She just couldn't take it anymore. I knew I was at fault, but I couldn't stand the rejection. Even after we separated, I couldn't bare the thought of any other guy going with her. I made life impossible for her. I would stop by the house almost every day to check on her. Once I kicked in a guy's door when I heard he was dating her. Finally she met a man who wasn't from Hampden. He was from India and seemed like a nice guy. I went over there one day and shook his hand. "I don't want anything bad to happen to Melonie," I told him.

In 1982 something bad did happen to Melonie, something I never expected in a million years. It was the first week in November and Charlie Jr. was six years old. Melonie was twenty-five. I was living in an East Baltimore neighborhood called Greektown, where I already had shacked up with another girl. But I was still checking on Melonie and Charlie Jr. every few days.

It was a Saturday night and I was back up in Hampden making my weekly stops to collect on loans, bookmaking and drugs. I parked my car and started to walk down the street. I saw Melonie sitting on the stoop of her parents' house. I knew instantly that something was wrong. Her face was drawn. She was either sick, or someone had hit her, I thought. I started to panic. "What's wrong?" I asked.

When she answered me, her speech wasn't right. But I could understand what she said. On Halloween night she had a mild stroke, she said. Her father had taken her to Johns Hopkins Hospital, but she still needed to go back for more tests. At first they thought it was caused by high blood pressure. I could hardly believe what she was telling me. Charlie Jr. was too young to understand what was going on. A month later she was diagnosed with lupus, the disease they call the "lone wolf." It was destroying the organs in her body. The medication made her sick and screwed up her head. She was on Tylox and high doses of prednisone. She was so doped up she couldn't talk. She would grab our little son's face with her hand and squeeze it as if she were trying to tell him something, but she couldn't get the words out.

She also had an ulcer that burst. The wound must have been two inches deep and five inches wide. It had to be packed three times a day, but it never healed. Melonie was sick for nine months. I spent hours almost every day at her parents' house and in the hospital sitting by her side, only going home to get fresh clothes. I was a better husband to her then, than when we were married. I even tried to win her back. But as she lay dying, she said, "I don't want your pity."

Finally she couldn't take it anymore. She had lost all her hair and was bleeding everywhere inside her body—even from her eyes. On October 9, 1983, Melonie passed away. I know she also died of a broken heart, and it was all my fault.

But I did keep one promise to her—that I would never take Charlie Jr. away from his grandparents. I promised to bring him up in Hampden to be close to her parents.

I kept my promise for twelve years—until the day FBI agents came in unmarked cars. They drew their guns outside my house long enough to keep me covered so I could run inside, grab some clothes and hustle out of town. Charlie Jr. was grown up by then and had his own family. He chose to stay behind, even though I pleaded with him to move with me. It wasn't the safest place to live for the son of a wanted man.

But even in those earlier years when I was living high and could have moved almost anywhere with the money I made, there was another reason I stayed in Hampden: I wanted to stay near Billy. Our partnership was crucial to our enterprises.

I reacted to Melonie's death by throwing myself into my work. For a normal person that might have been a healthy response. Of course, in my case, it was a dangerous one. I knew I was on the road to destruction, and I didn't give a damn.

I also became involved with several women at once, not really having deep feelings for any of them. I had a son named Jason by one of the women, who I had started seeing even before Melonie died. He was born two months after her death. Melonie's parents were also setting me up with dates. I was seeing so many women that I was dishing out money for abortions almost every month. I had made such a big investment in one particular abortion clinic that I thought I should be made part owner. Billy finally convinced me that the women were just shaking me down for money.

The first spring after Melonie's death I started to notice a young woman I had watched grow up in Hampden. She was nineteen, already married and had a young daughter. I remember seeing her around the neighborhood when she was a young teenager and thinking that she was going to grow into a fantastic-looking woman. Her name was Gina.

Though I had seen her for years, there was something about her that spring that caught my eye. Maybe it was her innocence. She wasn't like all the other women I dated who always were going nightclubbing. I started putting out feelers to find out what I could about her and her husband, who was away in the navy. I'd be standing on a street corner and see her drive down the street. I'd catch her eye, then put my hand over my heart and move it like my heart was pounding right through my shirt. When she saw me, Gina would just smile and keep driving. Billy and the other guys would say, "Leave the girl alone. She's young and innocent. You'll just make her into another victim."

One day I was standing in front of my in-laws' house and Gina drove up the street. When she saw me pounding my hand over my heart, she stopped the car and motioned for me to come over to the window. For the first time in my life, I was speechless with a woman. I sent over a guy from the neighborhood named Joey to see what she wanted.

"Why is he always pounding his hand over his heart?" she asked. Joey, not one of the smartest guys in Hampden, told her he wasn't sure, but he thought I liked her. "You'd have to ask Charlie," he said. So Gina told Joey to get me to come over to her car. I was surprised how nervous I was. I hesitated at first, but Joey said, "You have to be a fool if you don't go over to that car."

When I finally got to her car, she asked the question again. "Why do you always make that pounding motion every time I drive past you?"

"Because I love you," I said. Without hesitation Gina shot back, "I am married and have a daughter and I don't fool around on my husband." I ignored her comment and tried to get a date. No luck. She just drove away.

After she was gone, I started plotting to see her again. When I wasn't working the streets or going out with other girls, I somehow found time to spy on Gina. I discovered that she often visited a friend down the street from Melonie's parents. I would show up and work my way casually down the block, talking to all the neighbors on the way. This was easy, since it was a street of little row-houses, with everybody living close together. Then I finally got up the courage to talk to her. I told her there was no way her husband was being faithful to her when he was overseas for six months at a time. "He's probably been in whorehouses at every port of call," I said. She got mad at me and was really upset. Just as I was striking out, I got lucky. Gina's husband had sent a letter bragging to a friend about visiting a whorehouse while overseas. Gina eventually got her hands on the letter. The next time I saw her she looked upset and withdrawn. I finally convinced her to go out and get a bite to eat with me.

I took her to a very inexpensive steak house. I didn't want to scare her with some high-priced place. She had already told me she heard Billy and I and all our friends were rich gangsters. I denied it. "I just work for the city housing department," I said. At least that part was true.

She finally agreed to start seeing me. I didn't care if it was only to get even with her husband. I respected her in a way I didn't respect the other girls I went out with. Finally our relationship began to blossom—until it was time for her husband to come home. She had told me all along that she wanted to make a go of it with her husband, to come clean about our affair and to ask him to come clean with his. About a week before he was due home, Gina told me she couldn't see me anymore. I acted like I didn't care, but deep down I was crushed. I think Gina was in love with me, too, but she was stuck between a rock and a hard place. Billy knew I was devastated. He said, "She is the best thing that ever happened to you since Melonie."

I started going with another girl who was studying law. Once night Gina drove by my house just as the girl and I were leaving my house to go to an after-hours club I operated with Billy. Later that night Billy and I had a torch job on a car to make a quick $500 each. But instead, we drove around looking for Gina in Billy's canary yellow Lincoln. I couldn't focus on anything but Gina. We finally caught up to her at the Royal Farm Store on Keswick Road. I got out of Billy's car and jumped into the passenger seat of Gina's car. She thought I was a stranger who had come to rob her. When she realized it was me, she punched me in the face not once, but twice. I can still hear Billy bellowing out his car window. "Hit the son of a bitch again, Gina."

I finally got her to calm down and stop punching me. Then she threw me out of the car. I guess you can say we were both more than a little confused. She was family oriented and wanted to make her marriage work. She even went to church on Sundays. It was easier for me. I just told her I would take care of her and her baby. After Gina kicked me out of her car, Billy and I headed out to Cockeysville in the suburbs and did our torch job.

Gina apologized a few days later for punching me. She said she wouldn't be seeing me again and that she was headed down to Norfolk to meet her husband's ship when it came in. I told her I loved her and that I'd still be here if she ever changed her mind. Not long after that, I heard that Gina confessed to her husband about our affair. Her husband didn't take the news very well and had even shoved her during an argument.

The Saturday night after I heard the news, I was in Showalters bar in Hampden. A few other wiseguys were there waiting for shit to happen. In walked Gina's stepfather, Bill. He loved Gina as if she were his biological child. Bill had a reputation as a fighter, so I expected he and I might get into a good fight that night. But I was really waiting for Gina's husband to show up and confront me. I had my speech already worked out. I'd tell him that I would step aside out of respect for Gina if that's what she truly wanted. But if he got all ignorant with me, I had every intention of knocking the sailor out. While we waited, her father asked me, "What are your intentions?"

I told him, "I would provide for her, love her and take care of her and her daughter." Gina's dad knew I was sincere, so we waited together for her husband to show. But he never did. Within a few weeks Gina and I were picking out furniture for our new house.

Chapter 5

Busted

In the spring of 1986 I was relaxing with a neighbor in his yard, across the alley from my house. His name was Bubby and he was Melonie's uncle. Bubby was also an honest city cop who always suspected I was up to no good, but I never talked to him about my scams.

It was late afternoon as we sat at his picnic table smoking cigarettes and shooting the breeze. Two strangers drove up in an older model red car and parked it in front of my house. One guy looked like a biker and the other, a heavyset guy, looked like Joe College. When one of them opened the gate to my yard, I stood up and took notice.

"I wonder who they are," I said.

"They look like cops to me," said Bubby.

"No way, Bubby. They're probably selling something," I said.

"They don't look like salesmen to me. I'm telling you, Charlie, they're cops," said Bubby. "If you're so sure they're salesmen, why don't you go over and see what they're selling."

"Hell no, then they'll try to get me to buy whatever they're selling. And if they are cops, I sure don't want to go over in case they want to lock me up," I said.

We carefully watched them from Bubby's yard, as if we were examining them through a magnifying glass. The heavyset guy knocked on my door a couple of times. After getting no answer, he wedged a little card in the door. By now I was crouching down at Bubby's picnic table, thinking maybe he was right. Maybe they were cops. As soon as they drove away, I ran over to my front door to get the card. It read, BALTIMORE COUNTY DETECTIVE JOE HERRING. On the back was a note: "Charlie, it is important that you give me a call."

I ran back over to Bubby's yard and showed him the card.

"I told you they were cops," he said. "What kind of trouble are you into now?" he asked.

"I'm not into nothing," I said.

"Then if you didn't do anything wrong, why don't you call the detectives in about an hour." I said I would, but of course I had no intention of calling them. And I wasn't about to tell Bubby the truth. He was a friend, but he also was an honest cop.

I already knew why the detectives were looking for me. I had heard that an old wiseguy named Dorsey Calp had been busted for bringing seventeen pounds of 90 percent pure cocaine up from Florida. He got caught coming through Baltimore's Harbor Tunnel on Interstate 895. Police found the dope stashed in the tire well of his Chevy Malibu.

I'd known Dorsey since I was about sixteen. He was sixty-one now, one of the older wiseguys I'd met when I worked in the building trades. Dorsey was busted along with another old wiseguy named Roy Calhoun. Roy was fifty-five and, like Dorsey, had been in and out of prison most of his life. He had taken me under his wing when I was a teenager. Since their arrests both wiseguys had jumped bail and the cops were looking for them. I had actually met up with Dorsey at a bar in Hampden after he skipped bail and gave him $3,500. He also got a false driver's license by borrowing someone else's Social Security number and address, putting on a toupee and telling the Motor Vehicle Department that he lost his original license.

I figured the detectives may have seen me with Dorsey and Roy before they were arrested and thought I knew something about the drug ring. Maybe the detectives hoped I'd slip up in an interview so they could tie up some loose ends in the investigation. I was pretty cocky at that point in my life. I was thirty and still believed I was invincible. I was sure I had been careful enough to cover my ass.

When Gina came home, I showed her the detective's card. I laughed about it to show her I wasn't afraid. I tossed the card on top of the refrigerator and tried to forget about it.

"If they had anything on me, they would have locked me up by now," I told her. But I could see in Gina's face that she was beginning to worry.

"Don't worry, they won't be back," I told her.

Then I heard someone shouting my name through the front door. It was a drug dealer friend of mine named Chick. He had found the same little card from Detective Joe Herring in his door, with the same little message to call him. He asked me what I thought of it and I said it was bullshit and not to worry about it. But I knew Chick had something to worry about. He had been going around acting like Scarface. He had everybody and their brother selling the shit for him, including a few neighborhood teens. I was probably grossing $7,000 a week from cocaine, but I can tell you Chick was probably making $20,000.

The next day when I came home from my job with the city housing department, Gina told me the detectives had returned. They told her I should call them before it was too late. They had also been to Chick's house. I told Chick they didn't have anything on us and they were just fishing. But I did say we should go to our lawyer, Donald Daneman, and get him to find out what was going on. Chick and I went downtown to Mr. Daneman's office and told him about the detective's visits. He called Detective Herring and made an appointment for us to talk to him at the Garrison Precinct in Northwest Baltimore County. I thought it was a stupid idea, but I decided to go along with my attorney's advice. Mr. Daneman said we were just going out to meet with the cops and tell them that if they had anything on the two of us, they should just show us. If they didn't have anything on us, he would make sure they didn't bother us again. About a week later we headed out to the suburbs for our meeting with the detective. I hoped everything would be cleared up, but it didn't turn out that way. The detectives didn't mess around. They said they had evidence that Chick and I were part of a drug conspiracy with Roy and Dorsey. The only way we could help ourselves was to cooperate. There was no way in hell I was going to be a snitch. And even if I was, it would be too risky. They might link me to the murder and start asking too many questions. Again I acted stupid and said, "I don't know about nothing." And that was it for me. The detectives then said, "Well, then, Charlie. You will be indicted before summer."

"Do what you have to do," I said. Then I stormed out of the room.

I left Mr. Daneman in the room with Chick and the detectives, but I could hear what was going on. Chick was getting all belligerent and started cursing at the cops. The next thing I know, Chick and Mr. Daneman are coming out of the room and Chick is still yelling "fuck you" to the detectives. Mr. Daneman thought I should calm Chick down, but I thought it was funny. Our lawyer told us we'd just have to wait now to see what moves the police were going to make next. I was still sure they didn't have anything on me, so I wasn't worried at all. But, of course, I was wrong. Not long after that, I heard through the wiseguy grapevine that I would be indicted in a couple of days. Even though the indictments are sealed when a grand jury hands them down, we always knew someone who could find out when they were coming down.

In early June 1986, I explained to Gina and to Melonie's mother that I would most likely be locked up in a day or two. Melonie's mom was really upset. She begged me to stay at her house so I wouldn't get arrested. I guess she thought I could just hide out in her house forever. Gina was also worried that my bail would be so high I would never get out before a trial, but I knew my bail wouldn't be high. It would be my first arrest on drug charges and my first felony arrest. I had been really lucky and I guess a little smarter than most of the guys.

They were always being locked up and doing time for something stupid like stealing horseshit, and I'm not using slang. I really did know two guys who got caught stealing horseshit. One of them, a guy named Ray, wanted to find some fertilizer for his mother's garden. He was in his thirties and still living with his mom. One day he'd promised to get her fertilizer, but it was about 3:00 A.M.— just after the bars closed—when he decided to go looking for it. He had his pockets full of hundred-dollar bills when he and a buddy named Jimmy grabbed a couple of shovels and drove up Falls Road out to the horse country north of the city.

Billy and I were invited to come along, but we decided to get some breakfast at the Sip & Bite Restaurant in Fells Point, instead. The next day we heard on the street that police caught them red-handed on somebody's horse farm shoveling manure into the trunk of Ray's Coupe DeVille Cadillac. When Ray went to court, the judge found he'd violated his probation from a previous charge and slapped him with five years for stealing the horseshit.

With wiseguys, we were always trying to get something for nothing, even if our pockets were filled with wads of hundreds. We also loved the thrill of getting away with something. Ray wasn't the only stupid one in the gang, though. Another time a bunch of wiseguys got hold of a stolen money order stamp with a three-inch pile of money orders. Instead of cashing them with fake ID the idiots used their own ID, and got caught, of course.

With all the crimes I'd committed, I always made sure that I covered my ass. And my rule of thumb was to keep my mouth shut about anything I did illegally—which just about covered most of my waking hours, except my work for the Baltimore housing department.

Instead of trying to hide from the indictment, I decided to stay home. I guess a part of me hoped that the word on the streets was bullshit. But, of course, it wasn't.

Snared

They came for me on June 11, 1986. It was around 5:50 A.M. As I lay in bed, I woke to the sound of a convoy of vehicles driving into my tiny street. I jumped out of bed and peeked out the window through the blind. There, just below my bedroom window, were a dozen unmarked police cars and a police cruiser. Gina was in a dead sleep when I woke her up.

"They're here" is all I had to say. She jumped out of bed and ran to her daughter's room. Her daughter, Mandy—who by then I considered my own daughter—was four years old. Charlie Jr. was staying at his grandparents' house. I took another glimpse out the blinds. I saw what looked like a platoon of detectives, with guns drawn, running toward my house and around to the back through the small alley. One detective already had jumped the fence.

"Don't break the door. I'll be right down," I yelled out the window. In the years I'd picked up carpentry skills, I knew that if police broke down the door, they'd probably destroy it, along with the jamb. Replacing it would cost me time and money. I rushed downstairs and opened the front door. There stood a half-dozen detectives and one uniformed cop. I recognized only one of the detectives. He had locked up some of my friends before.

"Charlie, I guess you know why we're here," he said.

I acted like I was stupid. "No, why?" I asked.

"There's been an indictment handed down for you by the Baltimore County Grand Jury. We have a warrant for your arrest," he said. By now, detectives were coming through my back door from the alley and within a few minutes my house was loaded with them. They had their guns all over me, including the lead detective who had a shotgun.

"Look, there's a small child in the house. She's upstairs with my girlfriend," I said. "They're in the bedroom and they're scared to death." I admit I was finally getting worried, too. This was my first indictment. And even though the indictment was for drug dealing, there still could have been other charges they weren't telling me about. If they wanted to, they could have put me away for life on just a few of the illegal scams I had going.

The detectives marched me up the stairs with a couple of cops ahead of me and a couple behind me. As we got to the top of the stairs, I could see Gina and Mandy were crying. Some of the detectives took them downstairs, while the others took me into the bedroom. I was only wearing pajama bottoms, so they let me get dressed. I had to point into the closet; then they handed me my clothes and watched me get dressed. They marched me back down the stairs and read me my Miranda rights, handcuffed me and placed me under arrest. I took it all in stride as I walked passed Gina and Mandy.

Since it was June, the neighbors had their windows open that morning. That meant they'd heard all the commotion and were now watching as I was led away. I wasn't embarrassed for myself. I knew this was the price of doing business as a wiseguy, but I was embarrassed for Gina. She was a good woman and had never been through anything like this before.

The detectives put me in the back of an unmarked car. I thought they were taking me to the city's Northern District police station, which was only two blocks up the street. I figured the county police would come down from the suburbs to get me, but they had something else in store for me.

"We have a special command post in Baltimore County just for you and your buddies," one cop said. "But if you want to help yourself out, you could talk to us," he added.

I just acted ignorant, but I started to worry. I had never heard of a special command post being set up for an arrest like this. A drug charge was bad enough, I thought, but what if they bring up the murder? After all, I was being arrested by the Baltimore County police in the same jurisdiction where the murder had occurred eight years before. Now that I thought about it, I actually was more worried about the murder than I was about the drug charges. No matter what they charged me with, I decided I wasn't going to talk. I would just act stupid. I also worried about bail. What if they set it at some ridiculous price? I quickly thought of all the people I knew who could put their houses up for me to make bail. I also worried about my legitimate job with the city's housing department. I might lose it. And it was a gravy job with little work. I barely had to show up. I hoped the media wouldn't get hold of the story.

I began to wonder how I'd gotten caught. I always covered my ass, I thought. I only had a couple of truly good friends who were selling cocaine for me, so I couldn't imagine one of them had snitched. I never sold just to anyone. And I was only selling about three or four ounces of coke a week. I never used my telephone, except once or twice using code words. The rest of the time I used pay phones to make the deal and get the drugs.

It was ironic, I thought, that I was being busted along with my wiseguy friends for cocaine dealing. If you talk to a wiseguy, he'll put down anybody who sells the stuff. But when it's available, the wiseguys will be the first ones to put up the money for it, as long as they don't have to touch the stuff. They'll deny ever using it, selling it or being around it. That's just the way it's always been.

When we got to the command post, I realized we were at the Baltimore County Police Academy, then located in a former school building in Dundalk, about three miles from where I grew up in North Point Village. I remembered playing baseball here before it was converted into the police academy. Some homecoming—in handcuffs! I realized how serious this was when I saw the TV cameras already set up outside as the guys were being brought in one at a time in unmarked police cars. Security was really tight. As we approached, I saw a helicopter flying over the academy. Uniformed police officers surrounded the areas so no media could get close to us. I had been locked up before for minor charges, once for assault and once for disorderly conduct when I was younger. I had never seen anything like this, however; it was right out of a movie.

The police took me into the gymnasium. There I saw what looked like a human assembly line. Men having their handcuffs unlocked, then being escorted by detectives from one table to another, where there were stacks of booklets being handed to them. I didn't recognize one face in the entire gym. I later learned that several of my friends had gone into hiding and wouldn't be arrested until later that day—or a few days later. There must have been a hundred uniformed police, detectives and prosecutors and more than a dozen people like me. The detectives who brought me then took me from table to table to pick up copies of the indictment and booklets full of wiretap transcripts, which my lawyer would need.

Next, they said, I would be told my bail and we'd be through for the morning. They took off my handcuffs. When I reached the bail table, I was told there was no bail set for me. I was about to shit myself. I thought they meant I would be held without bail, like somebody charged with first-degree murder. No, they said, there's no bail because you're being released on your own recognizance. I couldn't believe it. All this security and now they were letting me go home! I wanted to get out of there as fast as possible. I picked up my booklets of wiretap transcripts— I swear they weighed about forty pounds. I was so happy I was ready to ditch the papers and walk home. But then I learned a police car was already waiting to take me home. It was too good to be true. A uniformed police officer chauffeured me back to Hampden. The only thing he asked me on the way home was for the directions to my house. I arrived back home less than four hours after my arrest. When my chauffeur dropped me off, he said, "Good luck."

Before I shut the door to the cruiser, I turned to the cop. "I want you to go back and tell all the rest of the people down at the academy in Baltimore County that they have the nicest police department I've ever been through."

I was being polite, but I was also being sarcastic. Not only had they let a drug dealer walk free without bail, but they had just lost the key to an unsolved murder in their own backyard. Boy, was I relieved.

Within a few hours the drug bust was on the front page of the *Evening Sun*. The article said they had warrants to arrest thirty-two people. A county police spokesman said the arrests came after a seventeen-month investigation and that our drug ring had been importing six to ten kilos of cocaine each month from Florida. The cocaine had an annual street value of $18 to $20 million.

My name did not appear in the news until the next day, when the *Baltimore Sun* began its article by saying that those arrested included "a housewife, a teen-age clerk at a 7-Eleven store, a plumber and a city bureaucrat." And there I was at the very bottom of the article as one of the people being charged with cocaine distribution: "A city housing department foreman, Charles Henry Wilhelm, 30, of Bay Street."

After the county cop dropped me off, Gina was surprised to see me come through the door. She ran and gave me a hug, but she looked worried and scared.

"Charlie, you're going to prison," she said. I tried to calm her down. "If I was going to prison, they would have set some sort of bail for me," I said. "I'll probably end up with probation for a year or two with some sort of fine." Gina was young and naive in those days. And, of course, I took advantage of her by lying about my drug dealing. I told her I wasn't actually selling the cocaine. I was just putting up the money so my friends could buy it. And I told her that loaning the money to my friends wasn't breaking the law.

Once I was released, I wasn't too worried about the charges, but I was worried about losing my city job. It certainly wasn't because of the money. I only made about $18,000 a year. I could make that money on the side in just a few weeks if I really hustled. The city job, however, came with health benefits for my son, and the job was a great cover for my illegal activities.

As soon as I got in the house, I called my city supervisor, who worked in a different location from me. I lied like I'd done many times before and reported that I was at work. Then I called Billy. He already knew about my indictment and arrest and was hoping he wouldn't get caught, too. Twenty minutes later he was at my door. We started going over the hundreds of pages of wiretap transcripts I'd brought back from the police academy. Even though Billy had trouble reading, he was able to look for his name and my name. After a few hours of searching for my name, we only saw one or two phone conversations with me talking, but I wasn't saying anything directly about drugs. And none of the wiretapped conversations came from the house. I always used pay phones. But it appeared I'd slipped up once, calling Roy's home phone when it was tapped. Still, I never talked about drugs. We used a code. I'd call Roy's house several times a day when I knew he wasn't home. I'd leave messages with his mother, who was in her seventies. Every call stood for one ounce of cocaine I needed. When Roy got home, I'd call again and he'd say, "My mom said you called three times today." I'd say, "Yeah, that's right." It meant I needed three ounces of coke. His poor old mother had no clue what was going on.

Billy was relieved not to find his name anywhere in the transcripts, but I wasn't so lucky. In addition to the call to Roy's house, there was another document in which detectives said they had followed Roy and me to a restaurant on St. Paul Street, where they watched Roy and me exchange a bag. They said it was filled with cocaine.

To be honest, Roy and I had a pretty good deal going. I paid $1,100 an ounce for nearly pure cocaine. That was a good price in those days. I would whack it, or dilute it, with seven grams of a cutting agent. I had my guys selling only quarter grams for $25 each. I made $3,500 from each ounce. I gave my guys around $700 an ounce for selling it.

Billy was still worried. He brought up the murder. I could tell he was afraid some cop would squeeze the truth out of me.

"Don't insult me," I said. "If I was going to rat on you, I would have done it years ago. Look, Billy, you are my family. We've done a lot of nasty, dirty things together. We both should be in prison for a long time," I said.

"Just because I'm the one who got caught doesn't mean I'd bring you or anybody else down just so I can walk," I told him. And I really meant it.

"I know that, Charlie," he said. "I just want you to know where I'm coming from. "But to be on the safe side, I think we should stop being seen together for a while."

I felt a chill. I didn't like that. Here he was, acting like I was too hot to be around, when he was the one who committed murder—not me. But I let it go without saying anything. We agreed just to call each other every day, but go out in public together only once a week. He tried to make me feel better by promising to help Gina and the kids with money if I went to prison. That made me feel good. And it eased Gina's mind.

Billy and I then headed down to Mr. Daneman's office with the transcripts. We showed him only the pages mentioning me. The lawyer said I didn't have a thing to worry about if that's all the police had on me. Then Mr. Daneman said that Chick got hit with a large bail and was still in jail. He apparently hadn't been too careful. He had sold cocaine himself, without using "bumpers," or other people to sell the stuff for him, on the street. Even worse, he went to a party and sold an ounce to a federal Drug Enforcement Agent—not once, but twice.

After my arrest I was still working for the city, but I was transferred downtown, where I had to show up every day in one of the main offices so the supervisors could see me. The city bureaucrats, of course, had heard the news about my arrest and this was my punishment. If I was acquitted, I could keep my job, but if I was convicted, I would be fired. I was crushed. I really liked that job and I liked the people I worked with. It sure would help when I went to trial to show a judge and jury that I was a single, working father. It would show I had some stability in my life.

A few months later my lawyer asked a judge to throw out the wiretaps as evidence. Of course, that didn't work. Before the end of the year my trial was about to begin.Mr. Daneman told me he was still pretty sure he could get me off, but if I did get convicted, the most I'd get was a year or two of supervised probation.

Billy let me know that there was no way he'd show up for my trial. He didn't want to be seen associating with me. My father had died the year before of a heart attack at age fifty-seven. My mother wouldn't be coming, either. She was living with her sister and had been in bad health since she had open-heart surgery in 1975. The operation left her paralyzed on her left side with lots of other complications that included mental problems, which put her in a psychiatric ward a few times. I tried to hide my arrest and trial from her, but of course she knew. She blamed Billy for my being arrested and said he was nothing but trouble. I'm not sure why she blamed him, because he always treated my parents with complete respect and I did the same with his parents. I told her, "It's not Billy's fault. It's my own damn fault."

I also couldn't get my brother, Johnny, or my sister, Betty, to come to court with me. They both were leading straight lives and Betty in particular was very straitlaced. I asked her to be a character witness for me, but she said, "I'm not lying for you."

"All you have to do is tell the judge I'm not that bad a guy," I said. But Betty knew I was guilty and would never in a million years lie for me or anyone else. She even said that if she was asked questions in court about all the trouble I'd been in over the years—but never got caught for—she would tell the truth.

So, my support group in the courtroom quickly dwindled down to Gina and Melonie's parents. My trial lasted only a few days. I stood before a jury and Judge William J. Hinkel, one of the county's toughest judges. Mr. Daneman said he tried to get the case changed to a more lenient judge, but that didn't work. The prosecutors were well known for winning drug cases. The charges I faced—two felonies and two misdemeanors—carried a maximum sentence of eighty-eight years.

Trial By Jury

It didn't look good for me from day one. First the prosecutors brought in all the coke they found in Dorsey's car, wrapped in brown paper, and introduced it at my trial. Then they told the jury they'd broken the code that Roy and I used to communicate with over the phone. To top it off, President Reagan got on television the night before my trial and declared a war on drugs. I didn't feel so cocky anymore. So on the advice of my attorney, I did not testify on my own behalf. Juries are always suspicious when you don't testify at your own trial—even though the judge tells them that they can't hold it against you. But, of course, they do. I'm sure they wanted me to look them in the eyes and say, "I never sold drugs." I knew my silence would make them suspect I had something to hide. And, of course, I had plenty to hide.

When both sides rested their cases, the jury deliberated for all of forty minutes before they found me guilty of cocaine possession. Judge Hinkel set my bail at $25,000 and a sentencing date for February 25, 1987, which was Gina's birthday. Melonie's parents put up their house to bail me out until sentencing. Once the judge set bail, I knew I was in real trouble and might have to do jail time. I just hoped it wouldn't be ten or twenty years.

I went back home and went to my city job every day. I tried to stop all my criminal activities, though I still kept a small numbers book. As far as shylocking went, I laid low. I didn't even go with Billy to pick up money. I figured the juice I was owed was lost. I didn't want to take the chance of somebody picking up the phone and telling police I was shaking them down. I had about $10,000 or $15,000 stashed for a rainy day, but that wasn't a whole lot in my world.

I also had to worry about my son Charlie Jr. and what would happen to him if I went to prison. He was ten years old and I was his only parent, though Melonie's parents were helping me raise him. And I really loved Gina, but I knew there was no way I was going to ask her to wait for me if I got slammed with a long prison sentence.

Then there was Billy. I knew he was worrying that I might roll on him about the murder to get myself a lighter sentence. I thought whatever sentence I got, I'd never rat on anybody. Besides, if I was going to rat, I'd have to get another lawyer. Mr. Daneman was also Billy's lawyer and the only reason I kept him as my attorney was to prove my loyalty to Billy.

I tried to prepare Charlie Jr. in case I got a long prison sentence. He kept blaming the police for my arrest, but I never downed the cops in front of him. I told him the police just made a mistake. I also lied to him about selling drugs. I didn't want him to think it was all right to sell the shit, and I sure didn't want him following in my path when he got older. Even back then, I didn't want him to turn out like me, Billy and my other friends.

Mr. Daneman told me not to answer any incriminating questions when it came time to be interviewed by a presentence investigator. Just tell him to talk to your lawyer, he said. So when I sat down with the investigator, it didn't go very smoothly. The guy got frustrated because I wouldn't answer most of his questions, like whether I knew Roy or Dorsey. It was like I was giving him my name, rank and serial number. After about an hour the investigator was disgusted. "If you don't cooperate, I'm writing to the judge that I recommend you go to prison."

I just got arrogant back at him. "Screw you," I said. "I'm only doing what my attorney told me to do. You can write any goddamn thing you want; then you and the judge can both stick it up your asses." Then I walked out.

So, on February 25, 1986, someone got it stuck up his ass all right, but it wasn't the investigator and it wasn't the judge. The investigator actually recommended a lengthy probation for me. That was a surprise My sentencing guidelines, however, called for three to seven years in prison. As the judge started to hand out the sentence, he scared the shit out of me by saying he could give me ten years. But he knew I had a young son and that my ex–in-laws were helping to raise him. So he gave me eighteen months in the Baltimore County Detention Center rather than shipping me off to one of the state's prisons farther away. And he said he'd recommend work release if I qualified. At the sentencing Gina and Melonie's parents were devastated and were crying. As for me, I actually woke up for a few minutes and started to think about the consequences of my chosen profession. If this was the price of doing business, I guess I'd gotten off easy, especially considering all the crimes Billy and I had committed.

I had never been in prison for any length of time and I was facing the unknown, but I also knew half the inmates at the county jail. I knew I would be okay. I just had to worry about Charlie Jr., Gina and Melonie's parents, and how I was going to support them financially while I was away.

The Good Life

Within four hours I had exchanged my suit and over-coat for an orange prison jumpsuit and was locked in my pod at the Baltimore County Detention Center in Towson. The first night in jail was tough. It wasn't what I'd expected. In the bigger state prisons I'd heard you can move around, but here you were locked in a pod twenty-four hours a day. I'd heard wiseguys talk about how much fun they had in prison, but I didn't see any fun in sitting around doing nothing in an orange jumpsuit all day. I was thinking, *If this is fun, I would hate to see what a bad time is.* But I decided to try and make the best of the situation.

I got Gina to get hold of my boss at the city housing department. She convinced him to let me keep my job for just two more weeks, so I could qualify for work release. Then I went to find out if I knew any prisoners working in the kitchen. One of them was a guy named Buzzy who was doing time for selling PCP. Buzzy got me a job working in the kitchen, which meant I was out of my pod for twelve hours a day and eating like a king. What's more, Buzzy knew the guy who delivered the vegetables to the jail. He got the deliveryman to smuggle marijuana, cocaine or anything else we wanted.

It was easy to smuggle stuff into the jail. There was only one guard for about thirty prisoners. The guard was also the main cook. While he was busy making sure we were doing our assigned jobs so the food would get cooked on time, the truck driver was telling us what box to look into for the contraband. I swear it was easier than stealing horseshit!

My next move was to get my name on a list to be transferred over to the old jail just a few blocks away. This was a crumbling old building just a few blocks from the big county detention center. However, you could move around more easily than in the new detention center, where you were locked in a pod with thirty-five or forty inmates twenty-four hours a day. I wanted to get on work release so I could pretty much come and go as I pleased. I knew a guy whose brother was a guard, so I got the guard to tell the warden I'd be a good candidate for work release. In three days I was out of that tacky orange jumpsuit and back into regular clothes at the old jail. Now I was living on a tier with about 12 two-man cells; there was a TV in the center of the tier. It allowed me to move around and begin wheeling and dealing. There were about 150 prisoners and I swear I knew about 50 of them.

My first objective was to get on work release so I could spend my days outside. Before my two weeks with the city was up, I resigned before they could fire me officially. I know it sounds silly, but it really was a matter of dignity to me not to get fired. Still, with work release you had to show a paycheck to have proof that you were on a job; then the county would take half of your paycheck for room and board. Once you turned over your paycheck, you'd get a check back three days later with your room and board deducted. I called a friend of mine from the streets who had a small contracting company. He agreed to call the jail and tell them that I was working for him. He told them I made some ridiculous sum like $150 a week, so that I'd only have to pay the jail $75.

Sometimes I actually did work for the guy when he needed a hand. Most of the time, though, I hustled on the streets like before. Gina's dad would pick me up at the jail each morning at six o'clock. I'd go home and take a nap until 9:00 A.M. Then, I'd get into my Eldorado and start hustling. When I'd show up at one of my old haunts, the wiseguys couldn't believe that a convicted felon like me was being allowed to run the streets again. They thought it was hilarious. I was so sure of myself back then that I started selling coke again, maybe about an ounce a week. It was just enough to get me by financially and help Gina and Melonie's parents.

Billy and I met during the day and I could tell he still had his doubts about whether I was going to roll. He didn't say anything, but I knew him better than anyone and I could sense it. I also made sure I saw my son each day, which made him think jail must be easy, but I didn't want him to think that way. I wanted him to think jail was hard. I sure was a hypocrite, but I didn't want him growing up like me. Back in jail I had other hustles up my sleeve. I volunteered for trash detail. That way I could clean the warden's office after he left for the night. There on his desk I'd easily find the list of inmates who were being transferred from the other detention center. When I'd find a name I'd recognized, I'd ask the guards to have the guy placed on my tier.

It also helped to do favors for the guards now and then. I don't mean anything illegal, but if there was a loudmouthed prisoner the guards couldn't stand, I'd get my friends to shut him up. The guards loved that. The guards would then bend their rules for us. Though they stripsearched us every time we went in and out of jail for work release, to make sure we didn't have any drugs or weapons, they'd let us keep money. Sometimes I went back to jail with $5,000 in cash. That way we could play card games like jacks and seven-card-stud all night long, until it was time to go out on our "jobs." When they finally granted me weekend visits home, it got even better.

One time my lung collapsed. I told a guard I was having trouble breathing. Instead of calling an ambulance, the guard told *me* to call someone to take me to the hospital. I got Gina to pick me up in my Cadillac. She drove me to St. Joseph Hospital nearby. They didn't even bother to send a guard to follow us and make sure we were really going to the hospital. And I was there for seven days with no guards at the door! I even had a private room after my roommate died. I just had to call the jail to say I was still there.

Everybody came to visit me, including Billy. As soon as he got a look at me with the tube in my chest, he got a shit-eating grin on his face. "I'm so glad you're all right," he said. Then we looked one another dead in the eyes. I started to laugh. "You lying son of a bitch. You got here so fast, just to make sure I was dead," I said. I think a part of Billy was relieved I was okay, but he probably was thinking, *What would it hurt if maybe Charlie died.* He knew exactly what I meant. We were best friends and he wouldn't kill me because of what I knew about the murder. But if I died on my own, that would have been just fine with him. When I was released from the hospital, I went home for about eight hours before heading back to the jail.

In August I was paroled after spending six months in jail. I can't really say it was much of a punishment, though. Most of the time I had a ball, but now I had to find a real job because my parole officer would check up on me. So I went to work in the carpenters local working on the Jones Falls Expressway. Though I was given a paycheck, I don't remember doing any carpentry work. I spent most of my time on the job working as a wiseguy, lending money and doing book. And I still got my carpenter's check.

Billy and I were closer than ever. By going to jail and not rolling on him, I proved my loyalty. And as our friendship deepened, so did our partnership in crime. Our numbers racket and shylocking business was really booming. I was hurting more people than ever with no remorse whatsoever. As soon as I made money, I blew it by gambling or giving it away to friends. I also gave it to Gina and to Melonie's parents. One of our side businesses was torching cars for the thrill of it—and for the money of course. We were hired by an owner to burn a car so he could collect the insurance money. We figured it was an extra $500 for a half hour's work.

I also started a small contracting company, even though I couldn't get a license due to my felony conviction. And, of course, I thought nothing of paying off building inspectors to get good contracting jobs. Here's how I did it: Every Thursday at 8:30 A.M. the city would come out with a list of homeowners who got federal money to renovate their homes. Contractors would get the list, then go to the homeowners and place bids to do the work. The city would review the bids to make sure the contractors weren't trying to gouge the homeowner. Then the homeowner would select the lowest bid. No one could see the list before Thursday, except the inspectors—and me. I would grease an inspector's hand with about $500 to make sure I got the list early so I could bid on the best jobs first. I also got them to tell the homeowners to choose me as a contractor. Some of the inspectors would also tell me the bids of other contractors and I would make a lower bid and win the job.

With all the hustling, I stopped just long enough to get remarried. In October,1987 Gina and I tied the knot. It was a pretty nice affair and I got everything at a serious discount. I got the limos for free and the hall donated. I got a cut-rate price on the tuxedos and free booze from Showalters, the bar where I hung out with the other wiseguys. The band played for half its fee, though I had to pay for the church and the minister. Gina wore a white gown and a veil, which made her look even more innocent than when I first watched her driving through the neighborhood. I wore a white tux. Billy wore a black tux with a pink bow tie and a pink cummerbund—to match the bridesmaids' pink gowns and the pink carnations on the head table.

As my best man, Billy sat with us at the head table. I could tell something wasn't sitting right with him that day. Maybe he worried he was losing control of me to Gina. When it came time to make the toast, Billy picked up the microphone in one hand and lifted his champagne glass with the other. I expected him to make the kind of emotional toast you'd expect from a best friend, but he looked uncomfortable. When he wished Gina and me a happy life together, he just didn't have his heart in it.

Chapter 6

Second Thoughts

My mother died of congestive heart failure in 1988. Billy and I were pallbearers at the funeral. So were my brother, Johnny, and his friend Bruce Hall from our old neighborhood. While I was out robbing the world blind, Bruce had gone to college and had become an FBI agent and a forensic geologist. He could solve crimes by examining rocks and minerals for clues. Bruce worked out of the J. Edgar Hoover Building in Washington, DC; I scammed out of the alleys and sleazy bars of Baltimore. I found it mighty ironic: here we were at a funeral of cops and robbers!

On these family occasions when I'd see Bruce, I steered clear of him. I just didn't trust the guy. Even though he was my brother's best friend, he was still the FBI. I'm not sure how much he suspected about my enterprises. Every time he'd see me, though, he'd look me in the eye and say, "Charlie, if you ever need anybody to talk to, I'm always here."

It had been ten years since Mark Schwandtner was murdered. Nobody had been caught, but that didn't stop me from having nightmares. I didn't have them very often, but when I did, they were intense. All the dreams had a similar theme: I would get caught with Billy, John and Ronnie and we'd all get the same prison sentence. In these dreams I'd be sentenced for thirty or forty years in prison for a murder I didn't commit. And it wouldn't just be any prison. It would be the Maryland Penitentiary in downtown Baltimore, which is the most brutal prison in the state, with the most violent criminals.

After my mother's death, my brother and I stopped speaking to each other. Billy couldn't stand Johnny's friendship with Bruce and it would have caused too much friction in our partnership for me to be hanging around my brother. Billy used to call Johnny "that FBI snitch brother of yours." By 1990, with both parents dead, I had almost no contact with Johnny. My sister at least was civil to me, though she kept her distance and made it clear that she did not approve of my lifestyle. I told myself I didn't care. I had Gina and the kids. And I had Billy. He was my family.

I had a lot on my mind. Running an empire of scams was a pretty stressful life. I was rarely home to see my kids. I couldn't have told you what food they liked to eat back then. Even the birth of my third son, Justin, in 1988 didn't keep me home, though I made a little more time for him than I had for my other sons. I just loved coming home, going into Justin's room and watching him play.

My workdays would start early, if I wasn't up until four o'clock a.m. the night before. I'd head across town to Doughboy's, a bar tucked away on a grimy block of Clinton Street behind busy Pulaski Highway. From the outside, Doughboy's was nothing more than a tiny, windowless corner rowhouse across the street from an auto mechanic's garage. Without even a sign out front, it looked more like an abandoned building than a headquarters for organized crime, but opening the door was like going through a secret passage into another world. The walls of the next two rowhouses had been broken through, so the inside was actually a large hall. The place was a filter for everything that was going on in the underworld. Doughboy's got its name from its owner, a wiseguy and drug dealer named Ricky "Fat Ricky" Payne, who physically resembled the Pillsbury Doughboy.

By eleven in the morning, it would be buzzing with wiseguys and bookmakers. And I knew them all. Billy would arrive in his canary yellow Lincoln and we'd sit together while I ate my bacon, eggs and toast. We'd all be talking freely about drugs, guns and numbers. If a stranger happened to walk in, all talk would stop. The stranger would immediately know he'd come to the wrong place.

We came to Doughboy's, not only to make deals, but to keep up with the gossip about police raids and arrests. We knew if we let our guard down, we'd be in trouble. Some of our guys had direct connections to dirty cops who would tell them when there was "paper" out on the street. By "paper," we meant arrest or search warrants.

While the leaks from dirty cops were crucial for us to keep business going, we still had to worry about the good cops who were after us.

One of those honest detectives was a guy we actually respected. He worked in vice. His name was Detective Carroll Herold. On the streets we just called him Spanky. He was a legend among us wiseguys and bookmakers. He was a really sharp detective and I don't mean the way he dressed, because he sometimes didn't present himself much better than an auto mechanic. He was sharp because of the way he worked as an investigator. He was a heavyset guy with long gray hair and a beard. He reminded me of Peter Falk from the old *Columbo* TV show. He'd been tailing us and locking us up for years. Every wiseguy I know who'd gotten handcuffed by Spanky never said a bad word about him. They knew he was just doing his job.

Despite the nightmares and the stress from keeping ahead of the police, the thought of changing my life never entered my head. I still thought Billy and I were unstoppable.

The Slap

In 1990, however, something finally stopped Billy. He had slapped a convicted bookmaker called Sam "The Breadman" Merlo. The guy owed him more than $100,000 and wasn't paying his juice on time because he was gambling his money away at the racetrack. He was ducking Billy and that was a big mistake. Billy had gone out to a private club in Pikesville to get Sam's juice payments. But when he didn't come through, Billy slapped him in the face—in front of witnesses—making his face swell up and his ear ring.

Sam was a little middle-aged man who never had a violent bone in his body. Billy was in his late thirties and in really good shape. One of the witnesses called the FBI, and the next thing you know, Billy's been locked up for loan-sharking.

Sam was called before a federal grand jury to testify about the slap. Even though he was the victim, Sam was a most reluctant witness, to say the least. The grand jury transcripts show the guy stonewalling the prosecutors for hours. If you could ever believe the guy, he had completely lost his memory. Couldn't recall a single conversation he'd ever had with Billy. He drove the prosecutors crazy, refusing to answer their simplest questions about whether Billy threatened him if he testified.

Finally the government lawyers wore Sam down. He admitted that Billy had told him to "say the least you are supposed to say. . . . He wouldn't want me to say something that would do him tremendous harm." Sam also admitted that he'd borrowed more than $100,000 over the years from Billy and that Billy had offered to pay for Sam's lawyer. Sam insisted he did not fear Billy. They were old friends, he said. But finally he told the grand jury, "This man weighs two hundred pounds. If he wanted to do me bodily harm, he could kill me. It wouldn't even be a contest." So Billy was charged with witness tampering, along with loan-sharking.

I showed up for one day of the trial to prove my loyalty, even though Billy never came to my trial. When I got to federal court, the courtroom was packed with wiseguys proving their loyalty to him. I thought they were crazy. They were playing right into the FBI's hands. Here was a roomful of wiseguys for the government to look over so they could pick out who is who.

Naturally, Billy was convicted. While he waited to be sentenced, the judge released him on a $100,000 bond and placed him on electronic home monitoring for three months. It was the biggest favor a judge could do for a man in Billy's position. Now, instead of Billy traipsing all over town to collect on loans and bets, his wiseguys had to come to him. He stayed at his mother's house in Parkville, a working class suburb in Northeast Baltimore County. She had a big yard, big enough for Top 40 bands to entertain the wiseguys who visited.

The wiseguys paid homage to Billy by bringing steaks and crabmeat, which he packed into his mother's freezer. They also brought him prostitutes and other women, and he didn't pay for any of it himself. The guys even gave Billy a percentage of their take if they made a big score collecting on loans or bookmaking.

He was so cocky that he had an extra telephone line strung across the alley where he rented a garage. He turned it into a boxing gym so he could stay in shape.

The phone line was there just in case the home-monitoring people called.

The party came to a dead halt every afternoon when *Days of Our Lives* came on TV. Billy would kick everybody out of the house then and make them wait outside so he could watch his favorite soap opera alone. Even his mother would come outside with the rest of us. The guys would make fun of him, but Billy just laughed.

"What is wrong with all you guys?" he'd say. "You have no culture in your life and you are not domesticated."

Billy also had a thing for fortune-tellers. He would send out for gypsy ladies like other people send out for Chinese food. Some weeks he had his palm or cards read ten times. He was obsessed with seeing the future. He really believed in those phony fortune-tellers. He even made the other wiseguys have their fortunes told. They'd all be in the backyard at the picnic tables, having their palms read just to humor him.

One day a fortune-teller told Billy something bad was going to happen to him. "I already know," he told her. "I'm going to prison."

"No, this is something else that's going to happen to you in the future," said the gypsy. "Someone very close to you is going to hurt you."

I showed up at his house just after she left. "It's probably you," he said, laughing.

He was having a blast on home detention, but it didn't sit right with me. He got mad because I wasn't hanging out at his mother's house every waking minute like everybody else. I guess I hurt his feelings. One day he took off his home-monitoring ankle bracelet and drove over to my house. I said, "What ever happened to us not letting no one know our business? We're going to end up in prison for a long time." He said, "The guys are our business."

I loved Billy like a brother, but I didn't see the point

of bringing all the attention down on us by having everybody show up at his mother's for all the world to see, just when he was about to go off to federal prison.

Billy didn't get my logic. He was too busy playing the Godfather of Parkville. As his days of freedom got shorter, he began to hand off pieces of the business to different wiseguys. I was to run Joe's Tavern, a bar in Dundalk. I'd also take over bookmaking and loan-sharking accounts. He also told everybody if there were any problems, to report them to me or one of his girlfriends, the woman we called The Queen.

Billy would be gone for five years. While he was living in federal prisons in Texas, New York and Pennsylvania, he expected us to make regular visits to take orders from him. And he expected our enterprises to run smoothly. When he came out, he assumed everything would be the same as it was when he left. In our world, though, five years is a long time. Not much stays the same.

Scamming At Joe'S Tavern

Just before Billy left for federal prison in Texas in fall 1990, he bought a few bars for us to run, so this way he could launder his money while he was gone. Of course, he couldn't buy them legally, since he was a convicted felon. He just put the name of other people on the liquor license. Joe's Tavern was to be my responsibility. The liquor license showed the new owner was the mother of one of Billy's girlfriends. We paid $140,000 for the place, but for tax purposes the sale was reported as $40,000 so the seller could avoid paying taxes on the rest. Billy originally wanted me to run the bar with a man named Lew Benson. Lew was a Baltimore deputy sheriff who worked at the city courthouse, guarding courtrooms during criminal trials and escorting shackled defendants to and from the lockup. But I knew Lew as a bad guy in good-guy clothes. He was the only wiseguy I knew who got to wear a registered gun in public. I knew him as a loan shark who bragged about his friendship with Billy. He was also a well-known local boxer, which may explain why his nose looked like a head of cauliflower. For some reason, Billy changed his mind about Lew running Joe's Tavern and cut him out of the deal just before he left for prison. I was left to run the place with some other wiseguys, but that wasn't the last I'd see of Lew. We would one day cross paths in the most unlikely of places. And the sight of him—and his gun—would be just one of many heart-stopping moments in my life to come.

I first laid eyes on Joe's Tavern on December 6, 1990. It was located in a small, down-at-the-heels shopping center on Dundalk Avenue, just inside the city's east-side boundary. Behind it was a notorious public-housing complex called O'Donnell Heights. Driving by, the average person would think Joe's was a dive, but it turned out to be a gold mine.

That first morning I walked into Joe's, I looked up at the ceiling.

"What's this?" I asked the cleanup man. I pointed to about five bullet holes in the ceiling tiles.

"Police tried to shoot a couple of people over here and they had another shoot-out over there," he said, acting like the holes were just part of the decor.

Billy called that night from prison.

"How's it looking?" he asked.

"It's a winner here. We got a winner," I said. The place had a large bar, plus a lucrative package goods store where people could take out alcohol. It also had a Maryland Lottery machine, the perfect cover for bookmaking. If police ever questioned why we were talking numbers, we'd just tell them we were taking bets for the Maryland Lottery.

Joe's was also a big place, so I knew I could change the place around to bring in more money. Before long I was hiring live bands, such as Leapin' Larry and the Lizards, a country rock band, and charging an extra $2 a head at the door.

But that was just a warm-up. Sometimes I'd hire fifteen hookers and raffle them off to customers every fifteen minutes. I charged $25 for guys to get into Joe's, then sell them $5 raffle tickets. I'd have as many as two hundred guys in the place. I was making oodles of money. And to top that off, I was fixing the raffles so my friends would win the hookers. This would go on for three or four hours. The winners would get to go downstairs with the hookers. It was a regular whorehouse.

I was able to keep these enterprises going all night long, thanks to the liquor inspectors of Baltimore City. We'd pay them off with $500 to let us break liquor laws. Joe's was supposed to close at 2:00 A.M., but the bribes allowed us to keep open until 5:00 A.M. or even later. We also greased their palms by buying tickets to political fund-raisers for a couple of well-known senators. Sometimes we'd buy $1,000 worth of tickets for one fund-raiser. The liquor inspectors also served as our lookouts for the police. They would warn us when cops were on their way to raid the video poker machines. The police hoped to catch bar owners making illegal payouts to customers playing the poker machines, which are strictly for amusement, not gambling. The "pokers," as we called them, take quarters and bills like slot machines. You drop in your money, play the game, but no winnings come out. That's where we came in. From the bar we made illegal payouts to winners. It sure brought in a lot more business. In a busy eight-hour shift we'd pay out $1,000 in winnings, but take in as much as $5,000 or $6,000 in the pokers. Like many other bar owners in Baltimore, we were running a mini casino in a state where slot machine gambling was illegal. And with the liquor inspectors giving us advance notice of raids, it was an easy hustle to get away with. Bar owners could clean up their act and empty out the poker machines—so no money would be confiscated. By the time police showed up, we'd all be on our best behavior.

At Joe's I'd get a call from another wiseguy at his bar, telling me there was paper on the street for raids. I'd dump the machines and take all the cash out of the registers. I'd just leave $100 in each cash register so it wouldn't look so obvious. I'd throw all the cash in a bank bag and wrap it in a rubber band. Then I'd run out to the parking lot and throw it in the trunk of my Lincoln, which I was driving now instead of the Eldorado.

Behind the bar I also kept a list of pokers that paid out to gamblers. It showed how much I'd pay out each shift every day. I'd grab that list and hide that, too. The cops would show up and find nothing. Even if an undercover police officer had been hanging out in the bar and watching the payoffs, we'd have our lawyers get us off with probation and a small fine. But I'd still have my trunk full of money.

Though most of the bar owners and vending-machine owners got away with the scam, one company did get caught up in an eight-year court battle that ended in 1993. The company was nabbed by tax collectors for not paying taxes on the illegal payouts to gamblers. The company argued in court that the taxes on gross receipts from pokers should not include the money paid out to gamblers.

The company apparently hadn't paid taxes on the illegal "payouts" because the bartenders paying off the winners didn't work for the vending company. The case eventually was decided by the state's second-highest court—the court of special appeals. The court decided that the illegal cash payments must be included as part of the gross receipts for tax purposes. State tax collectors claimed the vending company owed $860,000 in back taxes over a twenty-seventh-month period for income from poker machines at fourteen locations. Multiply that by the hundreds of poker machines offering illegal payouts all over Baltimore. If tax collectors ever made a real crackdown, they could probably solve the city schools' money problems, or help an awful lot of drug addicts come clean.

Bar owners were also supposed to get licenses from the city for each poker machine, but we found a way around that law, too. When we heard the cops were on their way, we could quickly disguise an unlicensed poker machine. I'd call over to a vending-machine owner to grab some little metal licenses from legal machines and rush them over to Joe's. We'd tack them onto the unlicensed machines before the police came through the door.

We also managed to scam the state and the IRS out of tens of thousands of dollars in taxes. It was a lot easier than banking your money in offshore accounts. Since the poker machines were rarely monitored by the state, it was open season for us to skim thousands from the machines and rob the government. We were on an honor system with the Maryland comptroller's office to pay a percentage of our poker machine income as an amusement tax. It wasn't like anybody from the state ever checked the meters on the machines that showed how much money we took in. Even if they had, the meters were easy for us to manipulate.

The system also allowed us to rip off the IRS and the state on income taxes by lying about our income from the pokers and giving ourselves a discount. It was a fantastic system. It was like putting bank tellers on an honor system and never checking their accounts at the end of the week.

With half "empty" poker machines, we could save plenty on income taxes. When I ran Joe's Tavern, we skimmed every week. We grossed between $13,000 and

$16,000 each week and our net (after the illegal payouts to gamblers) was about $8,000 to $11,000. But we reported to the state that we netted $4,000 to $5,500 each week. Some weeks we didn't report anything. This went on year after year.

On the flip side we even found a way to manipulate empty poker machines for our benefit. If you're hustling drugs, shylocking or bookmaking, you need to find a way to show the government you earned the money legitimately. And there is no better way to spin bad money into good money than to buy some pokers and put them in the corner of a bar, restaurant or sub shop. You just keep them empty and tell the state you took in $10,000 or $20,000 in one week and pay taxes on that. Those little poker machines just washed that filthy money clean.

Joe's was a madhouse. Everybody was snorting cocaine, playing numbers and trying to win the jackpot on the poker machines. I started to notice one of the wiseguys working in the package goods store. He was taking an awful lot of orders for six-packs of beer over the phone. "Why the hell are we getting all these orders?" I asked him.

He said, "Guys are coming down here from Maryland Cup to pick up beer and cash their checks."

That was odd. Maryland Cup Corporation was almost an hour away. Finally I discovered that every time he took an order for a six-pack over the phone, it was a code for ordering 6 eight balls—or six quarter ounces of cocaine. My guy would put the six-pack in the bag, along with the coke. I laughed when he told me. I said, "You can't keep doing this, we're going to end up in prison." But I thought it was funny. You never knew what the guys were up to. It was crazy.

I also tried to keep up with collecting payments from loans Billy and I made, when I wasn't ordering beer and fighting off the thugs from the housing project who robbed people as they came out the door. I had to bust a few heads to get them to stop holding up my patrons. Once I even set a U.S. mailbox on fire, then called police to get the O'Donnell Heights guys busted for arson. Eventually they left my customers alone. We even developed some mutual respect when I paid their wives' gas and electric bills and gave some money to the school nearby.

Billy also had me keeping an eye on the Graceland Inn, another bar across the street that he controlled. And then I had to make sure the liquor board was under control. We had a lot of complaints about noise from neighbors and we were scheduled to appear at liquor board hearings. Luckily, our friendly liquor inspectors took care of the problem for us. We didn't even have to show up to plead our case.

I also had to be real friendly with the local police officers who patrolled the area and responded to complaints about Joe's. It's not very hard to co-opt a cop. First you offer him a free cup of coffee. When the weekend comes, you give him a free case of beer. At Christmastime you hand him $200 to buy something for his kids. When he's called in to respond to a complaint about noise or bar fights, he's real friendly about it.

Billy's Show

With all this going on, Billy was constantly calling me from prison to tell me how to run the business. First he pressured me to fire the barmaids who ran the place before we bought it. I said, "Billy, they're honest, dependable people." One barmaid, Miss Mary, had been there for eighteen years. I said, "If you bring in our own people, they'll rob the place."

He was also pressuring me to call in on loans that I considered uncollectible. There was one guy named Tommy. He owed us $8,000. His wife had left him with a three-year-old son. He was working as a maintenance man in a bank building. He had a mortgage to pay. I felt sorry for the guy, but Billy insisted I collect the entire $8,000. I said, "Where is the poor guy going to get the money?" It wasn't like Billy needed the dough.

I was also expected to visit Billy in prison once a month. At first I didn't have to go because convicted felons aren't allowed to visit federal prisoners. But when Billy got transferred from a prison in Texas to one in New York, he somehow fixed it so I got in. I didn't even have to fill out a visitor's form.

One morning I was ready to drive up to New York with a few other guys to visit Billy. We all had nice vehicles, so I figured one of us would drive. One of the guys named Jack came to my door. "Come on, let's go," he said. I looked out the door. There was a white stretch limo waiting to take us to visit Billy in federal prison.

"I'm not going," I said. "There's no way I'm driving up to federal prison in a limo. All we're going to do is shit in the federal government's face and we'll all go to jail."

When Billy called, I told him he wouldn't be seeing me that day. He said, "You son of a bitch." I hung up on him. We argued like that all the time. But it was the kind of arguing we always did—like we were brothers.

I started confiding in him that I thought Fat Ricky was stealing from Joe's. He was taking thousands of dollars in beer over to Doughboy's and dumping money out of the pokers for himself.

Billy called us up together for a visit.

I visited him in the newly built Allenwood Federal Prison in Pennsylvania. It had only been open for a few weeks and somehow Billy got himself transferred there. It was a strange meeting. We sat at a picnic table in the visiting area. Billy was making nice with Ricky, but yelling at me. He blamed me for failing to stop Ricky from stealing the beer and money. Of course, I had felt I couldn't do anything about the theft without approval from Billy. So I did nothing.

I said, "Wait a minute. I didn't rob nobody. Why are you yelling at me?" On the way home from Allenwood, Ricky said he couldn't believe that I got yelled at instead of him. "Billy should have been screaming at me," he said. Little did I know, it was all part of a plan Billy was hatching.

The Home Front

During these years I was home very little. Gina never wanted me to take over the bar. She said it would cause nothing but trouble because of my history of womanizing. She was right to distrust me, of course. I was wild enough without a bar to run as a cover for a whorehouse. But Gina started coming down to the bar with her friends and hanging out. Billy didn't like that. "I don't want her coming down that bar," he'd say. I wasn't sure why, but I sensed he never liked it when I was under Gina's thumb.

Gina and I argued every day. It got worse when she'd call down to the bar and find me gone. I might tell her I was taking a road trip. I wouldn't say where I was going, or for how long. Sometimes I wouldn't tell her anything. I'd just disappear for a few days. I'd head north with some of the guys up I-95 and go gambling in Atlantic City. We'd stop along the way to buy clothes at the White Marsh Mall. Once we walked into a strip club at Atlantic City and the guys were upset none of the girls were paying attention to us. I took out $20,000 in cash and put it on the table. It was wrapped in $2,000 bundles. I said, "Watch this." The next thing you know, there are women everywhere and I was giving them $100 tips.

Up until that time Billy and I had been a pretty good team. I trusted him more than I trusted my own family.

But in late 1994 when my grandmother died, I started to miss the family I'd left behind. I had actually started seeing my grandmother during the last months of her life, stopping by every few weeks to drop off a few hundred dollars for her medication. I had pretty much ignored her until it was almost too late. But at least I got to spend a little time with her in the end.

When my sister called me with the news of my grandmother's death, I was sad and frustrated with myself. I thought, *Why did I have to wait until she was so old to help her?* It was the way I was living. I didn't have any time for my own family. I only had time for my friends. My grandmother's name was Marie. She was my father's mother and was in her late seventies when she died. I hardly knew her.

There was a lot of tension at the funeral, as you can imagine. That first evening at the funeral parlor, my sister, Betty, immediately came up to me, but my brother, Johnny, wouldn't even make eye contact. He was across the room talking to Bruce Hall, who came over and politely wished me his condolences. My aunts, uncles and cousins were there, too, but I could feel their uneasiness because I was in the room. They probably were wondering when my friends were arriving with their gold chains, pinkie rings and expensive flowers.

It was the same uncertainty I'd sense when Billy and I would walk into a bar and people would just stare. We knew they were afraid of us. I used to like that feeling. Now it just made me feel like an outsider. When my friends did arrive, Bruce just acted like the same guy I grew up with. He never asked me anything about the guys who came into the parlor. But I could tell he felt uncomfortable being around my brother and me at the same time. He was stuck in the middle.

Betty asked me to come into the funeral director's office for a family meeting. There was Johnny, still refusing to look at me. My sister told me that our grandmother didn't have a life insurance policy to pay for the funeral. My grandmother had been living with an aunt and uncle, who were having hard times, so they couldn't help. Betty said she and Johnny were going to pitch in whatever money they could afford to help with the expenses. "If you could help, it would be appreciated," she told me. Johnny got up and left the room without speaking to me.

I told Betty I'd be glad to pay for the entire funeral. She thought that was not fair, since there were several other grandchildren who could pitch in. If they knew I was willing to pay for the whole funeral, they wouldn't offer anything. When they totaled up the donations, the pledge was $1,300 short, so I put up the $1,300 and gave it to my aunt. When Johnny found out, he came over to me and looked at me for the first time. "It was nice of you to put up the rest of the money," he said.

Then he surprised me. "Let's stop all this arguing," he said. He didn't agree with my way of life, he told me. "Why don't you get out of everything before you end up in prison for a long time," he said.

He also had something important he wanted to say about Billy.

"Billy just uses people," he said. Johnny had known Billy years before when the two were involved in karate. "I learned that Billy was only out for himself. I hope you learn that before it is too late," he said.

For the next two nights of calling hours at the funeral home, Johnny and I started to talk like brothers again. I felt great about our reunion. Even though Billy was like a brother to me, he couldn't replace my real brother. As visitors came to pay their respects, I introduced Johnny to my friends and he introduced me to his friends. When it came time for the wake, I paid Fat Ricky $500 to cater the affair. Some of the other wiseguys worked for free as wait-ers and servers. They cleaned up without charging us. That is one thing I will say about my old friends: when it came to something like a funeral for a relative, the wiseguys would walk to the top of Mount Everest for one of their own.

The Plot

A few months later, some strange things started to happen between Billy and me. In January 1995 I drove up to Allenwood again to see him. We had already figured out that the best time to visit was a weekday, when security was pretty loose. The visiting room was a small, L-shaped room with only a few guards. Billy had asked me to bring him a pair of Dock-sides because he didn't like the prison-issued shoes he had to wear with his prison khakis. So, I wore the Dock-siders—a size too big for me—into the prison and we switched shoes when the guards weren't looking.

Then he led me under the security camera so our conversation couldn't be caught on videotape. "I have something I want you to do," he whispered.

He fingered the gold chain around my neck and the twenty-dollar gold piece with forty-eight diamonds hanging from it. He carefully examined it. Then as nonchalantly as he could, he opened my coat and wrapped his arms around me. He began to feel around my waist and up my back. I couldn't believe it. My best friend in the world was patting me down. He was feeling for a wire. I was stunned.

He then ordered me to pull up my pant legs. I don't know if he suspected me of double-crossing him, or if he was just joking, but I felt very uncomfortable, like I was being violated. But I did as I was told. In all the years we had committed crimes together, not once had he patted me down. Until now.

"You've been in prison too long," I said, laughing. "You're starting to go over the rainbow."

He didn't say anything at first.

Then Billy started to talk business. He was angry, he said, because Fat Ricky was robbing the syndicate of tens of thousands of dollars in beer and poker machine income. He also believed that another associate, named Ronnie Jones, was robbing him, but I knew that wasn't true. Billy reminded me of how nice he'd been to Ricky on that previous visit when he reamed me out instead.

"I just wanted Ricky to think I wasn't mad at him, that's why I was yelling at you," he said. "When you're going to do something to somebody, you don't want him to suspect. You don't want him to know you're his enemy. You want to patronize him instead."

To Billy, being disloyal was the worst crime a wiseguy could commit, but he had a plan for getting even. He would wait until he was released from prison later that year. Then I would join him in a plot to kill both men. We would ambush one of the men, he said, at 4:30 A.M. on his way to Doughboy's. To throw off the police, we would wait six months to do the other guy.

To be honest, I was all for the plan at first. I knew Billy and I could do this and get away with it. After all, he had gotten away with murder before.

But when I got home, I started to have second thoughts. I had gotten this far in life without killing anybody. Why start now? As I said earlier in this book, once you cross that line of murder, it becomes easy to do it again, especially if you get away with the first one.

A month later, I paid Billy another visit in Allenwood. I hoped he had changed his mind, but he was still dead serious about his plot. I had been worried since that day Billy patted me down. I wondered what it meant. Clearly, he no longer trusted me. Would I get whacked next? I started to panic. My mind was going 110 miles an hour in a 50-mile-an-hour zone.

For the first time in more than twenty years, I was beginning to see myself as I really was. And I didn't like the man I'd become. For Billy and me, our lives were all about money and power. Billy always defended his actions against those who double-crossed him. Taking revenge, no matter how brutal, was simply a "matter of principle," he'd say. But I started to question his idea of "principle." Wasn't it really just a matter of greed?

I had finally reached a fork in the road. I could commit murder. Or I could find a way out.

Chapter 7

The Year Of Decision

By 1995 I was starting to have my first serious thoughts about escaping from my chosen profession. I was thirty-nine years old and I was tired of it all. There were guys everywhere I'd go. I'd have thirty wiseguys in my house. They'd be waiting at the doorstep when I got home. My Lincoln Continental was always filled with wiseguys. Everything was business. I'd have to worry about the police following me. Every car door I'd hear at night made my heart race. I always thought it was the police or the FBI. When I was younger, I liked outsmarting them. Now the thought of cops gave me nightmares. I didn't even like snorting cocaine anymore. It just made me sleepy.

I could never relax. If I wasn't worrying about the police, I was worrying about the bar. If I wasn't worrying about the bar, I was worrying about my messed-up home life. If it wasn't my home life, it was the bookmaking and the loan-sharking. And if it wasn't that, it was the murder I'd been covering up now for seventeen years. And if it wasn't the old murder, it was the two new murders Billy wanted me to commit. I was under a hell of a lot of stress, even for a wiseguy.

I was on the Baltimore Beltway one day during rush

hour. I had the car loaded with guys and ten grand in my pocket. We were stopped in heavy traffic. I turned to one of the guys and said, "You know, I envy all these people." He looked at me like I was nuts. "What are you talking about?" he said.

I said, "Look, they're all going home; they got a paycheck, they work for their money. I miss that. They have something to look forward to."

When you make money like we did, it meant nothing. If I spent $1,000 today, I'd just make $2,000 tomorrow.

My brother was one of those regular guys I envied. He sold medical supplies. And even though we were talking to each other for the first time in five years, there was still a big gap between our lifestyles. I often invited him down to Joe's on Sunday afternoons when I'd fix sausages and green peppers for the customers. Johnny never came, though.

"Billy wouldn't want me at the bar," he'd say.

"Don't worry about Billy," I'd answer. "He's just paranoid."

One Sunday I was at home cooking the sausages and peppers when one of my employees called from Joe's.

"Your brother's here with another guy," I heard over the phone.

Johnny got on the phone. "You'll never believe who's with me," he said.

"Who?" I asked.

"I have Bruce with me," he answered.

I told him I'd be right there. On the drive down to Joe's I was a nervous wreck. I thought, *You're in deep shit. An FBI agent is in the joint you run as a cover for bookmaking, gambling, prostitution, drug dealing and money laundering.*

I started to put together my strategy. As soon as I got to Joe's, I'd tell all the employees not to pay out winnings on the poker machines because a cop was in the bar. Next I'd call a couple of the wiseguys who sold numbers and drugs from our package goods store and tell them not to come to work until later. I also had to worry whether someone from the bar would snitch to Billy that my brother and his FBI friend came to see me.

Despite my panic, I was thrilled that Johnny had finally come to visit me at the bar. And I had always respected Bruce and how well he treated my family. When I got to Joe's, there were only about ten customers in the bar. I brought in the food and had a couple of employees start serving it. I saw Johnny and Bruce sitting at the bar. Before I greeted them, I wanted to get to the package goods store to warn the employees not to commit any crimes for a few hours.

Then I heard my brother yell, "Hey, Charlie, we're over here." We shook hands, exchanged greetings and started to talk about old times. We ate sausage and peppers and had a few drinks. I gave them a tour of the place. After a few hours of hanging out, we said our good-byes. Bruce didn't ask me one question about Billy or any other part of my life. I respected that. I admired the way Bruce and Johnny seemed so relaxed on a Sunday afternoon. I actually was jealous of them. My life wasn't like theirs. I could never relax.

Not surprisingly, I got a call from Billy the next day. He had heard my brother was at the bar with a guy named Bruce. Of course, he knew it was FBI agent Bruce Hall. Billy sounded mildly upset that Johnny had shown up at the bar, but he was furious about Bruce being there, too. Once again he summoned me up to Allenwood for a lecture.

When I arrived, I tried to smooth over the visit from Johnny and Bruce. Billy seemed to calm down after a while. But then he brought up my least favorite subject— murder. He just called it "that thing we talked about a couple of weeks ago." I tried to tell him "that thing" was a bad idea, but he was adamant. So for the second time I reluctantly agreed to help him do "the thing." On my way home I was sick to my stomach. One part of me wanted to be loyal to Billy and the wiseguy life. The other part of me wanted to run away.

I was really beginning to struggle with my conscience. The wiseguy life had not turned out as I'd imagined it would be when I was a young man tattooing my hand with the mark of a thief. Wouldn't I just end up in prison for a long time? How much longer would Gina put up with my shit? Should I help Billy kill Fat Ricky and Ronnie? What if my children turned out like me?

I wondered if there was any way to become a normal person. How could I right all the wrongs? It's not like I could just quit my job. How does a wiseguy quit his life without getting killed? I started wondering what would happen if I just turned myself in. How long would I go to prison? To turn myself in at Baltimore police headquarters would be too dangerous. There were too many dirty cops in this town. One of them might tell Billy. What would happen to my family? If I turned in Billy and the rest of the guys, what would happen to them and their families? I wasn't a religious Catholic, but I began to wonder if there really was a heaven and a hell. Where would I end up?

A Call For Help

Billy wasn't getting out of prison until November or December. That gave me some time to think. In the meantime I decided to get some advice. I immediately thought of Bruce.

I remember when he first became an FBI agent. He was at my brother's house just after graduating from the FBI Academy in Quantico, Virginia. He was about to leave for his first assignment in New Orleans. Bruce showed me his shiny new badge and FBI credentials. Then he told me, "If you ever feel the need to talk to me about anything, I will always be there to listen and to help you if I can."

I remembered those words now, and I especially remembered how sincere he was. Some people might tell you something like that, but you can tell they're just being friendly. In reality, they couldn't be bothered, but I could tell by Bruce's face that he meant it.

So I picked up the phone and called Johnny. I asked him to set up a meeting with him, Bruce and me. Johnny must have suspected why I asked for the meeting. He knew I was tired of my life and that I was up to my eyeballs in crimes. But he had no idea I was covering up for a 1978 murder, or that I was asked to commit murder. He didn't ask any questions. He just set up the meeting.

We met at the Wharf Rat, a bar in Fells Point, in East Baltimore. Bruce ordered us drinks, pizza and steamed shrimp. Bruce somehow knew how to make me feel real comfortable. We spent an hour talking about our families. Finally he asked me, "Charlie, isn't there something you wanted to talk to me about?"

I said yes but hardly knew where to begin. He then invited us to his apartment. Even though I had known him for twenty-five years, I found it odd that a federal agent was inviting me into his home. Though Bruce wasn't naive about my life, he didn't know exactly what our meeting was going to be about or how it was going to turn out. Neither did I. But his invitation was a sign that he trusted me. Maybe he believed I was different from other wiseguys. Maybe he saw something salvageable in me. I still had my guard up. Bruce was still an FBI agent and a big part of me didn't trust him.

We sat in his living room, overlooking the harbor. Bruce and Johnny sat on the sofa. I sat across from them.

After some more small talk Bruce asked me what I'd come to discuss.

"I have a friend who's in trouble," I began. Bruce carefully asked me questions about my imaginary "friend." I told him some of the trouble my friend was in and how I worried he might go to prison for a long time. "There's always room for your friend to change, as long as he hasn't committed any murders," said Bruce. I told him my friend hadn't killed anyone, but was covering up for an unsolved murder that three of his friends had committed a long time ago. I was careful not to give him any names. Before we got up to leave, Bruce told me that it sounded like my friend was in really deep trouble. "But your friend can help himself," said Bruce.

When we got to the door, I thanked Bruce for listening. Just as I put my hand on the knob to open the door, I heard him call my name.

I turned around to look him in the face.

"You go back and tell your friend to take his time thinking about whether he wants me to try to help him. But tell him not to wait until it's too late. And tell your friend that I'll still be here for him to talk to. I'll help him any way that I can."

I now could tell that Bruce knew that my friend was me. And once again I could tell from the look on his face that he was sincere.

For the next few months I thought every day about what Bruce said as I left his apartment. I continued to wear the mask of a wiseguy, but I could feel that part of me dying inside. In my heart I finally began to believe I wanted to leave that life behind. But how could I do that?

One day in May I visited Johnny at his house. He had a friend over, a guy who worked in private security named Ralph. The three of us ordered crabcake sandwiches for lunch from a nearby restaurant. I reached into my pockets for a few twenty-dollar bills, but my

pockets were bulging from so much cash, I could barely
get my hands inside. I slowly squeezed my fingers down
into each pocket to get the money. I kept my money
wrapped in bank wrappers by denominations of $20s,
$50s and $100s. I wrapped each bundle tightly in rubber
bands. After a few minutes of struggling, I got all the
money out and dumped it on Johnny's countertop.
There was more than $8,000. Johnny and Ralph looked
at the cash in amazement. "Wouldn't you like to have
that much money?" my brother asked his friend. "Charlie, you have enough green here to choke a horse."

"This money doesn't mean shit to me," I said. "I make
this much money every day of my life," I said. "I am so disgusted with my life. If I could just throw this money away
and be sure it would change my life, I'd do it."

Ralph gave me a peculiar look.

"If your life is that bad, you can change it," he said.

"You don't understand. I can't," I said.

"Yes, I do understand," said Ralph. Then he told me a
story. Ralph had some relatives who lived their lives as
members of the Hell's Angels motorcycle gang. They
eventually became disgusted with the gang and somehow
got out of the club alive. They now were living honest lives.

"I don't know how they did it, but they did it, and
that's all that counts," he said. While we ate our crab-
cakes, I thought about Ralph's story. It would stick in my
mind, like a little mental brick I was building in a wall between myself and my old life.

Being Tailed

In the weeks that followed, I began to notice cars following me. At first I thought I was just being paranoid, but
then I began to believe it. It could've been city detectives,
or even the FBI, but someone was following me. I started

to find ways to prove that I was being followed. I also figured out ways to throw them off. I'd be driving on the Baltimore Beltway and stop on the side of the road just before an exit. I'd count to forty, then take the exit. I knew if I was being followed by one or two tail cars, I had ditched both by then. After I took the exit, I'd get back on the Beltway, heading in the opposite direction. When I'd be driving in the city, I had several ways to throw off a tail. I would stop at a green traffic light, wait until it turned red, then drive like a bat out of hell.

Sometimes I'd drive the wrong way down a one-way street. If a car followed me, it was a sure bet that it was a cop. If I made a sudden U-turn and saw another car in my rearview mirror doing the same thing, that was also a dead giveaway. I was pretty good at throwing them off, but it didn't ease my anxiety. I was a wreck as it was.

I was getting so nervous that I began to check our trash. I'd set it out in front of my house the night before trash pickup. I'd open the lid and make a careful note of the item at the top of the pile—maybe a pizza box or a package from some of the kids' food. In the morning I'd get up before the trash trucks arrived and open the lid. If the top item was missing, I'd know someone was messing with my garbage.

I told Gina someone was stealing our trash. "You're just paranoid," she said. But I asked her, "Who would steal our trash other than the police?" I was careful not to put any paper from my bookmaking business in the can. I thought maybe it was a sign that it was time to get out. I figured I was being investigated for bookmaking. Some of the guys knew dirty cops in the city police department. They had gotten wind of an investigation. The cops were watching us for some reason, but I wasn't sure what. I knew any charge for illegal gambling in Maryland would just get me a slap on the wrist and a fine. My clerk, Linda, got busted once a year and was still in business, but that didn't give me much comfort.

I was so stressed out by July that I started to take it out on my wife. On July 4, my brother and his wife invited us to their house to eat crabs, a Maryland tradition on Independence Day. I'd been out late the night before and I didn't get home that morning until about 5:00 A.M., so I crashed on the couch. At 10:30 A.M. I heard Gina and Justin come down the steps. Mandy was at a relative's house and Charlie and his family were next door with his grandparents. I pretended I was asleep, but Gina knew the smallest creak in the house would wake me up. I didn't want to get up from the couch because I knew she was going to give me the fifth degree about being out all night. I didn't want to hear her ask me where I'd gone after Joe's closed.

I finally got up and went into the kitchen and acted like nothing was wrong, but I could tell Gina was furious. She had her Italian temper and she could be more stubborn than anyone I knew. I tried to break the ice by talking to Justin while he ate his breakfast. But then I heard the question. "What time did you get home last night?" she asked

"Early, about two A.M.," I said.

"You liar," she said.

I asked her if we could stop arguing just for today, since it was a holiday. "We should go out to Johnny's house and have a good time," I said.

Here we were, living a life with everything money could buy, but we were miserable. Gina was disgusted. She told me to take Justin and go to my brother's house without her. I thought, *To hell with her.*

I put Justin in the car, buckled his seat belt, and started to drive to my brother's house. I kept thinking about how screwed up my life was. I called Gina on my cell phone to make up with her, but she hung up on me.

She knew something had really been bothering me over the last six months, but she wasn't quite sure. I think she thought I was having an affair, but I wasn't. I hadn't told her about the two murders Billy asked me to commit. And she didn't know how bad I wanted to walk away from the wiseguy life. She didn't even know I'd met with Bruce. After she hung up on me several times, I decided to turn around and head back home.

When we got back to the house, I parked, unbuckled Justin's seat belt and carried him into the house. I set him down and went into the kitchen to talk to Gina. Justin asked me, "Why are you and Mommy arguing?"

Gina started to yell at me about my priorities being screwed up. I cared more about the bar and Billy than I cared about her and the kids, she said.

I defended Billy and the guys, but I told her things were going to change. "Do you know how many times I've heard that before?" she screamed. "Billy is never going to allow you to quit anything."

I picked up a kitchen chair and threw it into the living room. It landed in the center of a new glass coffee table and shattered it into a thousand pieces on the carpet. Gina and Justin ran upstairs crying. I followed Gina into the bedroom and the argument continued. I felt like I was reeling out of control. I was irrational and irritable from too much work and too little sleep. I knew our lives had hit rock bottom and I didn't need Gina to remind me of the truth. That was the problem with my wife. She always spoke the truth—even when she was in a rage.

As I stood in the doorway, I noticed a hard plastic cup filled with iced tea on the bureau. I picked up the cup and threw it in the direction of her knees, but didn't stay long enough to see where it landed. I turned to leave the room just as I heard a horrific scream, followed by a loud cry. I saw Gina holding her forehead.

"You split my head open," she cried.

"You're full of shit," I said. "I didn't hit your head." I thought she just wanted me to think I'd hit her in the head.

She was holding her forehead tight and I didn't see any blood. I had never hit her before—or thrown anything at her—and I didn't want to believe I'd actually hurt her.

Meanwhile, my seven-year-old son had just witnessed my attack. "What did you do to Mommy?" my little blond-haired boy cried.

There was so much screaming going on that he must have thought his world was crumbling. I didn't answer him because I didn't want to tell him I thought his mother was faking. I went downstairs and saw all the glass from the coffee table shattered all over Gina's perfectly decorated living room. I left her upstairs crying and went outside to cool off. I got in my car and sat there listening to the radio. After a few minutes I heard police sirens. I looked through my rearview mirror to see a couple of police cars coming up the street in my direction. I looked ahead of me and saw more cars coming toward me. I knew Gina would never call the police on me. With all the arguments we'd had over the years, she'd never called police. Police parked their cruisers and started running into my house. I got out of my car to go into the house to tell them my wife and I were just arguing.

A policeman stopped me at the door.

"Are you Charlie?" he asked.

"Yes," I said.

"You're under arrest."

"Good, you'll be doing me a favor."

I figured I was getting locked up for domestic violence. Maybe a neighbor heard glass breaking while we argued and called police. I was handcuffed and put in the back of the cruiser and taken to a local police lockup.

A Holiday In Jail

I figured as soon as I got there, I'd ask for a lieutenant I knew and get out quickly. But the lieutenant wasn't there. I was about to ask the desk sergeant to call him at home, but then I thought again. If I got to go home right away, we'd just start arguing again. So I sat in the lockup. My cell was five by eight feet. I had a stainless steel toilet, a sink and an oak slab for a bed, plus two cellmates. To be honest, I was perfectly content sitting in that bare cell, except I worried what Justin thought of the episode. For once, I had some peace and quiet. No phones, no calls from Billy in prison, no Joe's Tavern to worry about, no wiseguys everywhere I'd turn, no scores to make, no worries. I was relieved.

The cellblock was packed that day and everyone was complaining about being arrested on July 4. Except me. I knew a couple of the guys locked up in nearby cells, so I just shot the bull with them. There were five or six men who were locked up for domestic violence. Their bails had been set at $50,000. I didn't care about that, either. I figured when I got to see the court commissioner, I would just call Gina and she'd get the money together and bail me out. After about fourteen hours I got my charging documents from the turnkey at the lockup. I started to read the police report. It said Gina was taken to the hospital by ambulance. I was shocked. As I read on, I discovered that my seven-year-old son was the one who called the police. Gina and I had always taught Justin to dial 911 if there was an emergency.

Now I was really worried about my wife. I was allowed to make one phone call. Even though it was 3 A.M., I called Melonie's mother (Charlie Jr.'s grandmother) who lived next door to us. "How is Gina?" I asked. She told me Gina got seven or eight stitches in her head at the hospital. She was already back home with the kids.

Gina had also told her that she knew I really thought I'd only hit her in the leg. She was actually worried about me sitting in jail.

I was pretty anxious by the time I got to see a court commissioner at 5:00 A.M. I went into his office. He told me to have a seat. He began to read the police report. "Do you want to add anything to this report?" he asked me.

"Yes, I would," I said. "I admit to everything that I am charged with, except that I didn't intentionally hit my wife in the head with the cup. I meant to hit her in the legs. That cup was plastic. I didn't think it could really hurt anybody."

I told him I knew I was wrong and that when I got home, I was going to tell my wife I loved her and that I was sorry. I also knew I had to face my children and that made me feel like shit.

"I'm married to an Italian woman who is ten years younger than me," I told the commissioner. "Unless you are married to an Italian woman, you don't know how bad a temper they have. If you don't believe me, go live with my wife for a while," I said. I could see a tiny grin appear on the commissioner's face. He shook his head at me. I was prepared to get a bail of $50,000 to $100,000, which meant I had to put up 10 percent. But I guess the commissioner knew I wasn't trying to deny anything in the report. He released me on my own recognizance. I couldn't believe it. Melonie's dad picked me up and took me home.

As soon as Gina saw me, she started to laugh. She knew I didn't mean to hurt her. I laughed, too, and we hugged. We both knew the stress in our lives was the reason for our bloody fight. We agreed our lives had to change. I praised Justin for calling the police and told him he'd done the right thing. I thought this bad moment in my life was behind me. But it was a day that would be dredged up years later to chip away at my credibility at a time when I needed it most.

I headed back to Allenwood a few days later to visit Billy. He could tell I was under a lot of stress, but didn't know why. I knew if I told him I wanted to change my life, I'd probably get killed. I knew entirely too much to be trusted to walk away.

As soon as Billy saw me, he knew something was wrong.

"Are you all right?" he asked.

"Yeah, I've just been under a lot of stress with Gina and the bar."

Billy was never a big fan of Gina's.

"I don't know why you put up with her shit. She is just going to hold you back in life, Charlie," he said.

"Billy, I'm married to her and she has my child. I love her and we've been through a lot. You're not married. Your life is different," I said. Billy had three women in his life, and supported children he had with two of them. But he never let the women—or the children—get in the way of his wiseguy life. Business always came first.

"I don't want to lose Gina," I said. "With the bar, I'm never home. She's going to end up leaving me if I don't do something about it," I said.

"Okay. Here's what we'll do," he said. "You can get out of the bar." He agreed to put somebody else in charge until he got out of prison in a few months. I just had to show up for a few hours on Friday and Saturday night. He wanted the rowdy customers to see my face and know they'd get their heads busted if they got out of hand.

Billy was being so accommodating to me, but I knew his motive. Even though I'd been running Joe's Tavern for more than four years, I would get no profit from the business once I got out. He would keep all the money for himself. But that was okay with me. He also said I no longer had to pick up loan payments for him. He would have another guy do it for him.

"You just collect on your own loans," he said. "That way you won't have to be running around so much and you can spend more time with Gina. There's one more thing."

"What's that?"

"Keep the bookmaking going so I can take it over when I get out," he said. I agreed to do that.

He also told me he had paid off a "counselor" in prison so he'd get moved to a halfway house in Baltimore sooner than originally planned. I didn't know if he was telling me the truth or just bragging.

Our visit went much better than I'd expected. Billy had no idea that he had just made some decisions that would help me leave the wiseguy life behind.

A Real Vacation

Gina and I patched things up after our own version of July 4 fireworks. I'd been out of Joe's now for a few weeks, and didn't have to run around town collecting juice on Billy's loans. I was home more often.

I thought about my meeting with Bruce a lot more. Every now and then, I'd call him up at the FBI in Washington and ask him some more hypothetical questions about my friend in trouble.

We always went camping in Gettysburg around my birthday on the July 25. This year I was determined not to repeat my behavior of previous years. I'd always send my family ahead and show up a few days later. Then one of the guys would ruin the vacation by paging me and telling me to rush back to Baltimore to make a big score or to solve some problem.

This year I told Gina we were going to leave together

and spend some quality time as a family. I also had a very practical reason for getting out of town. I had gotten word from two of the wiseguys that there was paper on the streets and it was for bookmaking. I told Gina there was probably a warrant out for me, but I'd just get slapped on the wrist. She'd heard that one before. I'd told her the same thing almost ten years before when I ended up in the Baltimore County Detention Center for six months. But now I was worried our house would be raided and I'd be arrested before we had a chance to go camping.

The night before we left, I made sure I was home by nine o'clock, which is early for me.

Whatever juice I didn't collect on my loans, I'd pick up early the next morning. If I missed any then, I'd have to wait until I got home to pick up the rest. The money just wasn't so important to me anymore. When we got up the next morning to leave, my only worry was that the police would come before we had a chance to get out of town. If there was a warrant out for me, I'd just have my lawyer make arrangements for me to turn myself in when I got back in town.

I got up before the rest of the family, at about 6:00 A.M., and went out to collect on a few of my loans. By 7:00 A.M. my pager was going off, and when my pager wasn't buzzing, my cell phone was ringing. It was like a regular workday. Everybody was calling me to tell me about the warrants. Some guys were asking me when I was picking up their juice payments and dropping them off. It was crazy. By 9:30 A.M. I was back home. I turned off my cell phone, but forgot about my pager. Within ten minutes my pager was filled with telephone numbers of people trying to get hold of me. I refused to call them back. I ran into the house. "Gina, let's go," I said. I knew if we didn't hurry, one of the guys would be at our house to gum things up. I was totally stressed out.

Gina was moving as fast as she could. We were traveling in a caravan. My son Charlie was driving his 4Runner, Gina was driving her Dodge Caravan and I was the lead car in my Lincoln. We were running late when my pager went off again at 10:30 A.M. As we were about to leave, my clerk, Linda, drove up in her pickup truck and wanted to bullshit about the paper on the streets. Then I saw another wiseguy pull up in his Cadillac, motioning me to wait a minute. Linda was blocking me. My pager was going off yet again. I started yelling at her, "I don't have time for this shit."

I had had enough. I got out of the car and threw the pager down in the street. I got back in the car and gunned the engine. Then I ran over the pager. I put the Lincoln in reverse and ran it over again. I killed my pager! I was so tired and drained. Now I had Gina, Linda and the kids staring at me like I was a lunatic. Finally we started out for our trip. I drove for about a mile before I started to relax and believed I was really going on a vacation. For nine days I felt about as relaxed as a man could be in my position. It was my fortieth birthday and I was spending it exactly as I wanted—with my family.

Chapter 8

Tracking Charlie— A Detective's Saga

Detective Carroll Herold Jr. quietly spied on Charlie from his green van during a long surveillance in 1995. He patiently followed Charlie to his usual haunts and snapped Charlie's picture leaving his house carrying a bag of money and parking his car at Joe's Tavern. While Charlie suspected he was being tailed, he had no clue that the vice cop was wiretapping his phone.

Apparently, neither did anybody else in his syndicate. They never bothered to speak in code. Transcripts of the wiretaps showed them speaking freely of numbers hitting and thousands of dollars owed to customers.

Tracking down illegal gamblers was Detective Herold's specialty. Like Charlie said, everyone knew him just as Spanky. His parents gave him the nickname when he was still a baby because they thought he looked like the character from the "Our Gang" movie serials. It was hard to see the resemblance now, with his gray beard and his silver hair combed back off his forehead.

Spanky was a rather eccentric police detective. He dressed for work in bib overalls or Hawaiian shirts, jeans and tennis shoes. By the time he started tracking Charlie down, he'd been working in the Baltimore Police Department for twenty-five years and had spent most of his time in vice, where he preferred to stay. Some of his superiors weren't too keen on his investigating "upstanding citizens" for running illegal lotteries or football pools. They thought it was a victimless crime, but Spanky believed otherwise. He thought the underworld of illicit gambling led to other crimes, specifically drugs and loan-sharking, and the gambling universe could be a violent place. He would one day hear about a man named Billy Isaacs, "who broke arms for grins."

Over the years Spanky developed a reputation as a cop who didn't trust other cops. He suspected some of them were a little too friendly to the people he was investigating. He didn't have proof, just strong suspicions. His mistrust in his fellow officers was deeply rooted in the Baltimore Police Department's infamous history. When Spanky was a young police officer in 1973, the department was hit by a scandal involving six police detectives—and two former officers—who were charged with accepting monthly payoffs to protect gambling rings. Not surprisingly, all the detectives worked in the police department's vice squad.

Needless to say, the vice squad was an unpopular place to work for years after the scandal, but Spanky was unfazed. Busting multimillion-dollar lotteries and other gambling schemes fascinated him. Early on he had evidence that people under investigation were being tipped off by police. Spanky once staged a raid in Highlandtown, an East Baltimore neighborhood that he called, "the vice capital of the world."

"We hit the doors, but nobody was there." All he found were rolls of paper from adding machines, still uncurling across the floor. The gamblers had left in an awful hurry, Spanky remembered. "It looked like somebody had just called them."

Another time he raided a bar on Fort Avenue, the street that leads to Fort McHenry. It was owned by the biggest bookmaker in South Baltimore. When Spanky got to the safe upstairs, it was wide open and empty, except for a note inside. "You're not going to find anything," it said.

Spanky never proved someone in the police department tipped off bookmakers in advance of the raids, but it was obvious to him. So he kept to himself, never knowing whom to trust. Some in the police department thought he was secretive, even paranoid, especially as they watched him at the end of every workday. Spanky would pack up all his files in boxes, put them on a cart and wheel them down the hall to his car. He took them home every night and brought them back each morning. To Spanky, this was just part of his "clean desk policy."

He was quite a sight, too, when he staged a series of gambling raids. He'd be wearing his gun, his handcuffs and one of his two lucky T-shirts. Each carried the emblem of a Fells Point bar. One shirt was from The Horse You Came In On. The other was from a bar called Turkey Joe's. Spanky would never dare stage a raid without wearing one of those T-shirts. And for extra luck, he never washed them. After scores of raids, year after year, his colleagues decided to play a practical joke on him. They gathered the smelly T-shirts into a large plastic bottle and sealed it with evidence tape, allowing Spanky's exclusive wardrobe to ripen for the last raids of his career before retirement. One of his partners wrote on the lid, "Warning, potent voodoo charms."

Spanky may have seemed a little strange to his colleagues, but as Charlie said, Spanky was truly a legend among the wiseguys of Baltimore, a cop who couldn't be bought. They knew he wanted to shut them down, but they also knew he would never plant evidence on them just to make himself look good. When Spanky busted you, it was for good reason. He played fair.

Listening In

Spanky and his partners heard and saw plenty from Charlie and his friends in 1995, mostly about their illegal lottery. Charlie's bookmaking empire was a whirlwind of activity, with Charlie cruising around town, doling out thousands of dollars in gambling winnings in brown paper bags while detectives watched nearby. Spanky secretly took snapshots of Charlie leav-

ing his house with a bag of money in his hand and parking his
Lincoln at Joe's Tavern.

In secret court documents, filed by police to keep their wiretaps
going, Spanky identified Charlie as a "pickup man"—the guy
close to the top of the gambling pyramid who's in charge of
handing out money to the winners.

In one call, for example, detectives reported, "Charlie calls
Linda at 889-2643 and tells her he has eighty-four hundred for
Hank and eight hundred for Rudy so far. Linda says they owe
Hank fourteen thousand. They discuss hits and how much to
give him." The many nicknames of the gambling underworld
pop up casually in conversations: Fat Ricky, Baldy, The Boss,
Preston, Goose and a man referred to only as G.

Spanky and his gang cast a wide net, listening to calls and observing comings and goings from places frequented by Baltimore's
more upstanding citizens: a funeral home on the county's east
side, a large manufacturing company in the northwest suburbs,
even a tony waterfront restaurant in yuppie Canton, Baltimore's
own "gold coast." They also kept close watch on the more
obvious locations of Baltimore's underworld—Joe's Tavern and
Doughboy's.

On June 8 at 5:43 P.M. detectives listened to a most unusual
conversation between Charlie Wilhelm and his brother, John. By
now, Spanky and other city detectives had gotten used to the
same names mentioned repeatedly on the phones. But that day
they heard new names and wondered whom the Wilhelm brothers were talking about.

    John: What did God want?
    Charlie: Well, about you and Bruce.
    John: No.
    Charlie: Yeah.
    John: What for?
    Charlie: He's not going to talk with you; he's not going
to be friends with you, uh, he don't want me to bring you

*down the bar . . . He said that, um, he knows I was out
with you.*

John: He's just trying to reach you.

*Charlie (laughs): John, he knows, I mean, I told him;
look, I said I ain't had Bruce down that bar . . . and I
said as far as Bruce, I do my thing, he does his thing. I
said I'm not throwing nothing up in his face...*

John: Yeah, stay away from him.

Spanky was stumped. Who the hell is this? he wondered. The
name Bruce had never been mentioned before on the wiretaps, and
neither had the nickname "God."

During the same phone conversation John turned to Charlie's recent visit to see Billy in Allenwood Federal Prison in
Pennsylvania.

*Charlie: Listen to this . . . I tell you how much drag
they got, John, they paid a counselor off in that prison.*

John: They paid a what?

*Charlie: A counselor off—he's getting his release date
in two weeks.*

John: Oh really.

*Charlie: Oh yeah, it cost him a thousand dollars,
(laughs). He says everybody in there is on the take, this
place. He makes sure he stands underneath the cameras
'cause he watches the cameras, and anyway the direction
[of] the cameras, he went the opposite direction and he
stood underneath.*"

Spanky had no idea where this God was being held in prison.
There was also something else that Spanky couldn't pin
down. There was at least one phone call made from Charlie's
house to a phone at the FBI headquarters in Washington, DC.
It would be more than a year before he figured that one out.

Despite all the activity observed by police detectives, they continued to have trouble breaking into the heart of the gambling
ring to get to the top moneymen in control. They filed repeated
secret pleadings to a Baltimore circuit court judge named John

Prevas—a former drug prosecutor himself and an authority on wiretaps—asking permission to extend wiretap orders because other investigative techniques were of little use. Exhausting every other technique was a legal prerequisite to obtain—and maintain—a wiretap. And detectives believed they had tried everything else and failed. The byzantine structure of the illegal lottery had fire walls between every layer. It was cleverly designed to keep members of the same operation from ever coming face-to-face with each other. The less contact, the less likelihood that members of the organization could snitch on each other. Bettors never came close to the people who controlled the operation. By the 1990s, with the use of the fax machine, clerks taking in the bets had little physical contact with the pickup man or the lay-off guys at the top.

The gambling organization, wrote Spanky and his partner, Stephen Duffey, in their plea to Prevas, "has gone to great lengths to eliminate the chance of being discovered by conventional means.

"Every lawful investigative technique was tried, or considered and not tried, because of the inherent danger, in an attempt to gather evidence against the criminal enterprise which is being controlled by Charlie Wilhelm [and others]."

Spanky and Duffey wrote to Judge Prevas of their frustration: Informant debriefings didn't work; witnesses were unavailable to interview. They could not find anyone inside the organization to be a confidential informant. Even snooping through trash was considered a rotten investigative tool. Spanky was a veteran trash examiner, even before the days of latex gloves. He loved his job so much, he wasn't even bothered by the stink of dirty diapers. As long as there was a chance of finding even a snippet of evidence, he happily kept foraging. One time, he found gambling papers, torn into tiny pieces and mashed inside an aluminum foil package of fish scraps. He pieced the foul puzzle back together and photocopied the evidence to make it whole again. But now, he found sifting through trash of Charlie's crime organization gave him nothing useful.

Sending in an undercover police officer to infiltrate the or-

*ganization was also a long shot in an organization highly
suspicious of newcomers. It would be risky, both to the safety
of the police officer and to the progress already made in the
investigation. Police had already overheard one of Charlie's
clerks, a woman named Linda, say that Charlie spotted
Spanky in Joe's Tavern in April. Spanky, said Linda, was
down at the bar, having a few drinks, looking around, then
leaving. "He ain't no dummy," said the veteran bookmaking
clerk of the veteran vice detective. Spanky was a cop who had
personally handcuffed Linda more than once.*

*The detectives also argued to the judge that the analysis of
telephone records, court and motor vehicle records "all failed to
accumulate enough evidence to prosecute the principal subjects
of this investigation. Due to the highly secretive nature of this
organization, to protect the gambling operation, it is apparent
that they have been successful in cloaking [their] narcotics activity as well. . . ."*

*To make matters worse, detectives stumbled across a new road-
block by summer. This one was potentially more devastating to
their investigation than any obstruction Charlie's wiseguys
could ever invent.*

The Proof

*They discovered it without warning on July 13 at 10:22 A.M.
Spanky was meeting with other police officials and city prosecutors in a room in the Baltimore State's Attorney's Office on
North Calvert Street. They were planning their day's activities
when a young police detective named Molly Feather poked her
head out of the adjacent "listening room" and interrupted.*

*She'd been wearing headphones, listening to a wiretap of
Doughboy's. Fat Ricky, who operated Doughboy's tavern, was
on the line talking to Charlie.*

*"Spanky, I think you ought to come here and listen to this,"
said Detective Feather.*

The young detective played the tape back for Spanky and the others.

> Ricky: There's something big getting ready to happen.
> Charlie: Like what?
> Ricky: I don't know, they been in a room for two days.
> Charlie: Is that right?
> Ricky: Suppose to come out on the street today after lunch.
> Charlie: After lunch?
> Ricky: And this come from some guy who paid big money for information.

Spanky and company had no raid planned for that day, but the call put them on high alert, nonetheless. It played perfectly into Spanky's long-held suspicions of the Baltimore Police Department. Was a police official leaking information to the targets of Spanky's investigation?

Two minutes after Charlie's talk with Fat Ricky, Charlie left this message on Linda's answering machine: "Big bust in city and county today, starting at one P.M."

Charlie turned around and called another neighbor in Hampden. "I'll get everything out," the friend said.

Police overheard Charlie calling Joe's Tavern the next day. He instructed a barmaid named Miss Mary to hand over any envelopes that came in to another manager at the bar. Then Charlie told her he wouldn't be coming in for a while. He was taking a last-minute vacation. He'd be back in a week and a half.

On August 20 a man calling himself Giovanni called Doughboy's and left a message with the barmaid to tell Fat Ricky, "Things are supposed to happen in the morning."

Spanky panicked. The "things" were the police department's raids on fifty-two gambling targets. This time he really had planned the raids in the morning. Luckily for the police, the barmaid never gave Fat Ricky the message. And the call gave

Spanky's crew time to change plans. The raids had been planned for midmorning. Instead, they would strike just after dawn.

But the next morning, just before eleven o'clock, Giovanni finally got in touch with Fat Ricky. (He didn't know the raids already had taken place.) He referred to "fifty" search warrants to be served that morning.

Spanky was amazed at the accuracy of Giovanni's information.

"Cripes, it was like they were in the room with us. They knew everything we were going to do."

Spanky's investigation suddenly took on a new urgency. He had a leak to plug in his own police department. He now had confirmation of his long-held suspicions of his fellow men and women in blue. At least one police officer in a position to know Spanky's operation was probably taking bribes from Charlie's syndicate in exchange for advance warning of raids. The confirmation made Spanky lose faith in everything he believed a police officer should stand for, but he also felt relief. There was now hope that the culture of denial in the Baltimore Police Department would change finally. The police made emergency plans to "tickle the wire," hoping to flush out the leak by stirring up conversations and getting the dirty cop on the line.

They called several police districts, letting them know there were pending raids, when none were actually scheduled. That caused more phone conversations about "raids" among Charlie's wiseguys, but no police official ever came on the line.

Spanky's supervisors took over the investigation of the leak, leaving Spanky to pursue Charlie and dozens of other gamblers. Eventually the FBI, with Charlie's help, would take the case over from the Baltimore police. But catching the leak—and making an arrest of a police official—would prove to be one of their most difficult and elusive investigations.

Chapter 9

Coming Clean

Before I left for the camping trip, I tried to dump any evidence of bookmaking in case the house was raided while we were gone. I gathered up my "keep list" of one hundred regular bettors, along with their code names. I hid them at a friend's place. I was pretty confident I had cleared my house of evidence. When we got home, I discovered the police hadn't shown up. The warning must have been a false alarm—not that I let my guard down. At that point my brain was on high alert.

On August 21 I was asleep just after dawn. I woke to the sound of a car door slamming outside. Then I heard another door slam. Then another. Before I even opened my eyes, I knew they had finally come. The raid was on.

We lived in a little Baltimore rowhouse on Keswick Road in Hampden. It was next door to Melonie's parents' house. We had no front yard, so our doors opened right onto the sidewalk, letting the sounds from the street come right through our windows. In the back I'd built a big deck that both our houses shared. Inside, I spent $100,000 renovating and decorating. The kitchen cabinets were solid oak with $1,000 worth of trim around the doors. We had a fifty-two-inch TV in our little living room. Gina had spent a lot of money decorating it with blue carpet and fancy matching curtains. The sofa was a blue-and-purple color she called mauve. And she kept every inch of the house spotless.

At least the police didn't break down my front door. I paid $1,900 for that door—and that was half the retail price. They just walked right in. I never locked it. Why should I lock my door when I knew every thief in the neighborhood? The police wore jackets that said POLICE in big letters. Their guns were drawn, but they held them down by their sides. Spanky Herold wasn't with them: he was around the corner raiding Linda's house. I pulled on the pants I had on the night before, too panicked to notice the bulges of cash in my pockets. I came racing down the narrow stairs. My Rotweiler, Von, was barking like crazy.

The police started backing out the door, cussing the dog so badly that Gina worried they might shoot him. "You better get that fucking dog," they yelled. I grabbed the dog by the collar and put him out back. The police ordered Gina to get the kids downstairs. My grown son, Charlie Jr., was living in the club basement at the time with his girlfriend and their newborn baby, my first grandchild. Charlie had already gone to work, but Heather and the baby were awakened by the ruckus. Police also herded them into the living room.

The police officers weren't mean, but nonetheless, my family was pretty scared. I didn't try to outsmart them, either. I was just too whipped. "Don't mess up my kids' rooms," I said. "My money's in the sock drawer in my bedroom." I remembered stashing $4,000 there. I reached into my pocket and handed them $813. They asked if I had a safe. I took them to the basement. When we got there, I couldn't remember the combination. Then I thought of an old trick some burglar friends had taught me. The weakest part of a safe is on the bottom. I grabbed a crowbar, turned the safe upside down and went to work, peeling it open. Inside there were a bunch of keep and weekly sheets from bookmaking that I'd forgotten to hide. I had completely forgotten they were there. I must have put them in the safe on one of my late nights when I was shit-faced drunk. I had been looking all over the place for these damn sheets for months. And now, here they were, just when I didn't want to find them. When I stood up, I started to laugh at my own stupidity. The police laughed, too.

Upstairs, they made me sit at the kitchen table, which wasn't far from the sofa. Still, I felt stranded from my family. One of the police officers ordered my family to stand up so he could take their pictures. That got Gina real mad. She was already pretty angry at me for getting us in this mess and she was mad at herself for allowing it to happen. "Am I under arrest?" she asked the officer?

No, was the answer.

"Then why are you taking our pictures?" she asked. She didn't get an answer.

Then I saw my youngest son's face. Justin was only seven. Tears streamed down his little, frightened face. I will never forget that look. It's still etched in my memory like a photo from the Vietnam War. I thought, "What kind of father would allow his son, or any of his children, to go through this type of ordeal?"

Gina put her arm around him and told him everything would be all right. With the detectives guarding me, I couldn't even leave my chair to comfort him. So I just reassured him from the kitchen that everything would be okay. I felt like we'd hit rock bottom. Gina felt like our family was totally out of control.

After searching the house, police gathered up the money, the bag of bookmaking slips from the safe, a caller ID box, a cell phone, a calculator and my Baltimore Gas and Electric bill. They were finished by 7:20

A.M. They didn't arrest me that morning. Apparently, the raid on my house was just one of several evidence gathering raids they staged that morning. I didn't learn until much later that the police were less interested in busting the likes of me than they were with finding the big-money layoff guys at the top of our organizations. As you can imagine, they were also preoccupied with finding the leak in the police department who was botching their investigation.

The Last Straw

After they left, Gina and I agreed we couldn't go on like this anymore. The next day I told her I was thinking of going to the FBI and turning myself in. I called Bruce and set up another meeting. This time I would make it official. My friend in trouble would be me. This made Gina very nervous. "You could go to prison for a long time," she said. "And your friends will try to kill you. Why can't you just walk away?" she asked.

"I can't," I said. Nothing about my life would ever be that simple. And to prove my point, who should come home a few days later? Billy, of course. He was finally back in Baltimore after spending five years in federal prisons. He was to spend the last few months at the Volunteers of America halfway house in West Baltimore. His timing couldn't have been worse.

Billy was released at about 7:30 A.M. from Allenwood in Pennsylvania. It was about a three-hour drive to Baltimore. He was at my house by lunchtime. I was out front, power washing my awnings. It was a bright, sunny day and several neighbors were also washing their cars. Billy pulled up in The Queen's light blue 1987 Toyota Camry. I guess he didn't want to drive the new $43,000 black Corvette he bought just before he went to prison. He actually bought a red Corvette first, drove it around town a bit, but didn't like the color. So he took it back, like somebody else would return a pair of pants, and exchanged it for the black one. But on the day he got out of prison, he didn't want to draw attention to himself and have the FBI following him. So, instead, here was Billy, a guy who could afford the most expensive cars—and lawyers—in town, driving a car with 200,000 miles on it. The Queen had begged Billy to let her buy a new car, even with her own money, but he had refused while he was in prison. It was just one more way he could control her.

I wasn't surprised to see him. I knew he was getting released that day, but I figured he would go to see his two daughters before he came to see me. I guess not. He looked glad to see me. He was in a great mood and he immediately took up with me where we left off, kidding and cutting up. I tried hard not to show my paranoia around him. I felt like a piece of shit talking to him. Here I was, thinking about putting him in prison for God only knew how much time. All I could do was put on a mask and try to act like I was still enthused with the life we led. But I worried he would see through me.

As we talked, I could see the neighbors stopping to stare. Billy was like a celebrity in Hampden. Even people who didn't care for him were going door-to-door, whispering to their neighbors, "Billy Isaacs is out of prison."

That day he told me we were going to get even with everybody who ever did anything to us. And we were going to take control of all the illegal operations he headed up before he went to prison. He didn't mention his plan for us to murder Ricky and Ronnie. At least I was thankful for that. An old part of me was glad to see Billy come home, but a new voice inside my head warned me to keep my distance.

Those days after the raid went by in a blur, but I do recall one unusual conversation I had when word got out

about the search of my house. I was having a drink at
Buckley's, a little corner bar in Remington, a neighborhood just south of Hampden. I got into a conversation
with a neighborhood woman I'd known for years. Her
name was Pat Wheeler and she was friendly with a lot of
people I knew and was even at my wedding to Gina. Pat
worked as a secretary for the U.S. Attorney's Office
downtown and she had occasionally bragged about having access to sensitive criminal information. She'd even
offered to leak details of criminal investigations to Billy
and me over the years, but I'd never taken her up on the
offer. Now she had just heard about the raid and offered
to find out if the FBI was involved in the gambling investigation, along with the Baltimore police. "Thanks,
but stay out of it," I told her. I figured I could probably
get off easy from a local charge for gambling. But I also
had my mind made up to go to the FBI, so I wouldn't
need her help. Of course, I didn't tell her that. Within
a week I was on my way to Washington, DC, and was in
such a state of anxiety that I'd already forgotten about
my conversation with Pat.

The Long Train Ride

The day of my trip I was paranoid about being followed by some of the guys, especially since Billy was
home now. I refused even to take the train from Penn
Station in midtown Baltimore in case I bumped into
someone I knew. Instead, my brother, Johnny, and I met
up at the Baltimore-Washington International Airport,
south of the city, and got on a train from there.

It was a day of overwhelming desperation and despair
for me. As I looked out the train window, I could see the
houses and the trees race by, just as my life had rushed
recklessly past me for the last twenty years. I wondered

how I could have lived such a wild life, and yet have missed so much. I had a thousand questions running through my mind. What would happen to my family if I went to prison? Would my friends go to prison? Who would support their children if they did? I asked myself how I ended up like this. If nothing else, I hoped I would finally get some relief knowing that I was about to end my criminal life.

"Everything will be all right," said Johnny. I knew he meant well, but his words didn't reassure me. Nothing he said calmed me down. My hands were perspiring badly, but it wasn't from the summer heat. I still wore my $20 gold piece on a chain around my neck. I used to love that gold piece. But today I hid it under my shirt. I guess I was embarrassed by the greedy life it represented.

When we arrived in Washington, DC, we walked down Pennsylvania Avenue and turned the corner, where we found a small security kiosk. Then we walked down a long sidewalk that cut an opening toward the entrance of the hulking, sandy-colored building that bore the name of J. Edgar Hoover. There on the wall near the entrance was an inscription, a quote from J. Edgar Hoover himself: "The most effective weapon against crime is cooperation . . . The efforts of all law enforcement agencies with the support and understanding of the American People."

I looked at the word, "cooperation." I was about to become a cooperating witness, a nice word for "informant" or "snitch."

My knees almost buckled. I asked myself several times, "Is this what you really want to do?" I was a stand-up guy. I had stood through many battles and hardships with my wiseguy friends. They were my family—especially Billy. I had heeded Billy's words all these years: "Nobody talks, everybody walks." I even kept the murder secret when I went to jail for drugs almost ten years before. I could have snitched to get a lighter sentence, but I was loyal to the core. Not anymore. In just a few minutes I would wipe out twenty years of friendships by implicating my entire crime family.

I felt especially bad for two of the men involved in the Mark Schwandtner murder. Both had changed their lives in the eighteen years since the killing. John Derry had become a plumber. Ronnie Rogers, who had driven the others with the victim to the murder scene, but waited in the car during the killing, had moved to another state and changed his life, too. I felt bad for their families. But I believed if my life was going to change, I had to tell the truth about the murder. And that meant implicating the killers.

I truly believed that going to the FBI was the only way I could change my life for good. If I just walked away, like my wife had asked me to, I'd never be able to stay away forever. Someday I'd be back making the same old scores. If Billy didn't drag me back, I'd be back on my own. As tired as I was of that life, I knew I was still an addict for the money and the power. Going to the FBI, I was like an alcoholic throwing away the bottle. And at that moment I was too tired and remorseful to do anything but walk straight ahead.

My stomach was tied in knots as I asked myself, "When is enough, enough?"

I walked through the front door of the Federal Bureau of Investigation and changed my life.

We gave our drivers' licenses to the security workers. They called upstairs to Bruce, who was expecting us. He came down to meet us as we were issued visitor's passes. He shook my hand and greeted us as if we were just friends about to get a tour. But we all knew I wasn't there to sightsee. Bruce had even told his supervisor I was coming and would likely confess my crimes to him.

The sham we had going about my friend in trouble was now gone. We walked through a turnstile and started down a long hallway with cream-colored walls. We got on an elevator and went to another floor, traveling through many locked doors that Bruce seemed to open magically with sensors in his security badge. Bruce was a supervisory special agent in the FBI's materials-analysis unit. His specialty was examining soil, glass and building materials for evidence of crimes.

We finally entered a maze of areas where he and the other scientists work. It was filled with large microscopes and huge, complicated instruments I didn't recognize. They probably cost millions of dollars. Bruce started giving us his tour. I could tell it was his way of making me feel comfortable.

"Here's the chemistry unit," he said, showing us where the organic chemists break down compounds where drugs are hidden. He showed us examples of bottles that contained a malt beverage, where cocaine was dissolved in the drink. The drug could later be extracted by reconstituting it. It just showed how creative a criminal can be, not that I didn't already know that.

He also showed us through the fibers unit, the trace evidence unit, the explosives unit and the metallurgy group. It all looked so high-tech to me. What interested me the most, though, was the lowest-tech display of all—duct tape. "Not all duct tape is created equal," said Bruce, showing us the many textures, shades and even colors of duct tape. Scientists could identify a type of duct tape by counting the number of fibers per inch and comparing it to other types of tape. He told us how FBI scientists could examine the cut end of a piece of duct tape that might be wrapped around a dead body and match the cut end of a roll of duct tape in a suspect's car, for example. It was amazing what they could do.

My Confession

We finally found our way to Bruce's corner office, with windows that overlooked E and Ninth Streets. It was filled with government-issued cabinets made of steel and glass. The bookshelves were filled with books I'd never seen before. He had books on chemistry, mineralogy, physics and geology. On a workbench were several microscopes, along with samples of soil, glass and rocks. Bruce often traveled around the world to investigate cases and testify at trials. During his career he had handled one thousand criminal cases. He helped put a captain of John Gotti's Mafia family in prison by taking dirt dug from the graves where five bodies were found in Staten Island and tracing the soil to a shovel in the captain's home.

He helped solve a murder of a Michigan woman by testifying that the concrete blocks used to sink her body matched a concrete block in the killer's house. He also investigated Unabomber Theodore Kaczynski by attempting to trace glass tubing used in the bombs to tubing factories around the country. He also testified at the highly publicized trial in Wyoming where two men were convicted of beating a gay man named Matthew Shepard and leaving him to die. Bruce had examined a soil sample from the bumper of the vehicle driven by the suspects and testified that it likely came from soil at the murder scene.

After the 1992 standoff at Ruby Ridge, Idaho, Bruce was brought in to examine evidence regarding the killing by an FBI sniper of Vicky Weaver, the wife of white separatist Randy Weaver. Bruce testified that the agent did not have an unobstructed view of the woman, who was standing behind a door. He traced the trajectory of the bullet and showed how it went through the door window, leaving a mirror-image hole through a closed curtain. The sniper, said Bruce, could not necessarily have seen Vicky Weaver standing behind the door.

WISED UP   159

He also was part of a team investigating the suicide of Clinton White House official Vincent Foster, whose body was found in a Washington Park. Suspicions that his body was dumped in the park after he was murdered were ruled out after Bruce's analysis. He discovered the soil on Foster's shoes matched the soil on the park trail. That meant Foster likely walked into the park before his death.

Bruce even confirmed the type of fertilizer used in the 1995 Oklahoma City bombing.

Now, in his office, he showed me his collection of dark-colored rocks from Mount Rainier in Washington State. This was Bruce's domain. It showed how far he'd come from our days as kids in North Point Village. As for me, I might as well have been on Mars.

I'm sure he could tell I was out of my element. He finally sat me down. "I know we've talked about your friend," he said. "Now take a deep breath, Charlie. Are you sure you want to do this?" he asked.

"Yes, I'm sure," I said.

Bruce made it very clear that, even though we were old friends, he wasn't cutting me any slack. "You can't tell me something that I shouldn't know. You can't tell me you were involved in a crime and then take it back," he said. "I also can't promise you that you won't go to prison." But he did promise to give me moral support, no matter what happened. "I'll do everything I can to shepherd you through this experience," he said.

Bruce didn't really know what my crimes were. He'd never asked through all the years of funerals when he helped bury my parents and my grandmother. But he knew I'd been "out of pocket" for twenty years. A man could get into a lot of trouble in twenty years.

When I started to talk, he didn't act surprised. I probably sounded like a volcanic eruption. My story came out in rapid fire. There was just so much to tell. The bookmaking, the shylocking, the drugs, the video poker machines, the money laundering, the corrupt police and, of course, the murder I was covering up and the murders I was asked to commit. Here I was, in the place Bruce called "the Vatican of law enforcement," making the most important confession of my life.

I was pretty nervous, but I hoped he could tell I was sincere. Bruce acted like he was in control. He held out his paper so I could see the notes he was taking. He wanted me to trust him. But I didn't know that he also was sizing me up. He was making sure I wasn't "reverse interviewing" him. For all he knew, the Baltimore FBI could have been investigating me and I was here to con information out of him. Maybe I was trying to find out how much trouble I was in with the FBI. If I had asked questions about the kinds of investigations conducted by the FBI, it would have been a tip-off. But I didn't ask those questions. And he seemed to believe me. When I was done, he began talking about my friends.

"Any one of those guys could have helped himself and done what you're doing, Charlie," said Bruce. "Place yourself on a ship with all the guys you've been associated with for the last twenty years. There is only one lifeboat," he said. When the meeting ended, the three of us went to dinner.

Afterward, Bruce drove Johnny and me back to our cars at the Baltimore airport. I got in my car and drove home alone. I didn't know what would happen to me next, but I felt some relief. I finally had said what was bottled up inside me for half my life.

Days went by as I waited to hear from Bruce. He had to spend some time checking out my stories to see if they were true. He also had to find out if I was already under investigation from the FBI.

At least I wasn't having nightmares. How could I? I wasn't sleeping enough to dream at all. I honestly believed I was going to prison for a long time. I told myself I had to accept responsibility for the slimeball I had become and for the crimes I had committed. I tried to keep my worries from Gina, but it wasn't easy. I didn't tell her I'd gone to Washington, DC, to see Bruce. I tried to act normal. But now I had even more to worry about than I did before my meeting with Bruce. I already had city police detectives following me. Who knows, maybe the FBI was following me, too. And what about my friends? If they discovered I'd met with the FBI, I wouldn't live long enough to go to prison.

In a week Bruce arranged a meeting for me with the Baltimore FBI office. I had told him I didn't trust any law enforcement officer in Baltimore. I knew there were dirty police in Baltimore. Maybe the Baltimore FBI agents were dirty, too. But Bruce assured me the Baltimore FBI agents I would be meeting with would never leak information to my wiseguy friends. Finally Bruce called me with instructions.

Facing The Enemy

On September 14, at 11:00 A.M., I was to go to a hotel room on the fifth floor of the Hampton Inn near the Baltimore-Washington International Airport. I was a nervous wreck on my way there. Any number of people could be tailing me. Even though I didn't notice any strange cars following me, I made U-turns in the streets on my way to the airport. When I got to the hotel parking lot, I circled my Lincoln round and round before I parked. Every person I saw looked like a police detective or an FBI agent.

I took the elevator to the fifth floor. My heart was pounding so fast and hard that I thought I actually could hear the beat echoing off the elevator walls. When I got off the elevator, I stopped for a few seconds. I had always prided myself in being able to control any situation. But now, there would be no shaving of points on some sport bet, no laying off a number if a bet got too heavy. There would be no threatening to beat up some poor slob for not making his juice payments. I had been at the top of the food chain of organized crime in Baltimore. Now I was at the bottom, turning over control of my life to people I considered my enemies.

I found the door to room 520. I heard several voices inside the meeting room. I took a deep breath. *This is it,* I thought. I knocked and the voices became silent. I heard footsteps. Bruce opened the door with a serious look on his face. Inside, there were three other FBI agents, Stephen Clary, Dan Dreibelbis and James Orr. I recognized Dreibelbis and Orr, who were sitting on a couple of lounge chairs. We had crossed paths before. But I had never met Clary, a white-haired man who sat at a long conference table. As we were introduced, I immediately started looking for hidden cameras and listening devices. Of course, I wouldn't have been able to tell if the room was bugged, but I looked anyway. I knew these guys were professionals.

They apparently didn't know what to make of me at first. They knew no one in the FBI was investigating me, so there was no reason for me to come to them on this day. A cornered criminal usually will show up with a lawyer to make a deal—shorter prison time in exchange for squealing on your crime family. But I came without a lawyer and didn't ask for any special treatment.

I sat down on a couch next to Bruce. My mouth was so dry from nervousness that I didn't know if I could get a word out. The other agents had already been briefed by Bruce so they knew what questions to ask.

Steve Clary did most of the talking. He was a blunt-talking, longtime FBI agent, the only guy in the room not wearing a suit jacket or a sport coat. And I immediately took a disliking to him.

"So, Charlie, Bruce said you wanted to talk to us."

"Yes," I said.

Bruce spoke up. "I need you to tell these folks the same thing that you told me in my office." So I repeated my story.

Unlike my meeting with Bruce at the J. Edgar Hoover Building, the atmosphere was not friendly. It was downright chilly. The agents here were on their guard, not knowing what to make of me, coming in on my own without a lawyer. Steve Clary hammered me with questions. He wanted dates, times and every detail you could imagine. There was something about his manner that told me he didn't trust me. He even laughed at me when I told him how much money Billy had piled up and how big organized crime had gotten in Baltimore, right under the FBI's nose.

Steve also asked Bruce some questions, almost as if he were interrogating a fellow agent. He wanted to know how long Bruce knew about my criminal involvement—as if Bruce had been covering up for me. I wondered if they were playing good cop/bad cop, with Bruce being the nice guy and Steve being the tough guy. Steve was careful not to divulge anything about the FBI's knowledge of my friends' crimes. When I'd mention a wiseguy's name, he gave me no indication how much the FBI knew about that person.

I could tell Steve was an experienced agent by the questions he asked. For one thing, he knew how shylocking worked. I was able to size him up pretty quickly. He would have made a great wiseguy, I thought. I would have to be out of my mind if I thought I could bullshit Steve Clary.

"What are you looking for?" asked Steve.

"I'm not looking for any deals," I said. "I just want out, even if it means I'll spend twenty years in prison." Out of fairness, I said, the other wiseguys should get the same prison sentence that I get.

I made it clear that I wanted my family protected. And I wanted the FBI to protect them, not the U.S. marshals, and certainly not the Baltimore police. I told Steve that I trusted Bruce and that Bruce had guaranteed no FBI agent in the Baltimore field office was dirty. Bruce had promised that the Baltimore FBI agents would not allow anything bad to happen to my family.

"Do you have a lawyer you'd like with you?" Steve asked. I answered no. He asked if I was in trouble with the law already. I told him about my house being raided by city police for bookmaking. I said I wasn't afraid of a bookmaking charge, because I knew I'd get away with a slap on the wrist.

"Have you ever killed anybody?" he asked. I answered no, though I told them about the two murders Billy wanted me to commit. And, of course, I told him about the unsolved murder of Mark Schwandtner. I told Steve all the details I could remember, that John Derry had hit the guy over the head with a baseball bat on a bridge above the Gunpowder Falls, that Billy went down and drowned him. Steve Clary wrote the details down in his stenographer's notebook. "Billy I, Ronnie Rogers, John Derry" and others, he wrote. "Billy and John beat—John took bat—hit victim . . . Guy wasn't dead . . . Ronnie up on the bank . . . Bleeding heavy—head split open. Had to drown him. Didn't take wallet. John throws the bat and his clothes into the Jones Falls. John and Billy's clothes had blood on it."

Steve even sketched a little map of the storm drain at Greenmount Avenue and Thirty-third Street where we stashed the bloody clothes. I talked for about two and a half hours. When I was done, I thought they were just going to arrest me. I was even more nervous and frightened than I was before I walked in the door, if it were possible. But they said I was free to leave. I was in total shock. Who would have thought in a million years that I could have walked out of that room that day? When I got home, I finally told Gina what was going on. She was scared to death that I was going to prison for a very long time—or that I would end up dead before the FBI had a chance to take me away.

I was relieved they had let me go. But I was still put off by Steve Clary's attitude. He didn't seem to believe me and that made me mad. I hadn't come this far and put my life on the line for an FBI agent to think I was lying. I told Bruce, "I'm not going to deal with the FBI if I have to talk to Steve Clary again. Get me somebody else."

Bruce tried to reason with me. He was familiar with my hot temper. "Come on, Charlie, give Steve another chance," said Bruce.

When I calmed down, I decided to follow Bruce's advice. I gave Steve another chance. I couldn't have known it then, but it would be the best second chance I ever gave anybody.

Days later I got a call from Bruce. I was instructed to go to a safe house, a secret location where agents went to meet with people like me. It was an ordinary apartment off Route 40 on Baltimore County's west side. It was just a regular suburban apartment with not so fashionable furniture from the 1960s—chairs and sofas with crude wooden frames that held cheap cushions. (On one of my subsequent visits one of the chairs collapsed with an agent in it.) I found the decor pretty depressing. The federal government wasn't wasting any tax dollars here. There was a small kitchen and living room and a few bedrooms. It was a place I would eventually become very familiar with.

The agents always reminded me never to touch the lamps. I figured the place was bugged to the max. They used to say they could hide me and my family here for a few days if things got too hectic. I knew Gina and the kids certainly wouldn't have liked to stay in that place for even one night. I'd say, "No thanks, we'll take our chances on the streets."

That first day, though, I wasn't thinking about the decor when I walked into that apartment. There was Bruce, Steve Clary and a few other agents. They'd also brought their supervisor, Mel Fleming. He was very nice to me. Of course, he had to be if he wanted to get any information out of me. Mel was a notorious tightwad with the government's money. The agents were always begging him for cash to run their undercover operations. You'd think it was Mel's own bank account, the way he held on to every penny of the government's money.

There was one other agent who wasn't at the previous meeting at the airport hotel. He was introduced as Special Agent Thomas J. McNamara. He was a regular-looking, averaged-size guy, a redhead in his late thirties who resembled the actor Ron Howard. Agent McNamara was a poker-faced agent and a lawyer, and—I would eventually learn—as honest and straitlaced as an FBI agent can be. Agent McNamara and Agent Clary told me they would be handling my case. McNamara would be my official handler. I would also be working side by side with Clary.

The two of them gave me my marching orders: I had to stop selling and taking drugs. I couldn't threaten or beat up anyone. I couldn't sell stolen goods and I had to give up shylocking. I could never lie to them. Before I did anything illegal, I was to contact them and they would decide whether I was allowed to do it. They also said if they ever discovered me doing anything illegal that they didn't know about, I would be arrested, just like anyone else. They told me I could keep the bookmaking going, only to make it look like I was still a wiseguy. And I had to report to McNamara or Clary, every day with word of what I was doing.

They knew I was scared to death that there might be corrupt FBI agents in Baltimore, or that local police assigned to work with the FBI might be dirty. They assured me all the officers they worked with were clean. But, just to put me at ease, they agreed never to speak my name in the Baltimore FBI headquarters in Woodlawn. Instead, McNamara picked a code name for me. It was Warlock, a name he came up with while watching reruns of the '60s TV show, *Bewitched* with his kids. When I called him, I was to use this name, instead of my real name.

The agents also gave me a code number. It was 520, the room number where I'd first met FBI agents at the Hampton Inn. Whenever we paged each other, we would use that number to identify ourselves. Before long, I gave McNamara his own nickname. I figured, my wiseguy friends had nicknames, why shouldn't my FBI handler? Out of habit I simply called him Tommy. He never really liked me calling him that. "That's a kid's nickname," he would say. "My name is Tom." But it stuck anyway. I still call him Tommy.

On a small slip of white paper, Steve Clary wrote down the phone numbers of all the agents—but left off their names—so I could get in touch with them anytime I needed them. I put the paper in my wallet for safekeeping. Within a week I was signing papers to have my Lincoln bugged with a tape recorder hidden in the trunk. I agreed to carry a tiny tape recorder when I met with my old friends. The agents also gave me a pager. Eventually they would get me a cell phone, but not until they set up a phony identity and credit so I could get the phone. I also agreed to let them tap my home phone so the FBI could listen to me talking to my friends. I guess I had been an actor all my life. I'd conned people out of money, sweet-talked or threatened them into paying their debts. I'd put on great acts of denial to police and lied to more people than I can remember. Now I was about to begin the most important role of my life. Could I fool Billy Isaacs and a few hundred other wiseguys?

Chapter 10

The Betrayal—
Working Undercover

Working for the FBI became exciting, just because of wearing a wire. When you lived the life Billy and I lived, our lives were exciting, too. If people owed us money, we had to figure out how to catch them. Now I was trying to catch my own guys. A few times I can honestly say I was scared to death, absolutely scared to death.

My first night on the job with the FBI was Halloween, 1995. Like all other trick-or-treaters, I would be in my own costume that night. I'd be wearing the "mask" of a loyal wiseguy. That night would also teach me a lot about the importance of teamwork with FBI agents, but I would also learn that even the best plans didn't always work out as we expected. The logistics of setting up criminals to fall into a trap doesn't always play out as neatly as a Hollywood movie.

Before I could meet up with Steve and Tommy, I had to spend the early evening with my family. Halloween was a big deal in my neighborhood. Every year there's a Hampden Halloween Parade through the main streets of the neighborhood. It was a huge event and families came from all over the city. Trophies were awarded by a panel of judges for the scariest, the prettiest and the most original costumes. My daughter, Mandy, won for the prettiest costume two years in a row. By 1995, though, she was getting a little old for trick-or-treating, so I took Justin door-to-door. I wouldn't miss Halloween—or marching in the parade—for any wiseguy or FBI agent. Usually, I would hand out toys to the kids in the neighborhood, in place of candy. I'd have cases of baby dolls and wrestling figures I'd get for one quarter of the original price. Some years I gave out dollar coins to some of the poor kids who lived near us. But, of course, this year I was under a vow of honesty with the FBI. In this case it meant an oath to pay retail, so I gave out candy, like everybody else.

Earlier that day I had received a page from a drug dealer named Mike Bush. He wanted to sell me five ounces of cocaine. I called Steve and told him about the deal, but there was a problem setting up surveillance. Mike was with Frankie Tamburello, a convicted drug dealer, in Ocean City and they wanted me to take a three-hour drive over the Chesapeake Bay Bridge to meet them to get the stuff. There was no way I wanted to drive to Ocean City and there was no way for the FBI to set up surveillance that quickly for the trip. I had to stall for time. I called Mike back several times with excuses. I recorded each conversation with Mike that I made from pay phones in Hampden to his cell phone.

I told him I had something important to do the next morning and needed to stay in Baltimore. Mike said he could easily solve my problem. He would send a small plane to pick me up at a private airport near White Marsh, a Northeast Baltimore suburb. I could make it to the ocean and back in time for my morning appointment, he said. Now I had to come up with another excuse. "Gina and I have been arguing a lot lately because I wasn't home for a couple of days," I told him. "I don't want to go down the ocean and make things worse at home," I lied.

Finally Mike had another idea. He'd have a guy named Dino come meet me in Baltimore after Halloween was over, so I took Justin trick-or-treating. Tommy was also taking his kids trick-or-treating; then we were going to meet up with Steve Clary by 8:30 P.M. to come up with our game plan for snaring Dino with the cocaine.

I was going absolutely nuts trying not to let Gina know what was going on. Of course, I had told her about going to the FBI, but I didn't tell her what my assignment was going to be with them. Even on that first day working undercover, I could tell my life was going to be moving way too fast—even for a wiseguy. But I had no other choice. I had signed on with the FBI so I could change my life. I didn't have any time to look back or second-guess myself. I just moved full tilt.

I met Tommy and Steve in Northeast Baltimore in the parking lot of a big book and gift store, Greetings and Readings. I was supposed to meet with Dino in the shopping center across the street. I used my cell phone, attached to a tape recorder, to call Mike's cell phone to let him know where I was. Frankie answered. Just as I started to have a conversation with him, my battery went dead. Tommy quickly handed me his battery so I could call Mike's cell phone again. Just as I was about to start talking, Tommy's battery went dead. Next we tried Steve's batteries, but they were dead, too. This was in the early days of handheld cell phones, when batteries often went dead. "Oh, Jesus, I can't believe we're going to miss this one," said Steve. It got very tense. But then he tried to relax me. There will always be another day to catch the likes of Mike Bush and some of the other big drug dealers. "They're greedy and they want to get rid of the stuff as fast as they can," said Steve. And I knew drug dealers were willing to front the stuff to unload it as fast as they could so they wouldn't get caught sitting on a big shipment.

Finally we walked over to the pay phones in the shopping center, but naturally, we couldn't get a dial tone. They were out of order. Here I was, my first night on the job as an FBI informant, and we couldn't find a working phone to set up a drug deal. *This never happens in the movies*, I thought. The FBI has all kinds of fancy gadgets and gizmos and they always work just fine on a Hollywood screen.

The three of us hurried across the street to find a working pay phone and I finally called Mike and Frankie back. There's a problem, said Frankie. He and Mike couldn't get hold of Dino. He said he'd call me back at the pay phone in a half hour. Meanwhile, Tommy used another pay phone to call an FBI agent named Kevin. When we hung up, Tommy asked me how I would feel about this agent going with me to make the drug score. He'd pretend to be another drug dealer. "I don't like the idea, but I'll think about it after I meet the guy," I said. I wanted to size him up before committing to working with him. Tommy described him as a biker guy and said Kevin was good at undercover work. He'd disguised himself as a biker and caught some of the members of the Hell's Angels in New York. I thought, *I can never work with someone who looks like a biker. He'd never pass for a wiseguy.*

While we were waiting for Mike to call back, a pickup truck pulled up. A man dressed as a biker or a construction worker got out and introduced himself to me as Agent Kevin Bonner. Though I didn't think much of his getup, there was something about Kevin's personality that caught my attention. He was calm and self-confident. He also seemed like a really nice, no-bullshit type of guy. As we talked, I thought, *This could work*. I agreed to consider working with him, but not on this night. I wanted to go it alone for now.

Finally Frankie called me back. Dino would meet me a
few miles away at the Superfresh supermarket at Harford
Road and Taylor Avenue. He'd be driving a Mustang.
Frankie had already told Dino that he couldn't miss my
Lincoln. Now it was past 11:00 P.M. when Steve, Tommy
and Kevin got me ready for my first undercover sting.
Steve patted me down to make sure I wasn't carrying any
drugs. It didn't upset me. It was all part of standard pro-
cedure to make sure I was clean of any contraband. The
three agents tailed me in their cars and parked in different spots in the Superfresh parking lot; each one could
see me from a different angle.

They gave me $2,400 as a partial payment for five
ounces of cocaine. I would still owe Dino $3,600. He got
out of his Mustang and got into my Lincoln. For the first
of many times, I secretly flipped on a toggle switch under
the dashboard to turn on the tape recorder hidden in the
trunk. I felt the same adrenaline rush I got from making
a big score as a wiseguy and getting away with it. And I
wasn't scared at all—just excited.

Dino was a little guy with dark hair, whom I'd never met
before. Our conversation didn't last long, but I made sure
I got it on tape. He asked if I was Charlie. I said yes. I asked
him how many ounces he was giving me. He handed me
the bag and that was it.

After Dino drove away, the agents searched me again.
Then they sent me home, but not before telling me I
had done a fantastic job. Their compliments made me
feel like I was part of the team. That meant a lot to me.

An Infamous Fraternity

That night was my baptism into an infamous fraternity
of informants. We all have our reasons for coming forward. The most notorious snitch in recent years was

Sammy "The Bull" Gravano. Sammy was in thick with the New York Mafia, working as a hit man and underboss for mob chief John Gotti. Sammy was under indictment in New York for a laundry list of crimes, which included murder, loan-sharking, illegal gambling and conspiracy to commit murder. But after his arrest he went to the U.S. attorneys in New York and testified against Gotti and dozens of others. His testimony made the government's case against the Mafia much stronger. And it was worth it to them to let Sammy off easy.

He only had to serve five years in prison; then he went into the federal witness protection program and moved to Arizona. With the new name of Johnny Moran, he ran a construction company. But it was his side business that got him into hot water. In 2000 he was busted along with his ex-wife, son and daughter for running a drug ring selling thirty thousand tablets a week of the drug ecstasy. His profits were more than $500,000. I guess Sammy couldn't stay away from the fast life. And it's a shame he had to teach his bad habits to his kids. What a jerk for throwing it all away. He had a chance to stay clean, to be a changed man. And he blew it. I guess he really just didn't have it in his heart to change his life around. I hoped I did.

Over the following days and weeks I ran around town like a madman, paying for drugs with the FBI's money and trying to catch bigger drug dealers than Dino. Dino was known as a "bumper" in the drug trade, a guy the FBI calls a "cushion," used to protect the big drug dealer from having a face-to-face meeting with the person buying the coke.

After that first night I started using Agent Kevin Bonner as my new drug-buying partner. He continued to dress like a biker or construction worker, but his wardrobe was the least of my worries. The FBI never gave him enough cash to make him look like a drug dealer—and certainly not a wiseguy. And Kevin, like the other agents, had no idea how to count money. I don't mean that they couldn't do math; I mean they couldn't count money fast like I could. One day the agents were counting cash to give me for an undercover drug buy. They were taking forever, counting real slowly, "Twenty . . . forty . . . sixty."

I finally grabbed the cash and said, "Let me count it for you." I counted money so fast, the green edges of the bills blurred. They were impressed. Every time a new agent came on the job, Tommy would say, "Hey, watch Charlie count money." I couldn't believe these guys. They never carried more than forty dollars of their own money with them at one time. I don't know how they survived.

I also got real nervous a few times when Kevin paid for meals with a credit card. No self-respecting wiseguy ever used a credit card. That's why we had wads of hundred-dollar bills choking our pockets. And if the credit card didn't give him away, his language should have. Kevin spoke educated English (the guy graduated from Georgetown University Law School). Naturally, wiseguys never use educated English because they're not educated. And they all cuss real bad and use street slang. If wiseguys went to college and law school like Kevin, they sure wouldn't be in this crazy line of work.

Luckily, Kevin was real smooth and confident and easily followed my lead. I couldn't believe it, but the guys fell for his con. It just goes to show how greedy they were. Some days I'd just sit back and watch Kevin, with our hidden tape recorder running, bullshitting with some of the bigger drug dealers. I'd think, *How fucking stupid can you guys be? Does Kevin need a badge to hit you on your forehead that says, "Wake up, I'm a cop"?*

During our first days together, Kevin and I set up drug deals all over Baltimore. We bought drugs in the parking lots of car dealerships, in downtown bars, outside a popular seafood store in the suburbs. And most of our setups went smoothly, without a hint of suspicion from the dealers.

But, of course, that wouldn't last.

A Voice In The Dark

After my first few weeks undercover, I had my first scare that the wiseguys had figured out my ruse. My family and I were asleep at about six o'clock in the morning. As usual, the front door was unlocked and my bedroom door, which faced the stairs, was open. I awoke to the sound of a voice at the top of the staircase. "Charlie, Charlie," the voice whispered. It was Billy. Gina didn't move. I knew she was scared to death. We both were terrified to think Billy already had found me out. It was bad enough that he might kill me, but we both worried he might hurt the kids, too.

Billy had been in my house hundreds of times and had walked through the unlocked door at all hours over the past twenty years. Now his presence gave me an eerie feeling. I decided to keep my cool, not wanting to jump the gun in case he hadn't figured me out. But I was also on my guard in case some of the other guys were hiding downstairs, ready to whack me at Billy's signal. I got dressed and followed him down the stairs, watching along the wall and the floor for shadows from the living-room light I'd left on. I listened for whispering and for footsteps on Gina's immaculate blue carpet.

When I got downstairs, I was relieved to find no one else there. I only had Billy to worry about. I kept my eyes focused on him at all times in case he was going to pull a gun out to whack me. I made sure I was only inches from him so I could grab a gun and wrestle it from him. That would give Gina enough time to call 911. Billy didn't have a weapon, but he had something else that was loaded. It was several pages of wiretap transcripts from the city police. (These are not public documents and to this day I have no idea how he got them.) He already had pages highlighted in light green. Someone must have read the transcripts for him, since he couldn't read very well. He'd found a conversation I'd had back in June with Johnny about Bruce. It was a conversation in which Johnny referred to Billy as God and I said Billy paid off a counselor in prison to get released early. The transcript only mentioned Bruce's first name, but Billy knew instantly it was FBI agent Bruce Hall.

Boy, am I ever in hot water on this one, I thought.

"Why were you talking to Bruce?" Billy asked. He also wanted to know why I would mention that he bribed "hacks," the word we used for prison guards.

I tried to put on my best con voice. I backpedaled and bullshitted as best I could. "I was just running my mouth to my brother, trying to sound like a big shot," I said. Somehow I got him to calm down, though I don't know how convincing I was that morning. Before he left my house, Billy told me he'd kill me if he ever found out through his sources that I was working for the FBI. I wish this was the only close call I had with Billy while I worked undercover. I didn't know if my nerves could take much more.

He may not have hurt me that morning, but I knew his warning was absolutely serious. I knew the wiseguys had someone inside the Baltimore Police Department on the take. I was afraid that, through the wiretaps, the dirty cop might find out I'd been cooperating with the FBI. I could have just dropped everything and left town that day. But I hadn't gotten any proof for the FBI about Mark Schwandtner's murder. I felt stuck in the middle.

As soon as Billy left my house, I called Bruce at home. He got hold of Tommy and the three of us met at a park near FBI headquarters out in Woodlawn. Tommy had

My family: the boy on the right with the smirk on his face
is me at age 8. *(Author's photo)*

My dad in his police uniform in the 1960s. *(Author's photo)*

Billy Isaacs (right) and me (middle) in our early days with Earl Fisher (left). Earl would one day testify that it was me— not Billy—who committed murder. He also told a jury he didn't know Billy. *(Author's photo)*

Melonie, my first wife, with our son, Charlie Jr., in 1979.
(Author's photo)

Billy makes his best man's toast at my wedding to Gina in 1987.
(Author's photo)

Gina and me shortly
after we were married.
(Author's photo)

Joe's Tavern. Not much to look at outside, but a goldmine inside.
(Courtesy of Bill Barry)

Me behind the bar running Joe's while Billy was in federal prison. *(Author's photo)*

Visiting Billy at Allenwood Federal Prison in Pennsylvania. *(Author's photo)*

Doughboy's, a great hangout for wiseguys. *(Courtesy of Bill Barry)*

"Fat Ricky" Payne, Doughboy's owner. The place
was named for his resemblance to the Pillsbury Doughboy.
(Author's photo)

Spanky snapped my Lincoln (behind the pole) just as I drove up to Joe's. *(Courtesy of the Baltimore City Police Department)*

Spanky in 2003, retired from the Baltimore Police Department.
(Courtesy of Bill Barry)

Here we are together after speaking to police detectives at the Baltimore Police Department in 2003.
(Courtesy of Spanky Herold)

FBI agent Steve Clary,
who handled some of
my biggest cases.
(Courtesy of the Clary family)

My handler, FBI agent
Thomas J. McNamara.
(Courtesy of Joan Jacobson)

FBI agent Bruce Hall,
my childhood friend who
helped me come clean.
(Courtesy of Bill Barry)

We moved to this house in Alabama in 1996.
It had my first lawn. *(Courtesy of John Funari)*

Me on a tractor. Another first. *(Courtesy of John Funari)*

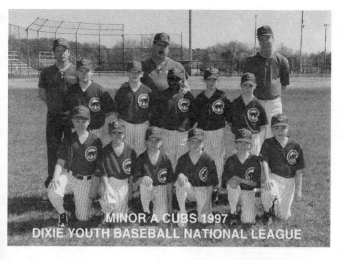

Some of the best times I had were coaching the Dixie Youth
Baseball League. I'm on the right in the back row.
(Courtesy of Mark Sanderson)

Father Joe Culotta at St. Ann
Catholic Church in Decatur
helped keep me sane.
(Courtesy of John Funari)

Gina's Uncle John,
who helped us settle
in Decatur.
(Courtesy of John Funari)

On a visit back to Baltimore I was stashed in a hotel under a phony name. But that didn't prevent a visit from my granddaughter, Melonie. *(Author photo)*

Another secret visit back to Maryland reunited me with my siblings. Left to right: Johnny, his wife Vicky, my brother-in-law Pete, my sister Betty, me and Gina. *(Author photo)*

Undercover city police detective Jim Cabezas as he looked on his taxi driver's license in the 1970s. *(Courtesy of Jim Cabezas)*

This card must be conspicuously displayed at all times

PUBLIC SERVICE COMMISSION

6142

JAMES I. CABEZAS

PASSENGERS
RECORD THE ABOVE NUMBER AND ENTER COMPLAINTS TO THE PUBLIC SERVICE COMMISSION—301 W. PRESTON STREET, BALTIMORE, MD. 21201

Jim in 2003 as chief
investigator for the
Maryland State Prosecutor.
(Courtesy of Bill Barry)

Mike McDonough, the
assistant state prosecutor who
investigated Baltimore liquor
board corruption with Jim.
(Courtesy Bill Barry)

Jim Gentry, assistant states
attorney who prosecuted
Billy Isaacs for murder.
(Courtesy Bill Barry)

Pete Johnson was a young investigator helping prosecute me for drug dealing in the 1980s. Ten years, later he was an assistant state attorney, and I was his star witness in the Isaacs trial. *(Courtesy of Bill Barry)*

Mark Schwandtner in the 1970s, shortly before he was killed.
(Courtesy of the Schwandtner family)

The railroad bridge over the Gunpowder Falls, where Mark was beaten, then thrown into the water. *(Courtesy of Bill Barry)*

The bridge from above. *(Courtesy of Bill Barry)*

My brother Johnny in 2003.
(Courtesy of Bill Barry)

Gina and me in 2003.
(Courtesy of Bill Barry)

Here I am eight years after
I decided to change my life.
(Courtesy of Bill Barry)

the same wiretap transcripts that Billy had and the three of us spent several hours sitting on benches by a pond in the blistering sun going through every page, underlining every statement about Bruce. His name was mentioned about a dozen times. Tommy wanted to get me and my family out of Baltimore right away. It's just too dangerous, he said. He knew Billy was a killer, and he was certainly getting paranoid enough to kill me. Like me, Tommy also was very worried about the leak in the city police department and what that officer might know about my job with the FBI. But I insisted on finishing what I had started with the government.

I didn't know it at the time, but Bruce had put his job on the line for me. When I went to turn myself in to him, he believed he was doing the right thing by helping me come clean. But our unusual relationship apparently caused suspicion inside the FBI. After all, how often does a career criminal turn himself in to an FBI forensic scientist whom he grew up with? And when his FBI phone number came across the penn register being tracked to my phone by the Baltimore police, it set off alarms. (A penn register is a device that records the phone numbers of all incoming and outgoing calls to your phone.)

The FBI must have wondered what a bookmaker and drug dealer like me was doing calling an FBI agent. Maybe they thought Bruce could be involved in criminal activity with me. There was an internal FBI investigation of Bruce, who had been a loyal agent and scientist for ten years by then. It's unsettling for me to think the FBI mistrusted Bruce. He was as dedicated as they came.

But I turned myself in during the time when the FBI was on high alert for corrupt agents. The agency had just been disgraced by a scandal in Boston, in which mobster James "Whitey" Bulger manipulated FBI agent John Connolly, his childhood friend, to cover up for his violent crimes while Bulger worked as an informant.

After Connolly retired from the FBI, he was convicted of racketeering and obstruction of justice and got a ten-year prison sentence. Bulger disappeared and got himself on the FBI's Most Wanted list.

Maybe the FBI was just being extra careful to root out corrupt agents back then. In Bruce's case he was cleared of any wrongdoing. He told me none of this at the time. He acted like his only concern was for my welfare. That just shows you what kind of a stand-up guy he is.

As for me, I thought I was towing the line pretty well in my new life. I had stopped taking drugs, stopped collecting juice on loans and hadn't threatened or hurt anybody since going to the FBI. But it wasn't always easy to keep my old life and new life separate. One day I was at the FBI headquarters with Tommy. He asked me to open the trunk of my Lincoln so he could make sure the hidden tape recorder was working. I popped the lid. Inside, the trunk was filled with imported crystal in the shape of swans and eagles. Big pieces. "What's this?" Tommy said, eyeing me.

"It's crystal," I said innocently. I had gotten the whole lot from a guy named Al in Little Italy. He got them hot off the docks.

"What are you going to do with it?"

"I'm gonna sell it," I said.

"Oh, no you're not. You've got to give it back," he ordered.

"How the hell am I supposed to give it back to Al?" I asked.

But that's exactly what I did. I went back to Little Italy with a song and dance about how I couldn't unload the damn swans and eagles.

I got into another jam in those first weeks, and this one almost cost me my life.

One afternoon I got home and took the mini tape recorder out of my pocket. Billy arrived at my door a few minutes later. "Get in the car, we're going for a drive," he said. This was not at all unusual. For years Billy and I would show up at each other's homes and simply say, "Get in the car, we're going for a drive." We'd never tell one another why, because it might be for a long drive somewhere one of us did not want to go. So, I was not alarmed that afternoon. We drove up to the Rotunda shopping center, several blocks from my house. We went in the back door, past the Radio Shack. Then Billy headed me toward the men's restroom.

Inside, he ordered me to strip. You have no idea how relieved I was to have just taken the tape recorder out of my pocket. Still, I was real nervous and put the best wiseguy face on that I could muster up. I pulled my pants down and lifted up my shirt. I laughed it off. "Now you strip, too," I said to Billy. I figured, fair is fair. He ignored my suggestion. I could tell that even though Billy found me clean, he still didn't trust me. He sensed something had changed about me. Disappointed that he couldn't confirm his suspicions, he took me back home.

As soon as he was gone, I dropped my guard and completely flipped out. I paged my FBI agents from a pay phone outside the 7-Eleven up the street. They could tell by my voice I was completely panicked. They did their best to calm me down. "Whatever you do, don't get in the car again with Billy," Steve warned. Tommy thought I should quit right there because it had gotten too dangerous. "I can't quit yet," I said. "I ain't got Billy yet."

As usual, Steve and Tommy were there to boost me up, but it was Bruce who gave me the courage to keep going.

You have to remember that Bruce is a scientist, as well as an FBI agent. And like a scientist, he analyzes everything to the last little detail. He would walk me through whatever crisis I was in at the moment and break it down, point by point. He would remind me that I was an adrenaline junkie and warn me not to get caught up in the moment, no matter how dangerous and exciting the job. He said he knew how I felt. Sometimes he would be caught up in an investigation he was doing and he just didn't want it to end. He would remind me my undercover work would be over soon. "When this is all said and done, make sure you're just the observer from the porch. You'll be retired. Just make sure you don't ever leave that porch again."

By the time he was through talking, my situation seemed almost bearable. He just had a way of making things not seem as bad as they really were.

Wiring The Walls

Once I got into my role with the FBI, I got a great idea for snagging the wiseguys. I used my last $40,000 to open a sub shop in Hampden on Thirty-sixth Street. I called it Eat-N-Run. I hoped I could use it to catch Billy or John Derry admitting to murder. If the FBI wired the place, maybe I could get one of the murderers to come in and talk in front of a hidden video camera. The FBI agreed to put in listening devices in the sub shop and a hidden camera in a fake alarm bell out back. It wasn't safe to install the hidden equipment during the day because the guys would wonder what was going on, but the FBI decided to install the fake bell and cameras inside during daylight. I could just tell the guys I was having an alarm system put in. Two FBI technicians named Art and Bruce came at ten o'clock in the morning dressed as alarm guys. They were the same ones who installed the tape recorder in my Lincoln. We acted like we didn't know each other. They introduced themselves with phony names and I pretended to know their boss. Wiseguys were already in the sub shop eating breakfast and drinking coffee. The guys wanted to know why I was having an alarm system put in. They knew nobody would bust into the place—all the neighborhood burglars already worked for us. I told the guys it was them I worried about. "You'd all eat for free and steal everything that isn't nailed down," I told them. "So I'm putting in cameras to watch you." They thought it was hilarious.

Art and Bruce started installing the fake bell in the rear of the shop. Around lunchtime Tommy showed up, acting like he was the owner of the alarm company. Tommy told me where they were going to install the cameras. The guys started joking about the cameras. Tommy and I were laughing, too. When I offered Tommy lunch, one of the guys said Tommy looked just like an FBI agent, young and clean-cut. "Hey, Charlie," shouted the wiseguy, "if you're offering this guy free lunch, he must be a cop or an FBI agent." You could have heard a pin drop. Tommy and I looked at each other for a split second. I turned to the wiseguy. "You're just saying that because you're such a cheapskate," I wisecracked. Finally everybody started joking again, and I breathed a sigh of relief.

It wasn't the first time I worried that Tommy looked too much like a cop. One day, when we driving through Hampden, I noticed his sunglasses.

"Tommy, these glasses have got to go," I said. "They look like police glasses."

I handed him a pair of $80 Oakley designer sunglasses.

"I can't take these," he said. "They're probably hot." I didn't say anything.

So, we reached a compromise. He took off his glasses and went without. It was just what you'd expect from an agent who wouldn't even take an illegal parking space.

The day after the technicians put in the fake camera, they returned to install the real thing, along with a VCR in the basement.

They met me at a nearby grocery store parking lot

after midnight, put their tools in my wife's van and went to the sub shop. That way, if any of the guys saw only my vehicle, it wouldn't raise any eyebrows. We had to install some of the listening devices outside the back of the building in the hose bib. And we had to tear down some of the wall paneling and put it back up by morning. If the guys noticed anything out of place, they would know something was fishy. We thought it was going to be an easy job just to run some wire over the drop ceiling and take out one piece of paneling.

We tried to drill a hole, but the concrete was so hard we gave up after three bits. Then we tried to fish the wire to the basement, but that didn't work because we didn't have a fish that electricians use. We were so desperate that I actually called a couple of guys and got them out of bed. When I told them what I was looking for, they thought I was in the middle of a burglary of my own and hung up on me. The FBI technicians had a good laugh over that one, but they knew we were running out of time.

I knew I was a good carpenter, so I suggested we take off most of the paneling on one wall and run the wire to the basement through a small hole. They worried I wouldn't get all the paneling back up in time for morning without any pieces cracking or breaking. After three hours of work, we were almost done. We were in the basement hooking up the VCR, hiding it under some boxes, when I heard a noise upstairs. I realized I forgot to lock the door when we came in. I went up the steps. There sat an old neighborhood wino who came in to get warm. We gave the old guy a cup of coffee. Then we convinced him to leave after promising not to call the police.

Catch Me If You Can

One morning Tommy paged me at eight-thirty. When I called him at the FBI office in Woodlawn, he said he needed me to identify a mug shot of Ronnie Rogers, the guy who waited in the car while John Derry and Billy killed Mark Schwandtner out on the railroad bridge. We agreed to meet at 1:30 P.M. up at the Rotunda shopping center, the same place where Billy frisked me in the men's room. I hung up and headed for the streets to see what the guys were up to. I stopped in Little Italy and shot the bull with some of the old guys in front of Sabatino's restaurant. Then I headed east for my morning ritual of eggs and bacon at Doughboy's. I was due later to meet a bookmaker named Baldy at Canton Square to pick up seven large ones he owed me.

At Doughboy's I shot the bull with Fat Ricky. While I ate breakfast, we noticed a stranger walk in who looked to me like he was pretending to be lost. He was a clean-cut white man in his mid thirties, wearing a baseball cap with a windbreaker over his shirt. It was a warm day; too warm to be wearing a windbreaker, I thought, unless you needed to hide a gun underneath it. The guy kept glancing at me and Ricky while he scanned the bar. Then he hurried outside.

Now, there's a detective who can't act, I thought. I told Ricky he looked like a cop. "You're just paranoid," he said. "Maybe the guy was casing the place to rob it later." No, I said. "He's too clean-cut to be a robber." I got ready to leave for my appointment with Baldy and said goodbye to Fat Ricky.

I had developed certain habits while living the wiseguy life. Number one: never sit with your back to a door. Number two: always scan the street up and down for strangers in parked cars. The side door to Doughboy's wasn't even closed behind me when I shot a look up Esther Street and saw a light brown Toyota Camry two blocks away. The car was pulled over at an angle, like the driver had tried to hide it in a hurry. Since there were no other parked cars to hide behind, it stuck out like a sore thumb. I closed the door slowly and looked carefully at the two men in the Camry. The driver was a balding, middle-aged man with glasses. In the passenger seat was the stranger who had just left the bar. Now I was sure the guy in the windbreaker was a cop.

First I thought maybe they were FBI agents tailing me to make sure I wasn't doing anything I wasn't supposed to do, but I knew FBI agents wouldn't be so careless in their surveillance. They must be city police, I told myself. And, of course, that made me extra nervous. Here I was, secretly helping the FBI investigate corruption in the city police department. I also figured the detectives in the parked Camry weren't just casing Doughboy's. If they were, they'd just drive past the bar and keep going. This was more serious. *Holy shit,* I thought. *I've got the police tailing me.* I tried to think fast. How could I get out of Doughboy's and lose the tail?

I turned around and went right back into Doughboy's. I needed to figure a way to get out of there to meet Baldy to get my $7,000. I had to have the money to pay off on some bookmaking hits. If the detectives pulled me over, they could get a search warrant and confiscate the money. Then I'd have nothing left to pay out on the hits. I had already spent my last $40,000 on the sub shop. I had stopped loan-sharking and drug dealing, under orders from the FBI.

This was the first time in my adult life I had to be careful about money. I was reluctant to accept the money the FBI pays informants, but finally I agreed to their $2,500 monthly payment after Tommy insisted I take it. I knew it would come back to haunt me when I testified against the wiseguys. Their lawyers would accuse me of ratting for the money. But in 1995 I needed it to support my family. I had bills piling up and I actually took my gas and electric bill and phone bills to the FBI agents to show them I wasn't blowing their money gambling.

When I walked back into the bar, Fat Ricky looked confused. "I thought you left," he said.

"I did, but either you or I have a problem, or we both have a problem."

I told him about the Camry up the street. "I was right about the guy in the windbreaker," I said.

He didn't believe me, until he came outside and looked for himself. "Okay, Charlie, I guess you're not so paranoid," he said.

I then came up with a game plan. I had to meet Baldy in ten minutes. And I couldn't call him to say I'd be late because Baldy never used a cell phone. He must have been the only bookmaker I knew who didn't use a cell phone. I also had to meet Tommy at 1:30 P.M. and I didn't want city detectives—who might be corrupt, for all I knew—following me to meet an FBI agent.

I told Ricky I needed another car. He gave me his keys. I put on an old baseball hat I got from one of the customers and threw on an old jacket I found lying in Fat Ricky's office. I went outside without looking around this time and got into Ricky's light blue Buick. I floored it and headed south on Clinton Street toward the harbor.

When I got to the corner of Baltimore Street, I looked in the rearview mirror. There was the Camry, flying down the street, trying to catch up with me. But I only saw the driver in the car. That meant the other detective was somewhere in a second car tailing me. Just as I turned to go east on Baltimore Street, I saw the wind-breaker cop in an unmarked Chevy Cavalier, turning in the opposite direction. He saw me and looked as sur-prised as I was. He started talking into his walkie-talkie.

When I got to the intersection of Baltimore and Highland Avenue, the Camry had caught up to me and was dead on my ass. When the light turned green, I made a U-turn in the middle of traffic. Horns started honking and pedestrians stared at me like I was a crazy person. Then I saw the Cavalier pass me, going in the other direction. I had lost them both, at least for a few minutes, I thought. I headed south again toward the water and made it to Canton Square free and clear. I ran into the video store where Baldy was waiting. "I don't have time to bullshit with you today. I have to go," I said. He handed me the money in a brown paper bag. I didn't even have time to count it before I was back in Fat Ricky's Buick.

I drove to the other side of the square and parked on a side street where I wouldn't be easily seen. I ran to a pay phone and called Tommy to cancel my meeting, but he didn't answer. I wanted somebody at the FBI to know what was going on in case I got caught by the city cops. I called Bruce collect at the J. Edgar Hoover Building in DC. He told me he would try to get hold of somebody in the Baltimore FBI office. In the meantime, he said, if I got stopped by the police, not to tell them anything about working with the FBI. "Just go with the flow," he said. "And call me back in fifteen minutes."

By then it was 12:45 P.M. I had forty-five minutes to meet with Tommy across town. At that point fifteen minutes felt like fifteen hours. I was a sitting duck, but I had to do something fast with the $7,000 in Fat Ricky's car. I heard the sound of a helicopter and looked up in the sky. The Baltimore police helicopter was circling in the area of Doughboy's. I was almost a mile away. Now was my chance to make it to Hampden and ditch the money.

When I got there, I parked the car on a tiny side street, where I used to live—out of view from any major road. I ran up the alley with the bag from Baldy and knocked on a friend's door. "Hold this for me for an hour," I said.

"No problem," she answered, without asking questions.

I then ran into a second house, where my brother-in-law lived. I knew he wouldn't be home, but the door would be unlocked. I grabbed the phone and called Bruce collect. "I thought the police got you, since I didn't hear back from you," he said. He had gotten hold of somebody at the Baltimore FBI office. Tommy was already on his way to meet me. Bruce thought it would be safe for me to meet him, since I had made it all the way to Hampden. The Rotunda was just blocks away.

As soon as I pulled into the Rotunda's parking lot, I noticed Tommy's car. I parked about eight spaces away and jumped out. Tommy was standing behind his car, holding a large yellow envelope.

"Bruce was trying to get in touch with you," I said. I then told him the whole saga of my morning.

"Whose car is that?" he asked.

"It's Fat Ricky's car," I said.

"Charlie, you haven't opened the trunk, have you?" he asked. I said no. "Good, don't. For all we know, Ricky could have a body in the trunk," he said, half joking.

Tommy then told me he believed *he* was being tailed by police on his way to meet me. The cops had probably seen us together before and had no idea Tommy was an FBI agent. They may have decided to follow him as a "freebie," somebody seen with a suspect whom police can track along on the same investigation.

"This is really getting crazy," I said. Here I was, working undercover for the FBI. City detectives are tracking me. The FBI is tracking the detectives. The detectives are tracking the FBI. Everybody is tailing everybody. And to complicate matters, I have to worry about what's in Fat Ricky's trunk. *This could only happen to me,* I thought.

"Charlie, let's hurry inside and get you to look at the mug shot," he said. We sat down at a table in a little café, just down the hall from the men's room where Billy strip-searched me just days before. I quickly identified Ronnie Rogers' mug shot and within a few minutes we were back in the parking lot. As we headed to our cars, both Tommy and I looked all over the place for the detectives. "Where are you going now?" he asked.

"I've got to go back to Doughboy's to get my Lincoln," I said.

He told me if the detectives caught me, not to tell them I was working for the FBI. Just go along with them, until the FBI can bail you out, he said. "And don't open the trunk," he repeated.

I told Tommy I had no problem getting arrested by the detectives, but I knew it would be a problem. Gina would be furious. I could hear her bitching that the FBI agents were supposed to protect me from the dirty cops and here they were allowing me to get arrested.

I headed back down Keswick Road and got my money back from my former neighbor. I took the money to my brother-in-law's house and hid it. I called Fat Ricky. He said the Camry had just returned and was parked a few blocks away. I got all cocky on the phone, playing the wiseguy role. "Those detectives are so stupid, they remind me of the movie *The Pink Panther*. They might as well be trying to hide behind telephone poles in broad daylight." I told Ricky I'd be there in twenty-five minutes.

When I got to the eastern edge of downtown, I noticed half a dozen unmarked cars pull out. Two were in front of me, two were alongside me and two were behind me. They were herding me like cattle. It was obvious they were taking me to their leaders waiting in the Camry at Doughboy's. As our convoy pulled up little Esther Street, I noticed Ricky and some other guys standing on the corner. They were laughing. "Boy, you must be a real

criminal to get all this attention," he said. I gave him a
thumbs-up and started to laugh, too. My day had been
so insane by then, it really was funny. I figured I had at
least outsmarted the cops by managing to pick up and
hide the $7,000 from Baldy, and I had met with an FBI
agent without being tailed.

As soon as I parked Ricky's car and turned off the engine, the Camry pulled up. "Charlie, keep your hands
on the steering wheel and don't move," said the driver,
the balding guy in the glasses. He had his gun pointed at
me. Next to him was the bad actor in the windbreaker.
They hurried over to the car with their guns pointing
right at me.

"I'm Sergeant Ritmiller and you must think you're a
real smart-ass. *The Pink Panther*, huh?" He said it in a real
arrogant way. I just looked up and smiled. But I was
thinking, *How the hell does he know what I said to Fat Ricky?*
I didn't think they still had a wiretap at Doughboy's after
we all got raided. He ordered me to get out of the car.
He had me behind the trunk, spread-eagle. He pulled
the back of my underwear so tight I thought my balls
had gone up my throat for a few seconds.

Before I knew it, the detectives had emptied my pockets and put the contents on top of Ricky's trunk. I looked
on the trunk and instantly saw my mistake. There was the
one thing I had forgotten to hide back in Hampden. My
wallet. Inside were all the phone numbers of the FBI
agents on a little piece of white paper in Steve Clary's
handwriting. No names, just numbers, but they were easy
enough for the police department to identify. Even
Bruce's number at the J. Edgar Hoover Building was on
the list. As Ritmiller searched the wallet, he pulled out the
paper.

"Whose numbers are these?" he asked.

"None of your business," I said. He put the paper in

his pocket. "You guys don't have a search warrant to take anything out of my wallet and keep it," I protested.

"Charlie," said Ritmiller, "I don't think you're in any position to tell us what we can or can't do at this point."

"I have rights and you can't take anything without a warrant," I said.

"Watch me," said Ritmiller.

I was in a panic. All he had to do was run a check on the numbers. If he or any of his partners were dirty, I was a dead man. They handcuffed me and sat me down on the curb behind Ricky's car.

"What's in the trunk?" one of them asked.

"I don't know. I haven't looked in the trunk. You guys know it's not my car," I said.

I imagined the worst by now. What if there were guns, drugs or swag (stolen goods) in there? I prayed for the trunk to be empty. My mind was racing to even worse scenarios. What if Ricky was secretly working for the detectives and he had told them about my *Pink Panther* movie comment? What if this was a trap?

Ritmiller turned to Ricky. "Hey, fat ass, get over here."

Ricky wandered over. "What's in the trunk?" the detective repeated.

"I don't know," he said.

"It's your car and you don't even know what's in the trunk?" asked the detective.

"I wasn't driving it," said Ricky. Great friend he was.

They unlocked my handcuffs, took the key and opened the trunk. I was hoping Ricky didn't put anything in the trunk and he was hoping I didn't put anything in the trunk.

Inside, there was just one pair of old shoes. We both laughed. Ritmiller turned to us.

"Laugh all you want. You and your buddy in that halfway house will eventually be charged with bribery and obstruction of justice." We knew he meant Billy. The charges must have been from things we said on the wire-taps.

Now the detectives wanted me to give them the keys to my Lincoln so they could search it. (I had left the keys with Fat Ricky when I took his Buick.) At least I knew there were no drugs, guns or swag in my trunk. Just a concealed tape recorder belonging to the FBI! How much worse could my day get? I refused to give them the keys.

"Get a search warrant," I said. They said they would, but then they noticed a bag on the back floor. They said they could see it was full of lists of illegal football pools. I gave in and told them they could have the bag without a warrant, but they could not search through the car. I started to get really mad. "You guys already took my wallet without a warrant. But if you search my car, there will be hell to pay and I don't give a shit what you do with me after that," I said.

I opened the door, grabbed the bag and handed it to them. They thought they finally had me. But the pools didn't have any markings on them. If bets were placed, there would be circles drawn around the teams chosen by the gamblers. But these lists were useless to the police, I gladly pointed out to them.

They took my phone numbers and my worthless football pools, but they let me leave. Thank God my trunk was safe. As soon as they left, I called Tommy. He couldn't believe that they took the phone numbers without a warrant. "They violated your civil rights," he said, adding that there was nothing we could do about it. Both of us were more worried that my cover was blown.

Those first weeks working undercover were insane. In that whirlwind of activity I was turning over dozens of tapes to Steve and Tommy. Every day there was a new twist and complication. Trying to catch wiseguys and pretend my heart was still into being a wiseguy was making me crazy. I thought, *You're either a good guy or a bad guy. How long can I pretend to be both?* I loved the adrenaline of both lives, but now I felt like I was starting to overdose on that adrenaline. There were just too many highs and lows. I'd be working on one case and already have to think ahead to the next case that might come along in just a half hour. And I had to concoct so many lies to my friends, I was having trouble keeping them all straight. Steve, Tommy and Bruce helped me think things through so I didn't get caught in a lie and get myself killed. We would practice the excuses I'd make to the guys, going over them again and again, so I could keep my stories straight.

In all the hectic weeks I was worried that I still hadn't pinned down either Billy or John Derry admitting to murder on tape. I still had plenty of work cut out for me—but there was one more thing I had forgotten to mention to the FBI. It had totally slipped my mind. To be honest, I had no idea I was sitting on a time bomb that could jeopardize the lives of FBI agents—not to mention my own.

Chapter 11

A Fox In The Hen House

I had been working for the FBI for about a month when, on November 17, we were meeting in the safe house west of Baltimore, sitting on the same old, tacky 1960s furniture. It was the usual crowd—Steve, Tommy, Bruce and assistant U.S. attorney Greg Welsh. They started talking to me about the witness protection program. To protect me and my family, I might need to move far away with a new identity. The idea of witness protection never sat right with me or with Gina. I imagined myself with some strange name, flipping hamburgers for the rest of my life far from Baltimore in a place with no crabs, no Tastykakes, no Utz potato chips. We'd never be able to call our relatives. The kids would never see their friends again. And we'd never be able to come home, even to visit. It was out of the question. But there was something else that also didn't sit right with me about it.

"Will my real name show up in your files if I go into witness protection?" I asked. It would, they said.

"Well, you got a problem in your office," I told Greg, Bruce, Tommy and Steve. "There's a leak in the U.S. Attorney's Office." I could tell by Greg's face that he didn't believe me. The others looked totally surprised.

"Who is the leak?" they all asked.

My mind started racing hard. I remembered Pat Wheeler, trying to be real chummy with me, sitting at the bar in Remington, offering to leak confidential documents from her job as a secretary at the U.S. Attorney's Office. She had never asked for money. She offered it as a favor. I always felt sorry for Pat. She was a lonely soul who just wanted to be part of the crowd. When she approached me in the past, I thought her offers were fantastic, even when I didn't really need her help. Imagine, a secretary in the U.S. Attorney's Office—with access to high-security computer data—casually offering to sneak out secret papers on federal investigations and give them to a career criminal like me.

At the time I thought she was a dream come true. But now I was on the other side. I realized she could become my worst nightmare. I really didn't want to rat on her, but I had no choice. I realized how easily she could find out who was rolling for the FBI and the federal prosecutors. If my name was in a file going into the witness protection program, Pat might whisper it to just one person in Hampden and the whole syndicate would know within hours. I'd be a dead man in a matter of days.

"Her name is Pat," I said. I was blanking out on her last name. To sound more believable, I mentioned the name of a prosecutor she once worked for. "I'm telling you, that girl's dirty," I said.

"Can you prove this, Charlie?" they asked.

"Yes," I told them, describing what she looked like.

"Is her last name Wheeler?" asked Greg.

"I'm almost positive that's it," I answered.

"Do you think she would get you some documents for money?" asked Steve.

"She'd do it for nothing, just for a favor," I said.

After Greg left the meeting, Steve turned to me and said, "You've got a good one this time, Charlie." I could tell Greg didn't believe Pat would leak information to me, but Steve did. He was all gung ho to have me catch Pat as soon as possible. He knew the damage she might cause. An FBI agent could get killed if she leaked information to a wiseguy.

Later that night I worried they still didn't believe me. I remembered that Pat was at my wedding. I had Gina pull out our wedding photos. Sure enough, there was Pat in one of the pictures. I called Steve to tell him I had a tape from conversations I had with Mike Bush and Frankie Tamburello. Steve met me twenty minutes later behind a bank in North Baltimore. I handed him the tape. Then I showed him the picture of Pat. "Every one at the federal prosecutor's office will believe me now," I said. Steve told me not to make any contact with Pat until he told me what to do. I agreed.

On the way home I started to take stock of my new life. I was already working on catching drug dealers, like Frankie Tamburello, and I was still trying to catch Billy confessing to the murder. I was trying to catch dirty cops. I had Baltimore detectives following me around half the time, not knowing I was working with the FBI. My car was wired up and my restaurant was wired with cameras and listening devices. I had an FBI cell phone to record phone conversations and I carried another miniature recording device on me at all times in case I was not in my car or in my restaurant.

Keeping track of all these electronic listening devices was pretty stressful on me. I was the kind of guy who had trouble hooking up a VCR. I was a hell of a carpenter and could build a house from the foundation up, but when it came to installing the smallest electronic gadget, I needed my wife or kids to do it for me.

One day I was sitting with Steve Clary in my favorite place behind the FBI field office—at the picnic table where I could smoke. We were making plans to go to

Ocean City to buy cocaine from Frankie Tamburello. Steve was a veteran agent with amazing investigative skills. I couldn't believe some of the plans he'd come up with for catching the guys. It was always a challenge working with Steve. He knew I was no electronics wizard. So what did he do while were sitting there? He got all excited and came up with an idea that would challenge me beyond my ability.

"Just sit there, Charlie. I'll be back in a minute," he said before heading inside.

When he came back, he had a big smile on his face.

"I think I have a toy that Frankie is going to love," he said.

The next thing I knew, he was getting into a blue 1980s Chevy or Oldsmobile. He drove it over to the picnic table. The car didn't look so great to me. I thought, *What the hell would Frankie want with this car?* He had a new Infinity Q car.

"Get in the car," said Steve.

I got behind the wheel.

He told me to turn it on. I did.

Then he gave me an odd set of instructions, without explaining why.

"Press the door lock," he said. I did that.

"Turn on the radio." I did that, too.

Then he had me switch the radio to a certain channel.

"Push in the cigarette lighter."

Then he finally told me to hit a toggle switch under the dash. The next thing I knew, the dashboard on the passenger side lifted up hydraulically and moved forward toward the seat. I had only seen stuff like this in James Bond movies. I couldn't believe it. There was enough room inside the dash to hide a couple of keys—or kilos—of coke. Better yet, the car was fitted with an FBI tracking system, so they could follow Frankie's every move.

Steve started to chuckle. "Frankie is going to love this car," he said.

"Yes, he is," I replied.

I had no trouble imagining how I would make up a fantastic tale for Frankie about how I found the car. But getting the hydraulic lift to work was another story.

Steve spent the next half hour trying to teach me which buttons to push to get it to pop up, but it was no use. I just couldn't remember the instructions. Steve wasn't smiling anymore. He got out of the car and walked over to the driver's side.

"Get out of the car, Charlie." He sounded like an angry father, disappointed in a son. "I can't believe you don't remember those buttons."

"Well, Steve, if you didn't give me so many other things to work with, I would be able to do this. I'm having a hard enough time keeping up with all the recorders you gave me," I said.

Finally he gave up on the idea of using the car. He told me, "Don't worry about it. We're going to catch Frankie, anyway."

I knew, too, that there were plenty of other ways to catch Frankie for drug dealing. But for the moment, I had to worry about catching Pat Wheeler.

A few days after I had dropped the bomb about Pat, the FBI told me to go to Pat and ask for her help. After making arrangements through a mutual friend to see her, I went back over to Buckley's bar on November 19. I asked Pat to come out to the car with me. "I need to talk to you," I said.

I slid into the driver's seat and nonchalantly flipped the toggle switch under the dash to turn on the tape recorder in the trunk. Following directions from the FBI, I made sure I referred back to our conversation just after the raid on my house when she offered to see if the FBI was involved. I asked her if she'd seen any recent information about me in the U.S. Attorney's Office. She said she hadn't.

"I will . . . I told you I would look for it," Pat offered. She told me her office had a computer printout of all active cases. She worked for a separate unit in the U.S. Attorney's Office, but there were "still ways I can look to see," she said.

Pat also said she might be working only for a few more days. The federal government was shutting down because it had run out of money due to a fight President Clinton was having with Congress over the budget. Pat would be furloughed without a paycheck. I asked her how she could get the document if she wasn't at work. She said she could still go down to her office in the federal courthouse and get whatever files she needed. I could even drive her there, she said. She also told me she would steal the whole file cabinet while the rest of her office was on furlough if she had to. I knew she was just bullshitting me on that one. But I also knew she was serious and would basically get whatever I wanted.

I asked her if she would look for information about some of my friends. I told her I was especially interested in finding out if Frankie Tamburello was a target of a federal investigation. All the guys thought they were going to be hit with a Racketeer Influenced and Corrupt Organizations (RICO) charge, I told her. I handed her a piece of paper with Frankie's name on it.

I also told her Frankie would pay her for the information. At first she said she didn't want any money, but I told her Frankie would be expecting to pay for it. The information would be considered very valuable on the street. I said I wasn't going to tell him where I was getting this information. I would get the money from him, and Pat and I could split it. If she didn't want any, I'd just keep it all. By this time I could see dollar signs in her eyes. Pat was about to open the door to leave when I handed her $20 to buy herself a few drinks. I told her to stay in touch. Then I mentioned that we would probably get $1,500 each from Frankie.

Lying In Wait

I knew the federal prosecutors were planting phony documents for her to find. All I had to do was wait. I gave her my pager number and told her to beep me when she found out something. I told her not to tell anyone about our meeting. Those FBI agents are sneaky, I said. They might get a third person to squeal on us. I was worried because our meeting was set up by a mutual friend who was a small-time cocaine dealer. I didn't want him getting in trouble because of Pat. She probably thought she was being careful, too. She told me never to call her at home.

As soon as I dropped Pat off at Buckley's, I called Steve on my FBI cell phone. I could tell by Steve's voice that he was excited about my conversation with Pat. He told me to meet him right away behind the bank on Roland Avenue. I got there first. I sat in the bank lot thinking, *Now the FBI will believe me.*

As soon as he pulled into the lot in his little white Pontiac, my heart started beating fast. I was so excited I got Pat on tape saying she'd get me confidential information. A part of me was sad, though, because I knew she had crossed the line and put me in the middle.

Steve told me to open the trunk so he could get the tape out. It was awfully cold as we were trying to take the tape out and put in a new one. When we finally got the new tape in, Steve asked me to go turn on the toggle switch under the dash. I clicked it on. "It's not working," he yelled from the trunk. He had just changed the batteries in the recorder the day before. The cold weather must have frozen the recorder.

Steve's face was filled with disappointment. He really wanted to catch Pat. He wondered if she had leaked information to criminals before. I was discouraged, too. I felt like I had failed at my new job. Steve asked me to get in his car. "Tell me exactly word for word what happened." I talked; he wrote. Then he said the notes weren't good enough without the tape. He looked at me with a straight face. "Go back and do it over again," he said.

"Over again? How am I going to do that?" I asked. I told Steve the next time I met with Pat, I'd make sure to use my little tape recorder in my pocket, in case the recorder in the trunk froze up again. He thought that was a good idea.

Luckily, I didn't have to repeat my conversation with Pat, because a week or so later, I got beeped. The number on my FBI pager was the pay phone at Buckley's. I called. Pat's friend, the coke dealer, answered. "Pat's here and wants to see you," he said. I called Steve and told him the news. "Don't forget the backup recorder," he said.

It was still really cold outside. I drove over to Buckley's and saw through the window that Pat was sitting with her friend up front. I waited in the car. When she came out, she was all excited. She said she saw some paperwork come across her desk and there were grand jury subpoenas for telephone records involving me, Frankie Tamburello and some others.

I asked her to see if she could get the papers. She said she would.

As soon as she was gone, I called Steve from the car. I drove up Roland Avenue, past the mansions of Roland Park, and turned into the bank parking lot by Roland Park Elementary–Middle School.

I popped open the trunk. Steve was already standing at the rear of the Lincoln, looking impatient. We pulled out the tape and put a new one in the recorder. "Did you use your backup recorder?" he asked. I told him I had. I got in the driver's side and flipped the toggle switch. "It worked," he shouted. We got into his car and again I gave him detail for detail what happened in my meeting with Pat. I handed him the mini tape recorder. He pulled out the tape, took a look at it and smiled. It worked, too. I initialed all the tapes and he played them in his car to make sure they worked.

"The prosecutors will believe me now," I said.

Steve started to laugh. He said they believed me all along, they were just shocked that their longtime secretary would leak information out of their office.

Steve told me again to wait to hear from Pat. "Let her make the next move," he said. We knew it might be a while before she came back from her furlough because of the federal budget crisis.

Using A Mule

I continued my undercover work, trying to catch my friends selling cocaine. But the beef between President Clinton and Congress was making my job more difficult. If there was no money to pay for federal workers' salaries, there certainly wasn't any cash lying around for the FBI to give me to buy drugs. One day Tommy came to me with an idea. He knew wiseguys liked flashy things like expensive jewelry and valuable coins. They especially liked them if you told them they were hot. The agents got hold of South African gold Krugerrand coins and Rolex watches, which had been confiscated by the FBI. Tommy asked me if I thought Frankie Tamburello and some of the others would buy the swag from me and Kevin. We could then turn around and use the cash to buy cocaine. In some cases we could just trade the swag directly for drugs. I thought it was a great idea. I knew if I were in Frankie's shoes, I would have taken the coins and the watches myself.

I was to sell these to my wiseguy friends, in exchange for money to buy cocaine. Kevin and I invented stories about how we stole them while committing burglaries. When we heard on the radio about a real burglary at the home of a state official, we claimed it was our heist to show where we got the loot.

In early December we were on the road in Ocean City, trying to catch Frankie Tamburello, the convicted drug dealer the FBI was eager to snag. We waited all day for his coke delivery to come down from New York. Finally it was 12:30 A.M. when he said he was on his way. I had both Tommy and Steve tailing me. Kevin couldn't be with us, since his wife was giving birth. I had a wire in my ear so I could tape-record any phone conversation with Frankie. Steve was driving on U.S. 1 behind me. My cell phone rang. It was Steve. "Charlie, there's a car coming up beside you in the next lane," he warned. I looked over and there was Frankie in a 4Runner. He rolled down his window and laughed. I ripped the wire out of my ear before he could see it. He yelled for me to follow him to a convenience store to make the deal.

Up until that day I had a lot of respect for Frankie. I felt bad about rolling on him and told the agents, though I promised to help them get him. They respected my feelings about him. But when I decided to go straight, I knew I had to turn on people I thought were hurting other people. Just by selling cocaine, Frankie was hurting people. But I didn't know what else he was doing to innocent people until that day in Ocean City.

I pulled into the parking lot. Frankie came out and told me he had to go into the store to bring someone else to meet me. As soon as they came out together, I could tell something was wrong with the man. His eyes were crossed and his face drooped. Frankie walked the guy over to my Lincoln and actually put the guy's own hand in his deep pockets and pull out a large bag of coke. He then told the guy to put the bag in my car. "He's retarded," Frankie said. Like I couldn't tell. He then told me the poor guy was his "mule." He used him to meet the Colombians to pick up drugs down the ocean and to make most of Frankie's deliveries. I was disgusted. It was like using a kid to deal drugs. I had sunk pretty low in my criminal life, but never that low.

As soon as Frankie was gone, I went to meet Tommy and Steve. "That Frankie is a piece of shit," I cussed as I got out of my car. "I can't believe he was using a retarded man as a mule." I asked the agents not to lock up the man. "It would be like locking up a six- or seven-year-old." The FBI never did arrest him for the coke deal, but they found out through their investigation that he only had the mental ability of a third grader. After that day I made it a point of going after Frankie and some of his coke dealer buddies. And I didn't feel one bit sorry for it.

A few weeks later I finally heard from Pat Wheeler. I got home from an undercover job at about 2:30 A.M. Gina was up when I got home. She said Pat's friend had been by a half hour earlier, looking for me. He said Pat had some papers for me. I knew exactly what he meant. Pat must have gone into her empty office when she was on furlough and stolen the documents. I tried to page Tommy and Steve, but I remembered the beepers didn't work down in Ocean City. They were too far away. Then I tried to call them on their cell phones, but I remembered the batteries were all used up trying to catch Frankie and Gussie Alexander, an elderly drug dealer, whose real name was Constantine.

I called the FBI office in Baltimore. "My name is Warlock," I said. I told the person manning the phone to get in touch with Steve or Tommy in the morning and tell one of them to call me. I knew Tommy would be there because he had to turn in the cocaine I bought from the guys. I finally got a call just before noon from Steve. I told him Pat had the papers. He told me to call him back as soon as I set up a meeting with Pat, but Steve warned me to wait for Pat to make the move to set up the meeting. I couldn't make it look like I was setting her up.

At about seven o'clock that night I was up at my sub shop trying to get John Derry on tape talking about the murder. It was even harder than I thought. We had spent so many years carefully *not* talking about the murder. Now it was a real trick, trying to bring it up without raising his suspicions. I called John, who was a plumber, and told him I had a problem with a toilet at the sub shop. I got him outside in the back, where the FBI had hidden the video camera in the phony alarm bell. I told John, "Billy's worried somebody's talking about the murder." I tried to draw John out, but he didn't say anything specific enough that was a clear confession. To make matters worse, there were other people walking by the camera, making the video unusable. The agents let me know I needed to do better than that if I was going to catch John or Billy.

While I was trying to pin John down, I got beeped. I recognized the number as the pay phone at Buckley's. I got real excited. I called Steve to let him know. "Get over to Buckley's right away," said Steve. He reminded me to take my mini recorder with me. As soon as I got to the bar, Pat came running out. She got into the Lincoln and I drove down Remington Avenue, pulling over a few blocks away. She grabbed some papers from her purse. She was laughing and looked pleased with herself that she had sneaked the documents out of her office. I started reading out loud, word for word, to make sure the tape recorder picked it up.

The papers had information about myself, Frankie and

several others in my crime family. Just as Pat had told me earlier, the documents showed that federal investigators had issued grand jury subpoenas for telephone records. I asked the name of the federal prosecutor. "Greg Welsh," she answered. I told her Frankie was hiding out in Florida and wanted to make sure he could come home for Christmas. But now he probably would stay down south. (Of course, I knew Frankie was really in Ocean City.) Pat warned that Frankie also should be careful on the phones. She said she'd keep an eye out for anything else she could find out about the case.

I told Pat she had given me great stuff. I asked her if I could have the papers to make copies, but she refused. She was afraid someone else might see them and figure out she was the leak. I told her it wasn't a problem. (I had read the document aloud on tape and I knew that was enough.) I drove Pat back to Buckley's; then I called Steve on the cell phone as soon as I was out of sight.

"Did she have the documents?" he asked. I said yes. We met at the bank again, and we went through the usual drill of checking the tapes and reporting what information I got. He was still really upset about Pat. He wanted to get her, bad. She was just too dangerous inside the justice department.

I met Pat a few more times over the following weeks leading up to Christmas. I was stalling for time. I couldn't believe my bad luck. I had promised her $1,500 at one of the few times in American history when the federal government had no money.

I told Steve we needed to get the money soon to pay off Pat. I didn't want her to start getting suspicious. I knew it wouldn't be easy to squeeze the money out of the FBI at a time like this, but it wasn't like I could pay her with some hot Rolex watches or South African gold coins.

Finally, on December 28, Tommy called me with good

news. The FBI finally gave him the money to bribe Pat. I met Tommy and Steve over at the Baltimore Zoo. They gave me the money in a plain white envelope, but it wasn't $1,500. It was only $1,000—all the FBI could scrape together. Tommy took it out of the envelope and we counted it together. I called Pat at home and told her to meet me. "I have something for you," I said. She sounded upset that I was calling her at home, but then she perked up when I told her about the money. An hour later I was sitting in my Lincoln with Pat on Remington Avenue near Buckley's, both of my tape recorders running. "You have yourself a nice little Christmas present," I said as I pulled out the envelope.

"Oh yeah? Thank you," she said.

I opened the envelope, took out the bills and counted them for Pat. I told her we were $500 short, but I'd get the balance for her another day. Her disappointment didn't last long.

"Oh Charlie, you serious?" she said.

I had finally sealed Pat's fate—and proved myself to the FBI in a way I had never imagined. And I had done it right under the FBI's nose. Tommy watched the whole transaction from his unmarked FBI sports car parked in a lot just a few yards away.

Bartering For Drugs

A few weeks later, on January 18, I met with the agents at the safe house to plan a major drug deal to buy one kilo of cocaine in Little Italy. This time, in addition to carrying a tape recorder, I would be wearing a wire so agents could listen to my conversations with Frankie and Gussie. As usual, I checked my rearview mirror as I pulled into the apartment complex to the safe house. I met with Steve, Tommy and Kevin, who would be my burglar buddy in the case. I took off my shirt so they could wrap the wire around my chest and tape the little listening device in the small of my back. The agents gave Kevin and me about thirty of the South African gold coins and a really nice Rolex watch. With the federal government still shut down, this would be the FBI's currency for the time being. Kevin and I were to sell the coins to Gussie so we could buy cocaine from Frankie. We knew Gussie was a rare-coin collector and that whacko, Frankie, loved flashy things like Rolex watches. Gussie and Frankie had already met Kevin on a few other occasions and I still couldn't get over how gullible they were. I never would have let a stranger like Kevin into our circle. But, as I said before, these guys were greedy.

The agents had already checked the value of the gold coins in the newspaper. The paper said they were worth $397 apiece. Steve said, "Tell Frankie and Gussie you're taking no less than three hundred fifty each."

I said, "No problem, but if they start wheeling and dealing, I'll go no lower than three twenty-five." Tommy got on the phone with his boss, Mel Fleming. (He's the guy who was very tight with the government's money.) Mel gave the okay, but said not to go any lower than $325 each for the coins and $2,000 for the watch. "No problem," I said.

We all headed to Little Italy, just east of downtown, not far from Baltimore's Inner Harbor. While Kevin and I were inside Velleggia's, one of Little Italy's oldest and best-known restaurants, Steve would be outside in a hidden vehicle with FBI technicians, listening to the whole deal. Tommy would be observing the deal from another table in the restaurant, along with Mike Downs, a Baltimore County detective who was working with the FBI at the time. Kevin and I also took our little tape recorders in our pockets for extra coverage.

It was about 11:00 A.M., so the place was empty. I was

worried about the wiseguys and what they'd think about two strangers sitting at a table nearby. I parked the Lincoln around the corner from the restaurant and Kevin and I sat for a minute, getting ourselves together. That gave the other agents time to set themselves up for surveillance. When we got inside, Frankie was already there. The three of us ordered lunch. I told Frankie I didn't have any of the $12,000 I owed him for cocaine he'd already fronted to me. "But I've got something better," I said.

"What?" asked Frankie.

"South African Gold Krugerrand coins and a Rolex watch."

Frankie seemed interested, but said we'd have to wait for Gussie. He'd know how much the coins and the watch were worth. While we were waiting for Gussie, I started buttering Italian bread and chewing it, not knowing how annoying it sounded on the wire. I loved that Italian bread, and I think I ate it throughout the whole deal, much to the irritation of the agents listening in.

Gussie arrived about twenty minutes later. He was about seventy years old. An old-time gangster, he was like a god in Little Italy. Everybody in town owed him money. And he had tons of money, but never dressed the part of a millionaire. He didn't even wear socks that morning. He came shuffling in wearing bedroom slippers. He paid gorgeous young women $500 just to drive him from his house in Ocean City to Baltimore in his Jaguar. Frankie looked at Gussie, then told Kevin and me that he thought the old goof was as high as a kite. Gussie also carried a bullet in his hand. Not a bullet for a gun, but a small device used to snort cocaine so he wouldn't be so conspicuous.

I started making a deal with Frankie to sell the coins for $325 apiece. The price of the watch was still up in the air. All of a sudden I noticed Kevin trying to catch my attention. He motioned toward the men's room and immediately I knew what he was thinking. He was worried the tape in his recorder was running out and he needed to put in a fresh tape. So did I. Even though I was wearing a wire, we needed the tapes for backup. Kevin headed to the men's room, making me very nervous. All we needed was for Gussie or Frankie to barge in and catch him with a tape recorder in his hand. A few minutes later I went into the men's room after him.

"Get the hell out of here," I said, panicking.

"Relax, be calm," said Kevin as he switched tapes. "We're going to get away with this." So I changed my tape, too, and we headed back to the table.

Gussie was so paranoid from doing the cocaine that he called me and Frankie into the back dining room. This way Kevin couldn't hear our discussion. Now I was on my own. As we started haggling in the dining room. I noticed the restaurant starting to fill up with wiseguys who heard about the coins and the watch. While Gussie was trying to negotiate with me, he was yelling at the other guys not to come into the dining room. But they'd better not leave the restaurant, either, he warned them. They all owed him juice and he wanted it.

I told Gussie I needed money to buy a kilo of coke from Frankie. First I said I'd take $350 a coin, but he refused. Then I came down to $325. He said no. I got tired of haggling back and forth. I finally told him I'd give him the coins for $270 each. I agreed to give him one hundred coins. That would be $27,000 for a kilo of coke. Gussie said he'd get the coke from Frankie and keep it at his house for me. Then he'd turn over the money to Frankie. Finally I told him we had a deal. I knew I was in deep shit. The FBI was listening to every word and I had just sold the government coins for a bargain-basement price.

Now there was the matter of the watch. Frankie pulled me off to the side and begged me to give him the watch for $1,000. I figured I was in so much trouble by now that it didn't matter if I gave the watch away. I agreed to dump it for $1,000.

Finally I went to get Kevin.

"How did it go?" he asked when we were outside.

"I have good news and bad news for you."

"Give me the good news first."

"I made a deal and they took the coins and the watch. We have to take one hundred coins to Gussie at his house and he'll have the coke."

Kevin got all excited. Then he remembered there was more.

"What's the bad news?"

I put my head down and spoke softly.

"I sold the hundred coins for twenty-seven thousand."

"And you sold the watch for two thousand?"

"No, I said, "I sold it for one thousand. Steve and Mel aren't going to be happy campers."

As soon as we got in the Lincoln, our beepers went off. Kevin called Steve on his cell phone and started to tell Steve what happened, not that he hadn't already heard it on the wire. I knew I'd be in trouble once we got back to the safe house. When Kevin and I walked in, there stood Tommy and Steve. Steve shook his head back and forth, but he said nothing. Tommy had a shit-eating grin on his face. Steve started to laugh. "How did you get from three-fifty to two-seventy?" he asked.

"I had good intentions," I said.

"Charlie, don't ever let me ask you to do any personal negotiating for me," he said. Tommy picked up the phone and called Mel with the news. He pulled the phone away from his ear, grinning. We all could hear Mel screaming over the line.

Chapter 12

To Catch a Killer

After the new year the federal government wanted to move in fast to arrest Pat Wheeler. The FBI agents told me that U.S. attorney Lynn Battaglia wanted it done right away. I understood how the United States attorney in Baltimore would want to eliminate one of their own who was selling secret criminal information to a wiseguy. But Pat's arrest would have blown my cover. The agents tried to hold it off as long as they could. In the meantime Pat was reassigned to a new job processing civil Freedom of Information Act requests. That took away her access to any sensitive criminal data without alerting her to the fact that she was about to be arrested. I knew I didn't have much time left, but I still wanted to try catching someone admitting to killing Mark Schwandtner.

One day I came home to find Billy in the kitchen talking to Gina. I knew she was very uncomfortable around him. Her knees almost buckled when she saw him come through the door, she told me later. I thought maybe I could take a chance and get him to talk about the murder. Gina was making pepper steak on the stove and I volunteered to run down the street to get some gravy at the convenience store. It gave me an opportunity to put on my coat with the recorder in the pocket.

When I came back, I sat in the warm kitchen with my coat on. I could tell Gina was worried that Billy was getting suspicious. By then, she knew enough about my undercover work with the FBI to have reason to worry. She also suspected Billy and I might have been involved in something as serious as murder, but I never told her any details. But now, Gina knew whatever I wanted Billy to talk about, it was dead serious and I was putting myself at great risk. I tried to get her to leave the room, so Billy could talk more freely, but she wouldn't budge. She was paralyzed with fear. She thought I was being careless and that Billy would pat me down any minute. Maybe I was careless, but I was desperate to help solve the murder and finish my work with the FBI. I got nowhere that day, but soon after, on February 4, I finally got a real chance to get something on tape that might bring the killers to trial.

Gina and I were just sitting down in front of the TV to watch a movie when the door opened and in walked Billy. He wore a white dress shirt, black dress slacks and a long black cashmere overcoat. Not your typical outfit for a felon living in a halfway house. I could sense Gina tense up immediately. She could barely stomach the sight of him. Billy tried to joke with her, but my wife wouldn't even crack a smile. I asked him what was up and he said he just needed to talk to me. He was on his way to dinner with friends and had to be back at the halfway house in a few hours. He didn't have much time. I knew he'd want to talk in private, so I took him downstairs to the basement. I wished I could have slipped on my coat with the tape recorder in it, but that would have been too obvious. The FBI hadn't bugged my house yet, so there was no way I could record our conversation. When we got downstairs, Billy unloaded on me.

"What the fuck is going on with you and John?" he

asked. I knew he was talking about John Derry. He must have heard about our conversation at the sub shop when I tried to get John to talk about the murder.

"I know you and John have been talking about the thing." The "thing," of course, was the murder. I tried to act surprised. "What the hell are you talking about?" I asked.

Billy got a real serious look on his face and said, "You know exactly what I'm talking about."

"I didn't bring it up to John," I lied. I told Billy that John had actually talked about the murder to an old wiseguy who had known about the killing for as long as I did. I blamed Billy for telling the old wiseguy in the first place. Then I defended myself.

"Look, I have never talked about the murder except when you sent me around to see John and Ronnie to warn them that 'nobody talks, everybody walks.'" Then I told him John had been at the sub shop doing some plumbing for me and John mentioned the wiseguy dredging up the murder. If Billy wanted to give anybody shit, it should be the old wiseguy, not me or John, I said.

Then I tried to turn the tables on him. "I've been your best friend for God only knows how long. You even patted me down and I didn't say anything about it," I said, trying to make him feel guilty about mistrusting me. Billy calmed down, but I could tell he still had his suspicions about me.

"We're going to stop this shit right now, once and for all with you and John talking," he said. "We're going up to John's house right now and I'm going to tell him the two of you no longer know one another from this day forward."

I said that was fine with me, but he should also tell the old wiseguy to keep his mouth shut, too. Billy said he would take care of him later. As we came up from the basement, an eerie feeling came over me again about Billy. He had patted me down twice—once when I visited him in federal prison and once up at the Rotunda shopping center. He had found the wiretap transcripts of me talking to my brother about an FBI agent. I had suspicions that he was being fed information from dirty Baltimore cops who may have told him I was a rat. It was a matter of time before he might try to whack me or have somebody else do the job for him. He was seeing me more and more as a liability than as his partner in crime.

I told Gina I'd be back in a while. While Billy said goodbye, I grabbed my heavy leather overcoat with the tape recorder in the pocket. Outside, Billy told me to walk on one side of Keswick Road, while he walked on the other. He told me to get in my car—which was parked a few blocks away—and pull up in front of another car he would be riding in. Then we'd head to John's house, which was about five minutes away.

I had no idea why we were walking on different sides of the street. Whatever the reason, I knew it couldn't be good. Maybe Billy had arranged for somebody to whack me in a drive-by shooting and he didn't want to be in the line of fire.

"What the hell are we doing?" I shouted.

"Just keep walking," he said.

It was a bone-chilling cold day, so we were the only ones walking on the street. I began to shiver, not just from the cold, but from the fear. I had been working undercover for the FBI since Halloween. Now it was nearly Valentine's Day and my nerves were shot. I began to wonder whether Billy was setting me up. Every time I saw a car come toward me, I prepared myself to jump from the sidewalk and hide behind a parked car. At the same time I couldn't allow Billy to see how frightened I was.

"Where's your car?" I yelled over to him.

"Just keep walking," he repeated.

Finally I saw my Lincoln parked up ahead. I wondered if he'd put a bomb under it. I bent down to see if there was anything under it. If Billy asked what I was doing, I'd just tell him I had an oil leak.

When I didn't see anything under the car, I got in. Billy walked on ahead to the parking lot of a 7-Eleven, where I noticed a white Lincoln parked with four people inside. Billy got in the backseat. Now I felt a whole lot safer with Billy in the other car and without a bomb under my car. I pulled out to the street and the other Lincoln followed me. I turned the toggle switch on to activate the tape recorder in the trunk, then switched on the tape recorder in my pocket. I talked into them, pretending to be singing to music on the radio, in case Billy could see my lips moving from the other car. I described the people in the other car and said where we were going.

While I hadn't been whacked, I still had plenty to worry about. I was so nervous I couldn't even read the correct tag number for the other Lincoln into the tape recorder. Later, when the FBI ran the license number, it came up for another car.

As we approached John's house, I knew that if Billy told John never to talk to me again, I could lose my last chance to pin Mark Schwandtner's killing on either of them. I tried to concoct a game plan. I knew Billy didn't know exactly which rowhouse was John's. Maybe if I took him to a house without any lights on, nobody would be home and he'd think he'd missed John. As we pulled up, I noticed the lights on at John's house, but the house next door was dark and looked deserted.

Billy got out of the car, but didn't say a word to me. "Why aren't we talking?" I asked. He just put his finger over his lips and didn't answer. We went up to the house next door to John's. I knocked as softly as I could. I didn't want John or his wife hearing the knock next door and come looking out the window so Billy could see them. Nobody came to the door. Billy used his huge paw and started beating on the door so loudly it could have woken up the entire block. When nobody came to the door, I thought I was in the clear. But finally an old woman opened it. "Is John home?" I asked. "John lives next door," she said.

It was a wonder Billy didn't see me shaking. If John answered his door, I knew my future would be decided in one of three ways: 1.) I would be killed. 2.) My family and I would have to disappear into the witness protection program. 3.) The FBI would send me to prison for a long time because I hadn't delivered the goods to them and hadn't signed any deal giving me immunity from prosecution.

I just stood on the neighbor's porch, feeling like I'd thrown in the towel. Billy hopped over the guardrail that divided the two houses and quickly knocked on John's door. A strange woman answered the door and I could see Billy talking to her. Then she closed the door.

"Let's go," said Billy abruptly.

"Where's John?" I asked.

"He and his wife went to dinner. He'll be back in an hour. That was the baby-sitter."

I breathed a sigh of relief and couldn't believe my few seconds of good luck. We started to walk back down the street.

"I'm going to eat," said Billy. "Then I'm coming back to see John." I told him to call me and I would come with him. "No, I'm going to see him by myself," said Billy.

He had to be back at the halfway house by 8:00 and it was already 5:30 P.M. I tried to convince him that he wouldn't have enough time to eat and get back in time for his curfew, but he was adamant about going back to John's house.

"Fuck the halfway house. I only have a few more weeks there, anyway," he said.

As I left John's Medfield neighborhood, Billy and his crew followed me down the street. Then they headed north and I headed south, turning off the tape recorder in my pocket and flipping off the toggle switch under the dash as soon as they were out of sight.

My state of panic returned immediately. What if John told Billy it was actually *me* who brought up the murder? Then Billy would have confirmation that I was a snitch.

As I drove the few minutes back to my house, I couldn't think of any game plan to get myself out of this mess. As soon as I got home, I paged Steve Clary. It was a Sunday and I always called Steve instead of Tommy on weekends because Tommy had small children and I didn't want to bother him. Steve's kids were grown and he said I could call him anytime.

I paged Steve, using my code 520, but adding 911 at the end of the page. In less than sixty seconds my phone rang.

"What's up, buddy?" asked Steve in a cheerful voice. I told him what happened and his voice immediately got serious and concerned. "Charlie, this may be the end. We may have to close up shop with you," he said. "It's a shame. You were so close."

Then all of a sudden something must have popped into Steve's head. He came up with a good idea, though it was pretty risky.

"Charlie, the only way we can get anything on the murder is for you to go back up to John's house now while Billy is at dinner."

I couldn't believe what he was asking me to do. I felt my heart drop to my stomach. "Where did Billy go to eat?" he asked. I told him it was a restaurant in Timonium, about a half hour away. "Good. Let's think this over," he said. "That gives you a window of opportunity to go back to John's house. You might have an hour before Billy has to be back at the halfway house."

I stalled for a minute. "I don't know when John will be home," I said.

"Charlie, I'm not telling you what to do, because I'm not in your shoes. If you say you're too worried to go back to John's in case Billy shows up, I will understand and everyone else at the FBI will understand because we know it is really risky," he said.

I started to apologize to Steve because I felt like a failure. "Charlie, you don't have to apologize, and don't feel bad. You've done a hell of a job. It's just a shame that Billy and John are going to get away with murder." Steve sure had a way of making everything seem like a challenge to me, while boosting my confidence at the same time.

"Okay, how do I do this without getting killed?" I asked.

"Are you sure you want to do this?" he asked.

"Yes, I have to."

He instructed me to drive back to John's house immediately.

"What if he isn't home?"

"Then wait for him. Take your cell phone, and if you see Billy, just leave."

"How do I get John to talk about the murder?"

"Tell him the truth, that you and Billy were just there and Billy chewed you out already and now wants to chew out John. John will then go on the defensive about Billy and may talk about the murder. If that doesn't work, then it'll just be too late."

Just before I hung up, Steve said, "Be real careful. Do not talk to Billy if he shows up. And if he tries to stop you, do not stop for him."

"What happens if Billy shows up and I'm already in the house with John?"

"Lure John outside somehow from the beginning so Billy can't catch you in the house," he said.

When I got back to John's house, the lights were still on. I turned on the tape recorder and knocked on his door.

His wife answered. She called for John, who came to the door immediately. He was a big man, almost as big as Billy. He came outside in the early-evening darkness, without me asking, and shut the door behind him. "What's going on?" he asked. The baby-sitter had described the two men who had come by earlier. John knew it was Billy and me.

Billy's on the warpath, I told him. He thinks we've been talking about the murder.

I didn't have to say any more before John opened his mouth. He started to describe the murder in pretty graphic detail. Here he was, eighteen years after the crime, laughing and bragging about how he and Billy killed this poor kid.

And he talked right into the hidden tape recorder:

"I popped the motherfucker . . . with a baseball bat."

"It was just me and Billy, right . . . Billy dropped him, he dropped him over there, like, just like a boulder used to drop off the fucking bridge."

I asked him, "What'd he drop him from, a bridge?"

"Fucking right. About twenty-five feet down," said John.

"Jesus Christ," I said.

John remembered how Billy had asked him, "You think I broke his neck?"

And John told him, "No, you dumb ass, Billy. You dropped him feet first. That motherfucker is going to wake up . . . and squeal on us."

"You think so?" Billy said.

"Yeah." John said, "You better go down."

"So," John told me, "Billy . . . went down that fucking water . . . then he threw him under again."

I couldn't believe he was reliving the murder. It was such a stroke of luck that I got him to talk. But then I couldn't get him to shut up. I started to worry Billy would drive up any minute. I was afraid every car light I'd see might be Billy.

I told myself, as soon as I saw that white Lincoln, I was running to my car and heading out of Dodge. John kept talking, telling about Ronnie Rogers waiting in the car and Billy's sister cleaning up the car later. He talked so long, I found myself telling him I had to go.

When I did, I flew down the street and called Steve on my cell phone. "Did you get it?" he asked.

"Yes, I got the whole confession. I couldn't get John to shut up."

He told me to meet him right away behind the Staples store on York Road. He had to make sure the tape took. "Don't go home because if Billy finds out you've been to John's house, he's going to be looking for you."

When I pulled into the parking lot, Steve was already there waiting with a shit- eating grin on his face. I got into his car. "Do you really think you got it?" he asked. Yes, I told him. He asked me to tell him exactly what happened, word for word. He wrote everything down as quickly as he could, but I was so excited he had to keep telling me to slow down. Then he asked for the tape recorder. I took it out of my pocket. He turned it on. John's voice was muffled through my heavy coat, but you could still hear what he was saying. Steve got a smile on his face from ear to ear.

"You got it all, Charlie. You've done a great job," he said. "But I think it is getting too dangerous now for your family. It's reached a point where they're going to have to leave in a few weeks."

Steve took the tape, punched the ends to protect it and wrote his name and date on it.

My adrenaline was flowing so high that I came up with a really stupid idea. By now, I told Steve, Billy had already been to John's house and was heading back to the halfway house. I wanted to find out what Billy said to John. Steve looked at me like I was nuts. "You can't do that, Charlie. It's too risky." I told him I didn't want to miss a chance to gather more evidence. He agreed to let me go, but gave me one last chance to change my mind. "Are you sure you want to do this?" he asked.

Looking back now, I wonder if I was smoking birdseed that night to do something so dangerous. My adrenaline was rushing so fast that I felt invincible.

I knocked on John's door with a fresh tape in the recorder. His wife answered and invited me down to the basement. When I got there, John appeared to be alone. I took one look at his face and knew he believed I had tricked him. I could tell Billy had already come and gone. "What did Billy say?" I asked.

Before I could say another word, John said, "Whatever I told you a little while ago was a lie." He rushed toward me, stuck his big hands inside my unzipped coat and felt around my waist for a wire. Like Billy, he assumed I'd be wearing a traditional wire, strapped around my chest with a microphone in the small of my back, like the one I wore in Little Italy.

To distract John, I began patting him down while he groped me. "Maybe you're wearing a wire," I said as we frisked each other. Just before he let go of me, John went to feel up under my shoulders. As his hand came down, he hit my little tape recorder in the outside pocket, but said nothing. He apparently didn't know what he'd touched. I backed up the stairs without saying good-bye. He knew he was had and I knew I had him. There was nothing more for either of us to say.

As soon as I got back in the Lincoln, I called Steve and let him know I was safe. He told me to go home and hide the recorder. "Stay in the house and don't go out."

From that moment I felt more vulnerable than any other time in my undercover life and I worried very much about my family's safety. Even though the FBI had Billy under surveillance, that didn't mean he couldn't get past them.

The next morning I met Steve and Tommy at the FBI

headquarters in Woodlawn. They played the second tape of John saying his confession was all a lie. We could actually hear John hitting the recorder with his hand as he frisked me.

Chapter 13

No Place To Hide

From the day I caught John confessing to murder, my life began to move in a fast-forward blur. Within a few days the FBI agents called Gina into their office to talk about the witness protection program. At 10:00 A.M. I drove Gina to the local headquarters. Instead of driving up to the entrance, Steve Clary had us meet him at a nearby convenience store. Gina and I got into Steve's car. He had on his best FBI face as he politely introduced himself to my wife. Gina and I could tell the meeting we were about to have would not be pleasant. When we arrived at the conference room, Tommy was there waiting for us with Steve Hess, who worked for the witness protection program. Steve Hess told Gina he was there to give her the option of going into the program with a new identity. Then Tommy and Steve Clary explained to her exactly what I'd been doing with the FBI—not that Gina didn't know some of the things I'd been up to. But I'd spared her many details so I wouldn't frighten her. Then they started to talk about Billy and his criminal past. They asked Gina, "Do you know how deeply Charlie was involved with Billy?"

She said, "Do you mean numbers?"

No, they said.

She asked, "Do you mean Joe's Tavern?"

Again they said no. "We mean murder," they said.

They then told her about Billy and John killing Mark Schwandtner. They slid a folder in front of Gina. Inside, they said, were photographs of the young man's beaten and drowned body. They wanted to show her what Billy was capable of doing. But she refused to look at the pictures. She just broke down crying and gave me an accusatory look. The woman I loved so deeply was looking at me like I was a monster. "I didn't kill anybody," I said, knowing I was still guilty of covering up for my friends. Tommy and Steve Clary even took up for me. Steve Hess tried to convince Gina that witness protection would be the safest place to be, but Gina wouldn't have any of it. To her, it would be the same as being "dead, scratched out, buried without a funeral. There's no way," she said.

After the meeting Steve Clary drove us back to our car. On the way home Gina wanted to know every crime I'd been involved in, down to the last little detail.

Though we decided not to use the witness protection program, we still knew we had to leave Baltimore. Gina had an uncle in Decatur, Alabama. His name was John Funari and he was the nicest, most kindhearted man you could ever meet. We thought we could move there with Uncle John's help and live under a false name for at least a while. But our true identities wouldn't be wiped out and we hoped we could eventually regain contact with our family.

This decision, as it turned out, would cause more problems than we imagined. We didn't realize that without new Social Security numbers or driver's licenses to go with our phony names, it would be difficult to find steady work.

As my family made plans to leave Baltimore, I tried to

find a way to tell my sister, Betty. My brother, of course, knew everything. But we had kept Betty in the dark. I told Johnny I didn't want my sister to wake up one day and find no trace of me or my family. So, in early February I went to Betty's house and told her and her husband what I'd been doing for the last four months. Betty was devastated and all she could do was cry. We made arrangements for a good-bye dinner at Jimmy's Seafood on the county's east side the following week. It was an emotional dinner with me, Gina, Betty and her husband, Johnny and his wife. I felt like I was on death row and was eating my last meal.

On February 14, 1996, Gina, Mandy and Justin left for Alabama. It was an especially sad day because they left without me. We had been building up our courage for months getting ready for this day, but it still wasn't easy. It was hardest on my four children. Even Charlie Jr., by then a grown man, took it hard. And he was the one staying behind. Charlie was the only one who knew about the move ahead of time. Though Gina wasn't his mother, she had helped raise him, along with Melonie's parents, Vernon and Shirley, who lived next door and still treated me like a son. I'd supplemented their income, helped pay for their medications and made repairs on their house. I knew I'd worry about them when I was gone.

I was leaving the house and the sub shop for Charlie Jr., if he wanted it. He also knew I was staying behind for at least a few weeks. Gina and I had talked generally with the kids about wanting to leave Baltimore and start a new life somewhere else. But it was almost impossible for us to prepare Mandy and Justin for this kind of move. Telling them was one of the hardest things we ever had to do. We couldn't give them much advance notice, and they couldn't say good-bye to a single friend. We gave Mandy the news two days before the move. We told her that once we left, we wouldn't be coming back. And once we got to Alabama, she couldn't call or write her friends. Try telling that to a thirteen-year-old girl. She cried for two days straight. We kept her home from school and wouldn't let her out of our sight. When she made phone calls, we listened to her conversations to make sure she didn't tell her friends she was leaving.

We kept Justin in school until the last day. When he was dismissed, I had a relative pick him up and bring him to Memorial Stadium about five miles from my house. I was waiting for him in the enormous, empty parking lot. When I told him about the move, I could see the confused expression on his face. He was only seven. He asked me what was wrong. He wanted to know why he was meeting me at the stadium, instead of the house with his mom. My heart really went out to him that day, especially when I said I wasn't moving with the family. I was staying behind for a few weeks. At that point he started crying hard. I tried to make it seem like a big adventure, but that didn't comfort him much. He wanted me to leave with him. Maybe he thought Gina and I were splitting up. After all, there had been a lot of tension in the house during the last few months.

Telling Charlie Jr., Mandy and Justin about our move was hard enough, but I felt especially bad about leaving behind my other son, Jason, who was born to a woman I'd hooked up with briefly after Melonie divorced me. By 1996 Jason was thirteen, old enough to understand why I was leaving. But his mother was a friend of Billy's, which made it too risky to tell the boy I was leaving town.

While we were getting ready for the move, Gina had been quietly packing boxes and hiding them in closets and under beds so the wiseguys, coming in and out of our house, wouldn't suspect. If anybody caught her packing, she told them she was getting the house ready to be painted.

Gina and I planned the move to make it look like she was leaving me, taking the kids and everything that wasn't nailed down. I put the word out a week in advance that I was going to Delaware to do a job that would make me $1,000 for the day. I left my house at 6:00 A.M. to make it look like I was heading to Delaware. Instead, I went to hide out at Johnny's house, out in the suburbs.

We used a rented Ryder truck for the move, which my brother rented for me in someone else's name. I couldn't use a moving company because one of the wiseguys owned a major moving company and might find out my family's destination. So my family was moved that day by four FBI agents posing as friends. One was Mel Fleming, Tommy and Steve's tightwad supervisor. There was also a woman agent who guarded Gina during the move. Neighbors came out and were immediately suspicious. Why was Gina moving out on me and who were these strangers moving her? My brother also showed up to help move, which almost ruined our cover. The neighbors and wiseguys would wonder why my brother was helping my wife leave me.

While they were loading the truck, I got a page from Tommy. "What is your brother doing at your house?" he asked, sounding irritated. He was really upset. I told Tommy that Johnny was supposed to be picking up my van keys for me. He should have run in and out. "Well, Mel wants him out of there now, before John blows the whole thing," said Tommy. I called the house and got the agents to put my brother on the phone. I tried to get Johnny out of there without hurting his feelings. I knew he was just trying to help. Outside, the woman agent stuck right by Gina's side the whole time, especially when neighbors came up to ask Gina what was going on. She just said she was leaving me.

Everyone started beeping me to tell me my wife was leaving me, but I didn't answer any page unless it had the code 520 on it. It was only much later that I learned some of my old friends were thinking of jumping the strange movers and flattening the tires. Boy, they would have been

in for a surprise. By 5:00 P.M. they were finished loading
the truck, and the agents followed it out of Hampden.
Gina and the kids finally got to my brother's house by 6:30
P.M. There was so much tension. The kids were crying,
Gina was crying. My sister and sister-in-law were there and
they were crying, too. I could feel the tears building up,
but I held them back. Gina was afraid of leaving me behind. She thought she'd never see me alive again. At one
point she refused to leave. She just couldn't handle it anymore. I tried to tell her things would get better in our new
life, but she was scared to death. I told her it was too dangerous to stay in Baltimore. She had to go.

Finally they left at 8:30 P.M. Uncle John drove the
truck, while Gina and the kids followed in the Dodge
Caravan. I knew I would spend the next thirteen hours
worried sick that someone had followed them. I couldn't
wait for the call telling me they had arrived safely.

Less than an hour after Gina left, I was heading home
when I got paged by my brother with 911 next to his
phone number. My first thoughts were that Gina was
being followed, or she was in an accident. I called
Johnny on my cell phone. "What's wrong?" I asked. He
said Charlie Jr. had just called from my house. Billy had
been there and wanted to know what was going on. I
called Charlie Jr. He said Billy asked him where I was.
Charlie Jr. said I was in Delaware and that Gina had left
me and wanted a divorce.

Billy told Charlie Jr. not to tell me he'd been there. He
offered my son a big wad of money, which he turned
down. Charlie sounded scared. I tried to tell him not to
worry. I told him to wait a half hour and then call Billy
and tell him I had just called. I told my son to get out of
the house and go next door to his grandparents' and
stay there until I got home.

I called Tommy to tell him about Billy's visit. He told me
to meet him right away. "Are you all right?" he asked. I said

yes, which, of course, was pretty far from the truth. When we met up, I gave him some tapes I had made from two drug dealers earlier in the day. Tommy told me that one of the other agents left what looked like a stereo and radio in the bathroom of my house. They were actually disguised recording devices. I could use them to make one last-ditch effort to get Billy to talk about the murder. Tommy and I both knew I had to get home before Billy showed up and started to snoop around. Tommy handed me the remotes to activate the recorders and I was on my way.

I already had a remote for my Lincoln, a remote for the camera and listening device at the sub shop. Now I had one for my house. Just try digging in your pants pocket to find the right remote control without somebody figuring out what you're doing. That's some trick.

I raced back to the house. When I was about eight miles away, I called Charlie Jr. "Did you call Billy?" I asked. Yes, he had. Billy had phoned ten minutes before from Joe's Tavern. He said he was leaving for my house right away. I tried to figure out how much time I had to get back to my house. I had to beat Billy there and still have a few minutes to set up the recorders and figure out how the remote control worked. I floored the Lincoln on the Jones Falls Expressway and hoped I wouldn't get stopped for speeding.

I got there first, parked in the alley across the street and ran inside before the neighbors saw me and started asking questions about my wife leaving. I locked the door behind me, ran up the steps and headed into the bathroom. The recorders weren't there. I ran to the bathroom in the basement. On the way I could hear someone using the key to unlock the door. I thought, *Oh shit, it's Billy.* The door opened, but it was Charlie Jr. "I'm sure glad it's you," I said. I told Charlie to leave and lock the door. He said he was afraid to leave me alone with Billy. He thought Billy would kill me.

I told my son to stand in the doorway next door at his grandparents' house. Wait for Billy to get to my front door, then say hi to him and shut the door. There was no way Billy would kill me once he knew Charlie Jr. saw him first. Billy would never leave a witness. After Charlie Jr. left, I hurried to the basement and found two boxes. I opened them up and got the recorders out.

Here was my problem: I had three floors in my house, but only two recorders. I had to guess where Billy would want to talk to me. I tried to think like him. He would come in, case the place to make sure nobody else was there. Then he would probably talk in the kitchen, but if he really wanted to be cautious, he would take me to the back part of the basement. So I put one recording device facing the kitchen and the other in the basement where Gina had left a lot of clothes and some furniture to make it look like she had moved in a hurry. I plugged them in, though I had no time to see if they worked. I pulled all the remotes out of my pocket, trying to figure out which one was which.

Then I set a hammer on the counter upstairs next to where I'd be sitting, just in case he was going to try to hurt me. I figured at this point I would just put the hammer through his head if he went for me. I knew I couldn't beat Billy with my fist. I'd worry about the consequences later. I've always said, "I'd rather be judged by twelve [jurors] than carried by six [pallbearers]."

I sat in the kitchen on the lawn furniture Gina left behind. The FBI agents had moved the table and chairs inside in case I needed a place to sit with Billy. I heard somebody trying to open the front door. As soon as I saw a tall shadow, I knew it was Billy. "Wait a minute," I yelled. I'd forgotten to turn on the recorders. I ran to the basement and pressed the remote to on. Then I ran back upstairs and pressed that recorder on, too. I slipped the remote in my pocket just before I opened the door. Billy wasn't alone. He was with his girlfriend, The Queen.

The good news was that he hadn't come to kill me. He would never commit murder in front of his girlfriend. He would have to try to whack me another day. The bad news is that he would also never talk about murder in front of The Queen. Another chance was blown. So much for the recorders. "Is anybody here?" Billy asked. I said no. As I expected, he put his finger over his lips and went upstairs without saying a word. Then he came downstairs and headed for the basement. While he searched the house to see if anyone was there, The Queen sat down in the kitchen. I sat down next to the hammer. She asked me what was going on with Gina. Billy came in and asked the same question. I told them Gina left with most of our stuff and the kids. I had no warning. Billy tried to act like he was worried about me blowing my marriage. He even offered me money. Billy, of course, had suspected a rat in our ranks for months. I knew his line of questioning was aimed at trying to figure out if it was me or somebody else.

"Do you know who the guys were who moved Gina?" he asked. I told him I didn't. He thought they might be U.S. marshals. Maybe Gina was afraid of me, he said, and she went to the feds. "No way," I said. "Did you ever tell her anything about your business?" he asked. Again I said no. Billy and The Queen stayed for another forty minutes asking me questions. I could tell he was trying to catch me in a lie. He and The Queen called my wife every name in the book. I had to play along with them. Man, that was a tough thing to do. I had put my wife through hell already and now I had to bad-mouth her to save my hide. I knew Billy wanted to see how I would react to his putting Gina down. I played it off real good. He tried to act like he was worried about me, but I knew he didn't give a shit about me. He was just trying to put the puzzle together about who was rolling to the feds.

"If you need anything, just let me know," he said. After they left, I waited fifteen minutes, then called Tommy. "Don't leave the house. It's too dangerous," he said. Then he ordered me to get some sleep and to be careful. Both orders were impossible to carry out. I didn't sleep a wink as I tried to get comfortable on the living-room floor. Every noise I heard outside made me jump up and think someone was coming to whack me. I also worried about Gina and the kids. I hadn't heard yet if they'd arrived safely in Alabama. As for being careful, it was impossible to be careful as long as I was in Baltimore. My days were numbered in my hometown.

Heading South

After that night I moved to my brother Johnny's house out in the suburbs, where I should have felt safer. Instead, I felt completely vulnerable. I also missed Gina and the kids terribly. On February 29—two weeks after Gina and the kids had left—I got up after one of many sleepless nights. I couldn't take the stress anymore. I decided this would be the day to leave.

I wanted Bruce to be the first to know. I drove downtown, hoping to catch him before he left for work in Washington, DC, but he had already gone. I decided to track him down in DC. As I drove through the streets of East Baltimore, not far from Doughboy's and my other old haunts, I saw a trash truck come up behind me. I recognized the driver. It was Billy's brother-in-law. He had spotted my Lincoln and was gunning for me. He had loaned me $10,000 back when I was a wiseguy and I hadn't finished paying him back. He probably also suspected me of being a snitch, like everybody else did, by then. I hit the gas and went flying down Fayette Street. I figured a Lincoln can certainly beat a garbage truck. But when I looked in the rearview mirror, he was still on my tail. I have never seen a garbage truck move so fast. Finally I took some narrow side streets and lost him. Then I got on Interstate 95 and headed to DC. I parked near the Capitol and got out of the car. It was bitter cold as I watched the heavy streams of rush-hour traffic. Everybody was going to work. They had a purpose. *This is what normal life is supposed to be about*, I thought. I called Bruce and told him I was quitting. He told me to come into his office. I was terrified of calling Tommy. He and the other agents had said all along that I probably wouldn't go to prison because I'd cooperated with the FBI. I trusted Tommy and Steve, but with no immunity deal, I still didn't trust the FBI as an institution to protect me. I figured once I quit my job as an informant, they would just lock me up. I got up my courage and paged Tommy.

"Look, Tommy, I quit. If you guys are going to do anything to me, do it now."

"What do you mean?" asked Tommy.

"Am I going to prison?" I asked.

"No," he said. "We're going to send you to your family."

He instructed me to meet him in Woodlawn later that day. I turned to say good-bye to Bruce and to thank him. But it was hard to find the right words. How do you say thank you to someone for saving your life and make it sound like you really mean it? We shook hands as Bruce told me the move to Alabama would work out okay. He said the two of us should stay in touch, but he also gave me a warning. "You are fortunate to have a second chance in life," he said. "Don't screw this up, Charlie. Don't make me look bad by going to Alabama and getting yourself into trouble down there."

I told him, "There's no way in the world I want to get in trouble after all I've been through. And I'd never do anything to make you look bad." I respected him too much.

On my way out I stopped at the FBI store and bought a few FBI baseball caps as souvenirs.

I headed back to Baltimore for what I thought would be my last day in my hometown. The first person I went to see was my old friend Bubby—Melonie's uncle—the honest cop who had moved to the southwestern edge of town, where I hoped not to run into any wiseguys. I'd known Bubby for years, but I'd never discussed my wiseguy profession with him—though, of course, he knew I was a drug dealer from the days in the 1980s when I was busted. He and his wife, also a police officer, were very upset when they heard Gina had left me. While they were working their police beats, they kept looking out for Gina's Dodge Caravan. They'd call every day to say, "We looked, but we can't find her."

Now I was at his doorstep to tell him the truth. As soon as he saw me, he said, "Gina must have been really pissed off at you to move the way she did with the kids." I pulled out one of the FBI hats. "Where'd you get this?" he asked.

"I'm not who you think I am," I said. Then I told him what I'd been doing for the last five months. "You son of a bitch," he said, smiling. "I can't believe you and Gina pulled this off. You had me and everybody else in town totally fooled."

He had been to the house and had seen Gina packing boxes. "I really thought you guys were having your house painted." I could tell he was really happy for me. "This is the best thing you ever did for yourself and your family," he said. I told him I didn't know if we'd ever meet up again. As I went to leave, he gave me a big bear hug.

From there I made a detour on my way to Woodlawn. I know I shouldn't have gone back into the city, but I was hardly thinking rationally. I drove to Hollins Market, one of the city markets on the west side. Gina had called from Alabama with the disturbing news that there were no Tastykakes down south—and no King syrup for pancakes. So I stocked up on $40 worth of peanut butter and chocolate Tastykakes, and got three giant cans of Utz potato chips. I figured they wouldn't have any reliable chips down south. Then I headed to the FBI. Tommy told me to leave my Lincoln there so they could take out the tape recorder and remove the toggle switch.

I got into an unmarked FBI car and we headed over to my house in Hampden to get my clothes. Tommy and Steve drove in one car, while I rode with some other agents. As we pulled up, the streets were empty, except for a little neighborhood boy named John-John and his grandmother. He was one of the poorest kids in the neighborhood and I remember always giving him toys on Halloween. "What's going on, Mr. Charlie?" he asked. His grandmother quickly pulled him down the street. She probably thought I was being arrested. One of the agents went inside with his gun drawn, just to check if Billy or somebody else was in the house. When he found it empty, he yelled, "All clear." I ran inside and grabbed whatever clothes I could and threw them in the backseat. Then we sped off back to Woodlawn.

When we arrived, my Lincoln was stripped and ready to go. Tommy took me around the FBI office to say good-bye to all the agents I had gotten to know. Before I knew it, Steve, Tommy, Mel, and Kevin Bonner—the agent I worked with undercover—were gathering around me to say good-bye. I really had grown close to them. I would miss Tommy and Steve the most. Steve was like a father figure, always scolding me when I fouled up a tape, challenging me to take one more chance, complimenting me when I did a good job. I would miss Tommy for his encyclopedic mind and his constant questions. He was the most dedicated student of my "wiseguy school" and soaked up every complicated detail of my old scams and the street slang that went with them. To this day he remembers everything I ever told him.

They all shook my hand and told me I'd done a fantastic job. They wished me luck and assured me that my family and I would make it in our new life. "You'll be safe in Alabama," said Tommy. He reminded me that we would see plenty of each other in the coming months. I'd be flying back to Baltimore to testify at trials and talk to investigators and prosecutors. "Call me when you get to Alabama," Tommy said, and handed me a cell phone and a sky pager to keep in touch.

I headed out to Johnny's house to say good-bye, then drove west in the snow, stopped in Frederick for King syrup before turning south toward Alabama. It took me nineteen hours because of whiteouts from snowstorms in the mountains. The Lincoln was so full of clothes and the cans of potato chips that I had to sleep sitting up behind the steering wheel when I stopped for breaks.

When I finally crossed the Tennessee River, over the Helen Keller Bridge near Decatur, I didn't even know where to find my new home. I stopped at a pay phone and called Gina's uncle John. He met me and I followed him into town. I decided to surprise Gina. I sneaked into the house through the front door without knocking. We had a new miniature Yorkie, named Mickey, who started yapping immediately. Gina and the kids came out to see what the dog was barking at. As soon as we saw each other, Gina and I both started crying. We grabbed each other and clung together for a long time. I was a very thankful man.

Chapter 14

No Ordinary Life

People think being a criminal and not getting caught is a hustle and a challenge, but try being an honest person. Now *there's* a hustle and a challenge. By March 1996 I was eight hundred miles from the wiseguys in Baltimore. It was just six months since I went to the FBI to rat out my friends so I could change my life. It certainly had changed. I went from living in a Baltimore rowhouse with no front lawn to a house near a wildlife refuge in Decatur. There were more wild animals than I've ever seen in my whole life. I was already in enough danger, worrying the wiseguys would find me here. Now I had to run from the cotton-mouths, alligators, bats and brown recluses. And I had a hell of a time trying to kill Alabama's funny-looking crickets and spiders.

Everything was new to me. Decatur was a laid-back town, with little traffic and less crime. I wondered how I would ever get used to it. Back home I would scan the *Baltimore Sun* for news of my friends' latest arrests. There was plenty of murder and corruption to read about. The *Decatur Daily* reported the theft of plants from somebody's yard. They had only a few homicides a year; in Baltimore there's almost one a day. One week the Decatur paper printed a running story about coyotes killing cats and small dogs. Gina sent me racing out every night, chasing down Mickey, our Yorkie, after he'd sneak out. I was probably the only nut running around town looking for a dog at 11:00 P.M. I hated that dog.

When spring came, I learned how to cut the grass for the first time. I borrowed Uncle John's lawn mower each week. I'd mow everybody's lawn on the street. I really enjoyed it. I certainly didn't enjoy the tornadoes—and the sirens that told you they were on the way. When we first heard them, we were scared to death. We all huddled in the bathroom with flashlights, pillows and blankets. It was such an eerie feeling. Whenever the kids were at a friend's house when the siren went off, Gina would make me go and get them right in the middle of the storm.

I didn't even feel at home going to an ordinary supermarket. The first time we went grocery shopping, I noticed everybody paying with personal checks or credit cards. I turned to Gina and said, "Everybody in this town must be in debt up to their ass." I lived in a cash world, where nobody paid with credit cards or checks. To this day I carry cash with me, but not in the thousands like the old days when I needed hundred-dollar bills on hand to buy hot stuff from boosters or to make a quick loan.

Decatur was so strange I might as well have been in a foreign country. Sometimes I'd ask myself, "What the hell are you doing here?" Still, I started out enjoying my new life. I worked hard at being a good father. When Charlie Jr. was young, I never took the time to be with him, though I kept him away from the wiseguy life. I never supported him in his schoolwork, never helped him with his homework. And I never went to his sport games. I always put business first. Even with my other kids, I never once sat down to play a simple game of Monopoly or Chutes and Ladders back in Baltimore. I decided not to make the same mistake twice.

Now we'd play some type of game every night. I thought we finally were becoming a true family. I signed up Justin for Little League and volunteered as a coach. I called the kids who played for me my "Bad News Bears." Some of them were the boys no other coach wanted. One boy was hyperactive, another cursed a blue streak and a third boy was just damn right ornery. But that didn't bother me. All the kids were funny and they taught me about life in the rural South. If a ball fouled off and went into the woods, they warned me, "Mr. Charlie, don't go near that bush because it's poison ivy." Or they'd say, "Watch where you step because there could be a snake." They weren't afraid of snakes, but they knew I was terrified of the most harmless garden snake.

Sometimes I felt stupid. Here they were—seven and nine years old—teaching me about wildlife and plants. While I could barely understand their Southern drawl, the boys would laugh at the way I talked and at the slang I used. If something went wrong, I'd say, "Have you been smoking birdseed?" Or I'd say, "You talking to me?" the way Robert De Niro said it in *Taxi Driver.* And they would always correct my pronunciation of Baltimore. I say it like a native does: "Balmer." But the boys would tell me, "Mr. Charlie, it's Bal-ti-more." At the end of the season I asked each boy to sign a ball for me. I still have them, protected under a plastic cover, on my bedroom bureau.

You'd think I'd find some peace of mind in a nice place like Decatur, feel a little bit safe. But it's hard to make a new life when you know people are out to kill you. Less than a month after I left Baltimore, Tommy called to say there was a contract out on me. The FBI got word from the street that a former Baltimore cop "gone bad" had hired two wiseguys to whack me. I guess it was to be expected. Within days of our arrival my cover as an

FBI informant was blown with the arrests of Gussie Alexander, Mike Bush, Frankie Tamburello, Fat Ricky Payne and two other drug dealers. They faced federal charges that would send most of them to prison for several years. Pat Wheeler was charged with bribery. News of her arrest was all over the Baltimore media.

The story broke in the *Baltimore Sun* on the front page for two days with the headlines, JUSTICE DEPARTMENT WORKER ACCUSED OF SELLING DATA and INFORMANT LINKED TO OTHER PROBES. Though I was never mentioned by name, the depth of my undercover work was laid out for all to see the day after Pat pleaded guilty to one count of bribery and admitted to selling me confidential information from criminal files. I imagined the wiseguys sitting around Doughboy's or Joe's Tavern reading about my secret, double-crossing life and calling me every name in the book. They were probably saying, "I can't believe he's done this to us."

The March 30 *Sun* story by reporter Scott Higham began:

> The case against a U.S. attorney's office secretary who sold information from case files grew out of a broad investigation that has resulted in a flurry of drug indictments and the arrests of four suspects in a 1978 murder. . . . The drug probe that snared Wheeler and the murder suspects began last year, when FBI agents started to investigate a ring of cocaine peddlers and organized crime figures operating out of Baltimore and Ocean City.
>
> Last fall, the informant met with FBI agents and federal prosecutors to tell them what he knew about the drug ring and other criminal enterprises in Maryland.
>
> "The FBI agents start to ask him what he knew and the witness said: 'I think we should talk about

the leak in your office,'" said first assistant U.S. Attorney Gary P. Jordan. "We felt like throwing up."

Pat Wheeler's arrest may have grabbed the biggest headlines, but for me the biggest news came from Baltimore County with the arrests of Billy, John Derry and Ronnie Rogers for the murder of Mark Schwandtner. Billy's sister, Susan Thompson, (formally Rogers) was charged as an accessory after the fact of murder because police said she helped the killers throw away bloody clothes.

I could only imagine what went through Billy's mind when police handcuffed him. I was relieved he was arrested so soon after I left town, but the relief lasted only two days. By then he was out on bail. All the others made bail, too. Gina was scared to death, and she was furious.

"Billy is running around free," she said. "He is having a good time. He is with his family. Where are we? We are eight hundred miles away, afraid to talk to our family. We have nothing. We are the ones who have to hide and be ashamed," she said. "The ones who are wrong still have their freedom." And she was right.

Billy's freedom gave me nightmares. In my dreams Billy beat me up so badly that I couldn't move. In one dream I actually felt like I was in a coma, but I knew everything going on around me. I could feel all the pain and hear everything he was saying while he was beating me. But I couldn't do anything about it. In another dream my family and I were being chased on foot by Billy, Gussie, Frankie and Mike. You name a Baltimore wiseguy and he was in my dreams. When we got caught, the wiseguys beat me up unmercifully while they held down my family. Gina screamed and the kids cried for them to stop. My seven-year-old son yelled, "Let my daddy go." But the wiseguys said, "We want your family to watch you die." Just as one of them held a gun to my head, I'd wake up.

Journaling

I was losing control of my life. And it had no purpose. When I was a wiseguy, my purpose was to make money and break laws. When I worked for the FBI, my purpose was to catch the bad guys. Now my life was empty and meaningless. One day I was pouring out my troubles to Bruce over the phone and he said, "Charlie, why don't you keep a journal. It would be a way to keep your thoughts together." And it would also help me when the FBI called with the same question they'd asked me before. I could look back in the journal to make sure my answers were consistent. So one day I sat down in the big kitchen of the little house we rented and started to write.

Since I wasn't used to writing, I started out just jotting down the phone calls I got from Tommy and the daily comings and goings of my family. Eventually I learned how to pour my troubled heart onto its pages.

My first entry began with the phone call from Tommy, that told me there was a contract out to whack me. We had come to Decatur to live a normal, ordinary life, but anyone reading my journal could tell we were a long way from normal.

The journal became something to look forward to every day. It was a release I found in nothing else. While I wrote, I actually felt in control. It became my new purpose in life. Sometimes I'd be driving down the road and think of something to put in the journal. I couldn't wait to get home to write it down. Lot of times I was so emotional while I wrote that my arm ached from putting too much pressure on the pen. Gina and the kids thought I was nuts for keeping a journal, but the writing helped ease the stress and loneliness on the many nights when I couldn't sleep. Sometimes it was just me, my pen and my paper.

While I was trying to act like a normal person, I was constantly thinking about Billy and all the people who were going to prison. Having little to do all day just made matters worse. Some people would like sitting home for six months, but I was used to hustling. I'd never been an idle man. It drove me nuts not to work. In my past life I only stopped working to sleep. Now I couldn't find honest work—and I could hardly sleep. I thought if I could get about six hours of straight sleep just one night, my mind would stop racing so fast. I was an ex-wiseguy, once known as a tough guy on the streets, but I sure wasn't tough anymore.

I wrote in my diary that I had heard of "post war syndrome." I later learned it was called post-traumatic stress disorder, and years later I was diagnosed with a chronic case of it. But then I wrote: "I wonder if there is such a thing as post criminal syndrome. I probably have just as much stress as if I was in a war."

I had constant flashbacks and panic attacks. At least war veterans are safe from the enemy once they come home. I didn't think I'd ever be safe, no matter how far I was from Baltimore.

It was nearly impossible to find work, given that Gina and I were using a phony last name—Williams. We had no papers with that name, except for the kids' school records altered by the FBI. Even without officially going into witness protection, the FBI promised to get us new IDs with the name Williams. But the new IDs never materialized. The FBI just kept putting me off, saying the new IDs would come soon. It was hard to change our lives without them. Employers wanted a résumé, a Social Security number and work references. Our situation caused more problems than I'd imagined. I wrote in my journal: "My tags run out on my van at the end of the month. The van is registered in Maryland. Now what do I do? Go out and steal a new set of tags every week? I don't think so."

The FBI continued supporting us with $2,500 a month. I wanted to find a job so I would no longer be on the federal dole. I knew defense attorneys would use it against me in the coming trials as a motive for snitching. But for now, I needed it.

While we waited for our new lives to materialize, we hoped no one would find us, but we heard bad news from Baltimore. Charlie Jr. and Gina's parents got threats in the mail. Each letter had a drawing of one person slicing another's throat. The knife blade had the name Wilhelm, while the attacker said, "Death becomes you." The FBI checked the letters for fingerprints, but they didn't match any prints of criminals in their computers. My son also found cheese on his doorstep. It's just another word for rat. There must have been a bounty on my head. One guy told my brother somebody could get rich if they found me.

I wrote in my journal: "People are saying they have spotted me everywhere. I have been spotted in Baltimore more than Elvis Presley has been spotted since his death. People are actually saying that they have spotted me walking around my old neighborhood, that they have seen a moving truck moving us back in our old house."

Tommy called and warned me to be careful. "How am I supposed to be careful when I have the only white Lincoln with a red top with Maryland tags in Decatur, Alabama?" I asked Tommy. He didn't have an answer.

I asked both principals at my children's new schools never to call their old schools back in Baltimore. I also gave my children my FBI code name, Warlock. I told the principals if anyone came to the school to pick them up, they should only be released if they are given that name.

Fear was always on my mind. When I grew more comfortable writing in the journal, I sat down to put my scary feelings on paper:

"Let me explain the different types of fear a family goes through when you're living this life. There is the fear of what the future holds, the fear of someone recognizing you and finding out who you really are. You fear people will kill your wife and kids—just to prove a point to you. You worry every time you drive somewhere so you constantly look in your rearview mirror to see if you're being followed. You worry a bomb will explode every time you turn on the ignition to your car. You worry your child will be kidnapped on the way to school. You fear innocent noises when you lay in bed at night. You fear a Molotov cocktail will crash through the window and land in your child's room. You're even too afraid to sit on your porch with your family in case there's a drive-by shooting. You most fear rainy nights. You know from experience those are the quietest nights—and the perfect time for your enemies to whack you. When I was in jail at least I had a release date. The confined life my family is living has no end."

Confessing

I started praying every night to God to help everyone who had touched my life, even the people who are out to get me and my family. It's not that I turned into some religious freak, but it was the first time in years I had gotten some faith back in my life. I was feeling down about the prospect of putting my best friend away in prison. And I was miserable not knowing my future. It was tearing me up. I needed to talk to someone who could help me cope.

I hadn't been to confession in years, but I figured it was as good a time as any to find a priest. There was only one Catholic church in that Bible Belt town. I drove by the old brick church a few times before calling. Then, exactly one month after my arrival, I got up the courage to call. Over the phone the priest at St. Ann Catholic Church sounded old and wise, maybe a man of sixty. Father Joe Culotta, however, was nothing like I expected. He was maybe around thirty-seven or thirty-eight, with one of the nicest voices I ever heard. He took me into his office and asked how he could help me. I felt so comfortable and relaxed with him. I said, "I'm a Catholic and I haven't been to confession or Holy Communion in twenty-four years, but I do believe in God."

He told me I could make a confession to him right then. I told him, "Father, I'll be here until next year making a confession of every sin I had ever committed." He told me that as long as I knew what the sins were and I wanted to be forgiven, that God would forgive me as long as I was remorseful. I was. I then went on to tell Father Joe about Mark Schwandtner getting killed. "His mother wants to know why it took so long for me to come forward," I said. I also told Father Joe about all the people I was putting away in prison, including Billy.

He told me it was ironic that I had come in that week. It was Holy Week when Christ had risen from the dead and started a new life. And, basically, I was doing the same. He also said I didn't choose everyone's path in life. The pain I was causing my old friends—and the pain I was causing my own family—had a purpose. It was to right a wrong. He asked me to pray for everyone who had touched my life, good or bad. And he asked me to pray for all the wiseguys' children. That part bothered me.

Sometimes through the confession I could barely talk from the sobbing and trying to hold back the tears. He told me to ask God to guide me and my family through this nightmare. Father Joe made a lot of sense that day. When I left the old brick church, I felt like a new man, except I had to make Holy Communion. So, on Palm Sunday I made my first Holy Communion in twenty-four years. I actually felt like a ton of bricks had been lifted off my shoulders and that there might be a place in Heaven for me after all.

I had finally begun to realize I had done something right in my life by becoming a rat and leaving material things behind. I wasn't proud about putting anyone's parents in prison, but I was proud that I saved lives by refusing to whack two people. I knew I had put a dent in a major drug organization in Baltimore. And I hoped maybe one person coming up the ranks of an organization might see it wasn't too late to get out.

Picking My Brain

Although Father Joe helped me see that I had done the right thing, he couldn't stop my nightmares, the flashbacks or the nagging worry that Billy was still free. The FBI wasn't too happy about it, either. The agents got to work to find a way to lock him up again. In July 1996 they flew me back to Baltimore to talk to prosecutors and detectives and to tell a federal grand jury how I collected juice on loans for Billy while he was in federal prison. Tommy picked me up at the Baltimore-Washington International Airport and drove me to the federal courthouse where Pat Wheeler used to work. We parked under the IRS building and walked down Lombard Street, in the heart of downtown Baltimore, just a block from the Inner Harbor.

As the traffic raced by, I wondered how many people might recognize me walking in broad daylight with an FBI agent. Luckily, I didn't see any familiar cars in the traffic. We went up to the U.S. Attorney's Office in a real secure area. Tommy rang the buzzer and said through the intercom that we had an appointment with assistant U.S. attorney Lisa Griffin. Lisa came out, introduced herself to me and took us back to a conference room. She asked me questions about my past and then started zeroing in on my association with Billy. I told her, "I knew everything about him, the way he thinks, the way he dresses, what type of music and hobbies he likes."

I also told Lisa that Billy didn't care for her. She had been one of the prosecutors who got him convicted for loan-sharking back in 1990. He had slapped a bookmaker who didn't pay his juice, then tried to shut him up so he wouldn't testify to a grand jury. Billy's threats hadn't worked and Lisa got the bookmaker to fess up to Billy's threats. Lisa asked me how Billy got all his money to start juicing loans. So I talked for about four hours, explaining how he used to swindle money out of other wiseguys.

Afterward Tommy checked me into a hotel under a false name and walked me to my room. When we opened the door, I was surprised how nice and big it was. "Tell Mel he did all right with this hotel," I told Tommy, knowing his supervisor would have a fit if he had any idea the federal government was paying for such a nice room. Tommy said if Mel knew I was staying in such a swanky hotel room, we would both hear from him.

That night I sneaked out with my brother, Johnny, so I could see my son and my granddaughter, as well as my sister, Betty. I also got to see my granddaughter walk for the first time.

The next morning Tommy picked me up and took me to Baltimore FBI headquarters to meet with a bunch of city police detectives. I wasn't too thrilled about meeting them. I still had a bad feeling about most city police because of the leak that still hadn't been plugged. When they came into the conference room, I didn't recognize any of them at first. Tommy introduced me to a major and a detective from the city's Internal Investigation Division. When Tommy got to the next introduction, I broke into a big smile. I immediately recognized the big, burly, gray-haired man as Spanky Herold, the honest city vice detective who followed me and tapped my phone in early 1995.

"Spanky, let me tell you, you are a legend among all the bookmakers and wiseguys on the street," I said.

Spanky and the others asked me about corruption in Baltimore City, including the sheriff's department, which guards the city courthouses. I told them about a deputy sheriff named Lew Benson, who was a well-known local professional boxer and loan shark. They asked me if I knew the identity of the dirty cop in the police department. I gave them a name, but I had never talked to the guy directly, so I couldn't prove he was the leak. I talked for hours before they let me go. Then they said something Tommy and Steve said many times before: "Charlie is a walking encyclopedia of organized crime in Baltimore."

Tommy picked me up the following morning to head to the grand jury in the federal courthouse. Lisa Griffin asked if I was ready to testify. I said yes, though I had butterflies in my stomach. I knew this was it. I might be putting Billy away for a good while with my testimony, but I had to do it. I couldn't go on living the way I was. They told me everything would be fine. I said, "Yeah, if I can keep the jurors awake." Tommy and Lisa said they didn't think there would be a problem. They said my testimony would probably be the most exciting story the grand jury had heard.

We walked into the grand jury room. I looked over all the people to make sure I didn't know any of them. Lisa started asking me questions. I answered by using a blackboard to write down the figures to explain how shylocking worked and how the point system added up. I felt like I was teaching a class.

I told them how I collected for Billy when he was in federal prisons in Pennsylvania and in New York. I told them we turned over the juice payments to The Queen, Billy's girlfriend. She then drove back to federal prison to update Billy on the payments. I also told them about Billy's black book of people who owed us money. The FBI never found it.

The jurors also asked me how we collected the money. I said we had to be stern and arrogant with the people who owed us. I told one guy to sell his wife's ass if he couldn't make the payments. I felt so bad for another guy that I secretly would make his juice payment to The Queen out of my own pocket.

"This sounds just like a movie," an older woman in the jury mumbled out loud.

"I wish it was, because I lived it and I'm still living it," I later wrote in my diary.

I choked up when the jury asked about the safety of my children and family. But in the end Lisa said I did real well with my testimony.

A Fish Out Of Water

I flew back to Decatur after my testimony. Trying to get on with our lives seemed impossible. It had been almost a year since the day my house was raided in Baltimore, and it had been five months since we resettled in the South. I still didn't have a steady job. I finally realized my days of testifying against my old friends were far from over. And my family didn't feel any safer than the day we arrived.

I worked at a pawnshop for a while but was fired because I didn't know how to use a computer. I did manual labor, but I injured my elbow. One of the few friends I made went into a catering business with me. I made Maryland pit beef and Philly cheese steaks, but I couldn't put the business in my name because the FBI still hadn't gotten us new identity papers. So, my partner took most of the money. The FBI said they would help me get a job. One agent down there even went with me on a job interview—to be a city building inspector. I scored well on the test, but they never called back. I didn't blame them for not hiring me. If somebody told you what I used to do for a living, would you hire me? Even if I could get a steady job, I would have to leave it to testify again in Baltimore. I felt like the FBI had drained me dry and there was nothing else to suck out of me. Gina said the FBI was using me.

I started second-guessing myself, wondering why I went to them in the first place without a lawyer and why I never got immunity from prosecution. In my journal I asked myself: "Who are the biggest cons—the wiseguys or the FBI?"

With the threats and contracts out on my life, Gina was scared to live with me. She thought she and the kids weren't safe. We argued a lot and she talked about leaving me. We sure could have used some counseling, but it wasn't like we could walk into a counselor's office and tell him what was going on in our lives. Who would believe such a fantastic story?

I knew if Gina decided to leave with the kids, I would be devastated.

One late night, as usual, I was the only one awake. I sat down at the kitchen table with my journal:

"I'm sitting here. It's 3 A.M. Gina is on the couch sleeping and the kids are in bed. I've looked for a bottle of painkillers that Gina had for her dental surgery but I can't find them. If I could find them I would eat every last one of them and end everybody's misery. Or else if I had a gun, I'd put it right in my mouth without hesitation and blow my brains out. I would let Billy and the rest of the guys win. Who cares!!

"Maybe by writing this, it's therapy for me to release stress and tension. And maybe it's my way of asking for help. I don't know !!"

The only time I calmed down was when I talked to Bruce. Unlike Tommy, who had to keep up our good relationship for his own benefit as an FBI agent, Bruce didn't have any motive for being my friend. Bruce convinced me that he would do everything in his power to keep any harm from coming to my family. I would talk his ear off on the phone when I was feeling low. Bruce always had high spirits and could help me snap out of a depression when I was having a bad day.

I kept trying to fit into life in Alabama. One day Uncle John invited me over to plant corn. I was really excited. I felt like John-Boy from *The Waltons*. I had never planted any vegetable before in my life and I imagined feeding my family from the land. Now, I'm not stupid about where food comes from. If you'd asked me about blue crabs from the Chesapeake Bay, I could show you how to pick a hard crab clean in minutes or how to prepare a soft shell-crab by cutting out the eyes, gills and flap in seconds before frying it. But the idea of planting seeds that grow food was a novelty.

Uncle John showed me the corn seeds, which looked like dried-up corn kernels. He told me we'd get four ears off every stalk we planted. He then went off to plant tomatoes and squash and left me with the corn seeds. "You'll be done in no time," he said.

After a half hour I noticed he already had finished planting and was back in the house, but I was still going at it.

He came to the door and yelled out to me, "Hey, Pollock,

what the hell is taking you so long?" I told him I was almost done.

Another half hour went by and I was still planting. The door opened again.

"Are you all right, Charlie?" asked Uncle John.

"Yeah, I'm fine. I'll be done in a few minutes," I said.

A third time he came out and asked me if I was sure I was okay.

Finally, after a few hours, I was finished. I came into the house, grabbed a cold soda from the refrigerator and downed it fast.

Uncle John was at the kitchen table with a cup of coffee. "What took you so long?" he asked.

"I would have been done earlier, but you kept bugging me and I lost count," I said.

"You lost count of what?" he asked.

"I counted every kernel of corn and multiplied it by four. But when you kept interrupting me, I forgot what number I was on and had to start all over again," I said. "But now I've got it. We'll have 2,334 ears of corn," I announced.

Well, that was all it took for Uncle John. He spit out his coffee onto the kitchen floor and started to laugh so hard he was in tears, doubled over.

Finally he said, "Are you telling me you were counting corn?"

I said, "Yeah, isn't that what you're supposed to do?"

It made sense for me to count. It was just like shylocking. The seeds were like a loan and the ears of corn would be the juice we would get in repayment.

There were plenty of other times in Alabama when I was a fish out of water. It took me quite a while to understand the difference between a steer and a bull. Uncle John explained it to me once and I thought I understood it. I thought a cow could give birth to three kinds of animals—a heifer, a bull and a steer. Finally he had to sit me down and tell me the facts of life. When Uncle John explained that a steer is actually a castrated bull, I couldn't believe it.

"Charlie, don't ask these kinds of questions to anybody else down here," he said. "They'll think you're nuts."

I knew by then my fantasy of being like John-Boy was over. If I ever tried to become a farmer, my family would starve.

Coming Unglued

Two months after I testified at the grand jury, Billy was still free. Gina and I were arguing all the time. She was depressed and cried for no reason. One minute she'd tell me she didn't love me; then she'd say she wasn't sure. She thought it would be safer if I moved out. I was so tired of arguing with her about the FBI. I called Tommy and Bruce to tell them my marriage was ending. Bruce said he had a safe house lined up for me. Tommy paged me. He said he was worried Gina would leave, then tell people back in Baltimore how to find me. I could tell Tommy was really concerned.

One night in late September I stayed up all night thinking about my life. When I lived on the streets back in Baltimore, I could deal with almost any situation. But now I couldn't even help my own wife and children out of their misery. I knew if our marriage broke up, it would be no ordinary separation, but nothing about my life was ordinary. Within a week I figured I would have to go into the witness protection program. Sometime after that, Gina and the kids also would have to enter the program in another city. And most likely, we'd be permanently separated from each other. I thought, *If I'm losing everything, so will Billy. If the government can't get him, then I will.*

The next day Gina and I had another blowup. By 9:00 P.M. she was helping me pack my clothes. She said, "The government doesn't care about us. You can stick the FBI up your ass." When Tommy called, Gina got on the phone and laid him out. She told him the FBI was full of shit. She really got on his case. I told Tommy, "I can't handle it anymore." He told me to leave so I wouldn't go off on Gina. I tried to convince Gina to stick it out. "We are so close to getting over the hump," I said, but she didn't want to hear it. Meanwhile, Justin was crying. Luckily, Mandy wasn't home. I hated the thought of never seeing my kids again and losing my marriage.

I got in the Lincoln with its expired Maryland tags and drove over to Uncle John's house to say good-bye. He and his wife, Pat, begged me to stay with them, but I said no. I started to think about how I was going to get even with Billy. I thought I'd drive all the way to Baltimore, walk into Sabatino's in Little Italy and tell the guys, "Let's get it on." They would call Billy within a matter of minutes. I guess I had a death wish. I certainly wasn't thinking rationally. On my way out the door, I grabbed a hammer.

I started driving north with a thousand thoughts going through my head. I couldn't even separate right from wrong. I had about $120 in my pocket. My old trusty Lincoln was loaded up with my clothes laid out on the red leather seats. I was worried about driving with dead tags, but I spent most of the time figuring out how I would "sneak" Billy and get away with it. ("Sneak" is another word we use for "kill.")

At about 2:00 A.M. I pulled into some rinky-dink hotel an hour north of Chattanooga for $20 a night. It was pretty dingy, but I couldn't afford anything else. I needed to save my money for gas and a little food. I was pretty strung out. I must have smoked two packs of Winstons since I'd left Decatur. I fell asleep at 3:00 A.M., but never went into a deep sleep. I was up again by 7:30 A.M. "How can I place a little fear in Billy? How can I turn the tide?" I asked myself.

I called Joe's Tavern in Baltimore. I knew he'd be there early collecting his money while the FBI agents slept. I still knew how his mind worked.

Billy answered the phone.

"Joe's," he said. I didn't say anything. "Joe's," he kept saying. I could hear the arrogance in his voice. I wondered if I was that arrogant when I was living that life.

I finally hung up. It made me sick to my stomach not to say something. I wanted to threaten him and tell him what a piece of shit he was, but then I remembered what Father Joe told me. My pain came from righting a wrong. I had come a long way toward changing my life. Did I want to blow it all now? I knew I would be jeopardizing all the cases I had helped the FBI develop. And I would be letting down Tommy, Steve, Kevin and all the other agents. Even more, I would be letting down Gina and the kids. How would they manage if I did something stupid and went to prison? Then I thought about Bruce. He was my beacon of light, the man who showed me the way out of a criminal life and convinced me I was doing the right thing. How could I let down Bruce?

The destructive side of me also knew if I said one word on that phone, it would be a warning to Billy that I was coming to sneak him. I knew I needed the element of surprise. I also knew he'd call his lawyer and say I was threatening him, then Billy would become the victim. I didn't bother to shave. I checked out of the hotel, lit up another cigarette and drove for two more hours. I tried to think how to get the message to Billy that I wasn't afraid of him. I wanted to tell him, "Leave my family alone." Billy knew if I was pushed, I'd do whatever it took.

I pulled into a truck stop, used the FBI's 800 number

to get an open line and called Joe's back. I knew Billy would be gone. Another guy answered the phone. I said, "Do you know who this is?"

He said, "Yes."

I said, "Tell Billy I'm back in Baltimore with my family and that we're tired of running." I hoped it would confuse Billy. He wouldn't know if I was trying to patch things up or if the FBI was setting him up.

Next I dialed my home number in Decatur. "I called Joe's," I told Gina. "I'm going to sneak Billy, chop his head off and stick it up his ass." I asked Gina if that's what she wanted. She was crying. She said she'd been trying to beep me. We could work things out, she said. The truck stop was so noisy I could hardly hear her. I hung up.

I jumped back in the Lincoln and started driving north on Interstate 81. I was about twenty miles north of Bristol, Virginia, when I got a page from my brother, Johnny. When I got him on the phone, he asked where I was.

"I'm in Baltimore," I lied. I knew Gina had probably told him I'd gone off the deep end. I didn't want him thinking I had turned back. "The wiseguys are really going to have something to worry about now," I told Johnny. He said Bruce was trying to beep me, too. I said I didn't get his page. If I had, Bruce is one person I would have called back. I told Johnny to tell Bruce that if the FBI wanted a good case against Billy, they should be at Joe's between 9:00 and 10:00 P.M.

"What are you going to do?" he asked.

"I'm going to pull my Lincoln right in Joe's parking lot and sit on the hood. When Billy comes after me, I'm going to hit him in the face with a hammer." I wasn't going to kill him, but I was going to hurt him pretty bad, then he'd really come after me and the FBI would have proof that he was out to get me. Even as I was saying this stuff, I knew he would call Bruce, and Bruce would call Tommy. Tommy would somehow cut me off before I did something stupid. I guess it was my way of asking for help. If you're going to sneak somebody, you sure don't give advanced warning, but I was impatient about Billy not being taken off the streets. I was tired of hiding.

After about ten minutes on the phone with Johnny, I told him I was coming to his house after I was through at Joe's. "Think about what you're doing," he said. I hung up. After another hour on the road I got beeped. It was Tommy. He'd punched in the FBI headquarters phone number with 911 behind it. *I'm in deep shit now*, I thought. But I didn't care. I pulled over at another truck stop, but not before he'd beeped me three more times. It was a beautiful, clear Saturday afternoon and here was Tommy going to his office to call me when he could be with his family. I knew he had a good excuse to get the state police to stop me. I was a sitting duck, driving with no registration and dead tags.

I called FBI headquarters. "Where are you?" Tommy asked.

"Baltimore." I lied again.

"Where?"

"The outskirts."

"Where?"

"Frederick," I said.

"Where in Frederick?" he asked.

"A hotel."

"What hotel?"

"I'm not telling."

"What do you think? That I'm going to lock you up if you tell me where you are?"

"If you're not locking me up, then why do you want to know where I'm at?"

"So I can talk to you before you do something stupid," he said.

He was trying to be stern with me, but I could also tell from his voice that he was worried.

I told Tommy I had called Joe's and that I was tired of hiding. I told him Gina and I were through. He tried to comfort me. He said he understood what I was going through. I told him, "All the textbooks in the world and everything you learned at Quantico couldn't teach you what I'm going through." He tried to understand. Then he asked me to come to FBI headquarters in Baltimore to talk things over. No, I told him. He then tried to threaten me. He said he'd get Washington to cut off my checks. "I don't care," I said. I told him the FBI had promised to get our new identities months ago. I had also asked them to get Gina some counseling. "We are just in limbo," I said.

He asked me if I actually talked to Billy at Joe's. "No, I'm not that stupid," I said. If he didn't believe me, I told him, I used the FBI's 800 number to make the call so he could get the recorded conversation. Then I told Tommy I was going to stay where I was for a while and cool off, then go to my brother's house. I promised not to do anything stupid. He sounded relieved and told me to call him Monday morning. I said I would.

I finally arrived at Johnny's at 8:00 P.M. I was so drained from the stress and lack of sleep, I collapsed on the single bed in the guest room. I got up early the next day and headed back home.

My mind was still a jumble over all the mess I nearly made. Gina and I patched things up. I promised to get her some counseling, even if we had to pay for it ourselves. I told her, "When the government is through with my knowledge, then we'll just be another statistic at Quantico."

Then I thought maybe we could get on with our lives. I realized I could have put everything in jeopardy by my insane plan—all the cases against all the guys, not to mention my own life.

Tommy called two weeks later. He finally had some good news. The FBI got Billy and The Queen for loan-sharking. Billy turned himself in to the U.S. marshals the day before. I said, "No shit. My wife will be glad to hear that." I asked how Billy reacted to his arrest. Tommy said Billy was real somber. He didn't have much to say. And this time he didn't get out on bail. I was relieved they finally got Billy, but there was a part of me that hurt. I thought, *What a way for the two of us to go down after all we've been through together.* I couldn't wait for this day to come and now I felt remorseful for putting him away.

Four weeks later, in November 1996, I picked up my plane ticket to head back to Baltimore to testify at my first trial against seventy-one-year-old Gussie Alexander. He was the only cocaine dealer I had to face at trial. All the others, including Frankie Tamburello, pleaded guilty. I was really on edge. If I'd slept twenty hours in a week, I was lucky. I thought about testifying in federal court. I knew the courtroom would be packed with reporters and wiseguys. I knew I'd feel a wounded pride, like I betrayed everyone forever. As usual, Tommy picked me up at the airport and told me I was to meet a new, young agent assigned to protect me during the trial.

First thing the next morning, the agent took me to the federal courthouse to listen to tapes I had recorded involving Gussie selling cocaine. While I listened to them, I realized what big risks I took at the time. But I also thought, *I could have done a better job. I should have asked better questions.* The tapes also made me realize how stupid and greedy the guys were to fall for my ruse and let an undercover FBI agent dressed like a biker, without *any* cash, come into the picture.

Prosecutors Lisa Griffin and Greg Welsh were starting

opening statements in the courtroom. I wasn't testifying
until the next day. All that night I kept waking up thinking about how many wiseguys were going to be there,
trying to intimidate me. I also knew that once the guys
started hearing my testimony, their assholes were going
to start puckering. The next morning the young agent
drove me back to the federal courthouse. I reviewed a
list of jurors to make sure I didn't know any of them.
Then I was taken to the courtroom. I saw Gussie first, sitting with his defense attorneys. I was real nervous. This
was my first time testifying against anyone in open court.
I was usually the one sitting in Gussie's seat, trying to
knock off a charge. Now I was really on the hot seat.

Gussie looked up at me from the defense table like we
were the best of friends. I guess he didn't want the judge
or the jury to think he had any animosity toward me.
And he acted dumbfounded about the drug charges
against him. He wanted the jury to think it was all a mis-
understanding. He was just an innocent old man, much
too old to get involved with drugs. The jury probably
didn't see the two goons he had in the back of the courtroom, but I did. They were eye-fucking me the whole
time I was on the stand.

I stayed on the witness stand all day telling how Gussie
sold coke to me in Ocean City and in Little Italy while I
was wearing a hidden tape recorder. The judge was in his
eighties and couldn't hear very well. That made me nervous. At one point the prosecutor entered a kilo of
cocaine into evidence. A few minutes later the judge
turned to me and asked what I did with the kilo. My
heart started racing real fast. I turned to Greg Welsh,
pointed and said, "I don't have it, he does." I worried
that the judge was senile. Maybe he thought I slid the
kilo under my seat. *This could only happen to me,* I thought.

My testimony took two more days, including hours of
cross-examination by defense attorneys asking about my

past life. Gussie's attorney probably expected me to lie, but I told the truth about everything. I was embarrassed by my criminal life and couldn't even look the jurors in the face.

A few days after I flew home, Tommy paged me. After deliberating for three hours, the jury convicted Gussie of dealing cocaine. That was great news, but then Tommy gave me the bad news. Gussie got out on bail while waiting to be sentenced. I knew Gussie was seventy-one years old. To the average person, he would seem harmless. But I knew if a wiseguy was one hundred years old, he'd still want revenge.

Tommy beeped me again two weeks later. Billy pleaded guilty to loan-sharking, but he only got three years. The Queen signed a paper admitting her guilt, but she got probation with the promise the charges would later be dropped. I said, "Tommy, if Billy isn't found guilty of murder, I'm in deep shit. The whole time he's in jail, he's going to be thinking of how to find me. You guys just keep sending him to college." In other words, Billy would learn from his mistakes.

Tommy said, "This is just the beginning of the sentences he'll serve."

I said, "Let's hope so."

The following February I had to head back to Baltimore for the pretrial hearing in the murder trials in Baltimore County. I knew this was just going to be like a dress rehearsal. The big trial against Billy was still months away. Still, I was so hyper it was almost unbearable. The anticipation of testifying was worse than actually being there. I asked Tommy if I could stay at Johnny's house, but Tommy said no. It would be safer to stash me in a hotel under a phony name. Maybe he had a sixth sense that something bad was going to happen.

Chapter 15

I Am My Brother's Keeper

Instead of flying to Baltimore for the pretrial hearing, I decided to drive. The FBI thought it was a good idea to change my travel habits, in case someone was following me. Even so, Tommy wasn't too happy that I was driving the Lincoln with expired Maryland tags.

I arrived on the first Sunday in February, feeling lonely and anxious. I needed someone to talk to, someone I could trust, someone who wouldn't judge me for all the mistakes I had made in my life. I simply needed somebody who wouldn't ask questions. I drove out to Woodlawn Cemetery, west of the city.

As I rode through the entrance, I could see the swans and ducks in the frigid waters of the little stream and pond. A feeling of peacefulness came over me—a rare sensation these days. The cemetery is a large one, but I knew which way to go, and quickly found my usual parking spot. I hadn't been here in a long time, but I still could have found the spot blindfolded.

I got out of the Lincoln, stuffed my bare hands in my pockets—I'd forgotten to bring gloves from Alabama—and looked down at the frozen grave before me. The granite headstone read: MELONIE WILHELM, JUNE 25,

1957–OCTOBER 9, 1983. Here was the grave of the woman who gave me my first son, the woman who divorced me for being such a scumbag, the woman who suffered a horrible disease and died at the age of twenty-six.

Why can't that be me? I thought.

There were no flowers on Melonie's grave, just dead grass under the headstone. I took my hands out of my pockets and started pulling up the grass to make it look a little neater. I did the same for her grandmother's grave nearby.

I hadn't been here in two years, so I had plenty to talk to her about.

"Melonie," I said. "You always told me that one day I was going to get into trouble that I couldn't get out of if I didn't straighten my life out." I then began to tell her where my life had gone in the last few years. Sometimes I communicated with her in silence and sometimes I spoke aloud. It was a complicated story, even speaking to a gravestone that can't ask questions.

When Melonie died, I was so grief-stricken and guilt-ridden, I hardly noticed anything around me at the funeral, though I remember Billy was there, along with many other wiseguys. All I wanted to do back then was to hug Charlie Jr. and love him. Do you know how hard it is to tell a seven-year-old that his mother is dead and is never coming back? Maybe that's why it was so hard for me, twelve years later, to tell Justin—also at age seven—that he was leaving Baltimore and might never come back. It brought flashbacks from Melonie's death.

Over the years after her death, I would ride out to her grave, sometimes at two or three o'clock in the morning. I would ask God why he took her and not me. At the top of my lungs I would scream, "If there is a god, then prove it and take me." When I got no answer, I would yell, "There isn't a god. He's just a myth."

Now I knew if there was such a thing as Heaven and

Hell, Melonie must be in Heaven and she must be an angel. Maybe she was my guardian angel. Even before 1995 I would go to her grave and talk to her when I was feeling down. Her grave was always a place I felt secure.

I asked her to look over my family and to look over our son, Charlie Jr. At the end of our visit I felt at peace. But as soon as I left the cemetery, my anxiety returned.

The next morning, after I had another sleepless night, Tommy picked me up at the hotel where he had stashed me. We stopped at the FBI office to pick up a young agent named Chris, who would be my bodyguard for the day. Then we headed up to the courthouse in Towson.

I had never been to the Towson Courthouse as a witness before. I had only been a defendant. I assumed I'd be brought in a secure back entrance like they have at the federal courthouse downtown. I couldn't imagine coming in contact with any of the people I had accused of murder before I walked into the courtroom, but I had no such luck. The Baltimore County Courthouse only has a back entrance for prisoners like Billy being brought into the lockups behind the courtrooms.

I knew this was not a good way to start my day in court. I got in line to go through the metal detector in the lobby. I looked dead in front me. There was John Derry. He was eye-fucking me the whole time. The agents grabbed me and rushed me into a separate elevator to the Baltimore County State's Attorney's Office. After a brief meeting, Chris took me back outside to the courtyard for a smoke. I looked up and there was one of the wiseguys coming into the courthouse. Chris kept his eyes on the guy until he was out of sight. I took a drag from my cigarette and threw it away. "It's going to be a rough day," I said.

We headed back upstairs to wait for the call from Jim Gentry, one of the assistant state's attorneys prosecuting the murder cases. About twenty minutes later we headed to a courtroom on the third floor. We were accompanied by Greg Welsh, the assistant U.S. attorney who prosecuted Frankie Tamburello, Fat Ricky Payne and the other wiseguy drug dealers I caught on tape. When we got to the courtroom, we met Steve Clary and Baltimore County police detective Mike Downs. It would have been a great reunion if I hadn't been so nervous about testifying.

As soon as we entered the courtroom, I could see it was packed with wiseguys. There must have been fifty guys I knew, not counting the women who came with them. Mark Schwandtner's family was also there, but I didn't notice them. We sat down in the back, so everybody had to turn around to stare at me. They shot daggers at me, of course. I quietly took in their threatening stares, then took a deep breath, steeled myself and looked over at the defense table, where all the defendants sat with their lawyers.

Just as I'd expected, there was Billy staring right at me with a look that said, "You motherfucker, you're going to get it." I made sure I didn't back down from his stare until he did. I felt like we were having a silent gunfight at the OK Corral. After a few minutes the judge asked all the witnesses to leave the courtroom, so I got up with the agents and went into the hall to be sequestered.

"Jesus Christ, they got some big boys in that courtroom," said Mike Downs after the courtroom door swung closed.

I said, "That's nothing. Wait till the full-blown trial if you want to see some goons."

Tommy said, "The FBI will have to bring in a SWAT team for your security."

Steve Clary looked concerned. He was angry I had to come in the back entrance of the courthouse, along with all the wiseguys. "I can't believe there is no other way for Charlie to come in and out of this building," said Steve.

Over the next few hours I waited in a room guarded by Chris while Tommy testified about his relationship with me as an informant. When it came time for the lunch break, the agents made sure the hallways were clear of the wiseguys before they let me out. After lunch we came walking down the hallway near the courtroom.

All of a sudden, a man sitting on a bench jumped up and yelled, "Charlie." Steve, Tommy and Greg grabbed hold of my arms and told me to keep moving. Chris stayed behind to question the man. After the agents sat me in a small room, Chris came in and asked me if I knew a man named William Smith. I said, "No. Did I do something with him? Or did I do something to hurt him?"

"No," said Chris. "The guy said he went to high school with you." I couldn't place the guy's name or his face, but it turned out he was there to testify against a man who robbed him.

Finally it was my turn to testify. I entered the courtroom and took the witness stand. I was so nervous, my asshole was puckering. You couldn't have squeezed a pin between the cheeks of my ass it was so tight. And my mouth was so dry I couldn't have gotten a word out without a drink of water. When the clerk handed me the water, though, I almost spilled it, I was shaking so badly.

Billy sat only about sixteen feet from me, so I tried not to look at him. Instead, I stared at the judge's attractive law clerk directly in front of me. Pete Johnson from the state's attorney's office started to ask me questions. I could barely get the words out. I tried to pull myself together so I wouldn't look stupid and give anybody in that courtroom the satisfaction of watching me clam up. Every time I began to panic, I just looked at the law clerk's legs and calmed down. I didn't look into the crowd of wiseguys once.

My testimony had mostly to do with the tape I made of

John Derry confessing to killing Mark and describing Billy's role in the killing. The defense attorneys were trying to get the tape thrown out as evidence. I wasn't there to testify about the murder. That would wait for the actual trial many months away. The lawyers hammered at me about the government's recording devices and how well the FBI agents supervised me when I used them. They also asked me about my criminal past to see if I would trip up and lie about it, but I freely admitted to my crimes. After two hours I was excused. I held my head high as I stepped down from the witness stand. But as I walked down the center aisle, I heard several voices muttering, "You fucking snitch."

I spent the next day at the FBI office in Woodlawn with Tommy and with Steve Hess from the Baltimore FBI's witness protection program. Steve yet again tried to talk me into going into the program, but again I declined. Tommy wanted to take me to lunch in a secluded place, but the other agents were going to eat at the atrium of the nearby Security Square mall. I told Tommy I thought the mall would be safe, so we went to the mall and I ate lunch surrounded by FBI agents.

Tommy took me back to my hotel around 4:30 P.M. I couldn't stop thinking about everything—the upcoming trial, Billy, the witness protection program and especially Mark Schwandtner's family. The hearing must have been emotional for Mark's mom. I guessed it dredged up all the old wounds for her.

I went to eat dinner at the hotel restaurant at 6:00 and was back at my room by 7:30 P.M. A few minutes later there was a knock on the door. I stood clear of the door and the window, then yelled, "Who is it?"

A woman's voice called out, "Security." I hesitated, then looked through the peephole and saw a guard I'd noticed earlier roaming the hallways of the hotel. I opened the door and she handed me a message. The note was marked "urgent." It had my brother's name and cell phone number to call. The time on the message was 7:10 P.M. I figured Johnny was just checking up on me and was worried when I didn't answer the phone in my room.

I dialed his cell phone.

"Hello," said Johnny.

"What's up?" I said.

He answered with a scream.

"You and your fucking Colombian friends, that's what's up. I'll never fucking come see you again."

"Calm down, Johnny, " I said. "I don't know what you're talking about."

"Your Cuban or Colombian friends caught me at a stop sign by my house and pulled a gun on me. And they had a message for me to give my snitch brother."

Apparently, the gunman in the passenger seat and the driver were brown-skinned men, so Johnny thought they were Cuban or Colombian drug dealers I used to hang with.

"What did you do when they pulled the gun?" I asked.

"I pulled out in the middle of traffic and almost hit a car. Then I took off to a gas station that had plenty of light and plenty of people."

"Calm down and call the police," I said.

"I'm trying to calm down and I already called the police," he said.

He was waiting for a Harford County sheriff's deputy to arrive. "Don't tell them anything about my situation," I said.

"I'm not," he answered.

Then I tried to comfort him.

"Johnny, if the Cubans or the Colombians wanted to kill you, they would have just shot you without warning. They were just trying intimidation tactics."

For some reason, that wasn't much of a consolation. I

asked him to describe the men. It was dark and raining, so he didn't get a good look at anything, except the gun. It was an automatic pistol and it was big, he said. Just then the deputy sheriff arrived at the gas station. Johnny told me to call Tommy right away. Before we hung up, I reminded him to calm down when he spoke with police.

I beeped Tommy several times with my code, 520, and the numbers 911 behind it, but got no response.

While I waited, my mind raced at a hundred miles an hour. How would I live with myself if someone I loved was killed because of me? I tried to put things in perspective and tell myself that the gunman was there just to warn Johnny. If he really wanted to kill my brother, he would have fired the gun. I was panicked. For more than a year I had dreaded that I would get whacked or someone in my family would get hurt. There had been so many contracts on my life and so many threats to my family, it was bound to happen. But now the real threat had come to my brother—and in the form of a gun— and it really hit home. If it wasn't for Johnny and Bruce, I would never have changed my life. And on this night my brother almost died for helping me do the right thing.

After about twenty minutes the phone rang. It was Johnny again, wanting to know the number for FBI headquarters so he could tell police to call Tommy. I was so stressed out that I couldn't remember the main number so I gave him Tommy's private number at his office. Johnny called back to say the deputy got Tommy's recording at his private number. I said, "Do you mean to tell me the police can't find the main phone number for the FBI headquarters?"

"I don't know," said Johnny. I could tell he was getting impatient with them.

Then, all of a sudden, I remembered the number.

As soon as I hung up, the phone rang again. Finally it was Tommy.

"What's wrong?" he asked. I told him about what happened to Johnny and that the deputy sheriff was with him.

He said, "Well, I guess that's who Deputy Sheriff Brooks is." He had just gotten a message from him.

"Don't leave your room under any circumstance. And don't answer the door for anyone," said my handler.

He called back twenty minutes later. He said Johnny was going to meet him at his office in the morning to describe the gunmen and look at mug shots.

I asked Tommy if he thought I was safe. Johnny had visited me at the hotel the night before. He could have been followed.

"Charlie, I think you're all right. The only reason the gunmen went for Johnny was because they couldn't find you. They thought you would be staying at your brother's house during the hearing," he said.

I remembered that I had wanted to stay with Johnny on this visit, but Tommy nixed the idea.

"I just had a gut feeling not to let you stay at your brother's house this time," he said.

"I'm sure glad you had that feeling," I said.

"You're right, because you would be dead. They would have just shot you," he said. I knew he was right.

Johnny called back and sounded much calmer, though he was still shaky. Deputy Sheriff Brooks had talked to Tommy and the county's deputy sheriffs were going to ride past his house several times to make sure there were no unusual people or vehicles hanging around. But Johnny was also afraid his wife would find out. He decided not to tell her—at least for the time being.

I told him, "Johnny, this was bound to happen eventually." Since I had gone to the FBI, Johnny would sometimes show up on the streets and ask questions about the wiseguys, like he was a federal agent or something.

I asked him again if he could describe the gunmen, but he could only remember the gun. "It was big," he kept saying.

I told him to go home, get some sleep and try to remember every little detail about the gunmen and their vehicle.

"I can sympathize with the way you feel, having a gun in your face. Now you know how I've been living, day in and day out," I said. Before I hung up, I told him I'd see him at the FBI office in the morning.

I called Gina back in Decatur to make sure she and the kids were all right. I asked if any strangers had come to the door. She said no.

She knew something was wrong, so I told her what happened to Johnny. She said she wanted me to hurry home as soon as possible so I'd be out of danger. She also told me to back off and stop cooperating with the government. I told her, "If I backed off, then nobody would be safe and we would really have to worry. This is what wiseguys thrive on—fear and intimidation." I also said police would be checking on Johnny's house. And I lied a little. I told her the FBI had guys in the parking lot of the hotel outside my window. I could hear her sigh of relief, so I knew it was a lie worth telling. Before we hung up she told me to be careful.

Next I called Charlie Jr. in my old neighborhood to make sure he was okay, but I didn't tell him what happened to Johnny. I knew if strangers had been to his door, he would have volunteered that information.

By the time we hung up, it was 10:30 P.M. Now I could worry about my own safety. I looked around my hotel room. Where could I sleep so I wouldn't get shot? As I've said before, the best time to sneak somebody is at night when it's pouring down rain. I was on the first floor over-looking the parking lot. There was a big window. And like most hotels, the bed was dead in front of the window. Somebody could easily shoot through the window and into the bed. I thought of sleeping in the bathtub, but it was too small. Then I pulled the pillows and covers off the bed onto the floor just under the window. If anybody started shooting, I would just get covered with broken glass.

Every noise I heard woke me up. I think I slept with one eye open. Around 3:00 A.M. my back was hurting, so I decided to take a chance on the bed. I said a prayer, asking God if something happened to me, would He take care of my family?

I got up at 5:30 A.M. and sat down at the hotel room's little table and started to write in my journal, jotting down every detail I could remember about the night before. It helped me unscramble my thoughts and gave me a little bit of control of my morning.

I was packed by 7:30 and waited for Tommy to pick me up about 9:00 A.M. I told Tommy it was just a matter of time before Johnny had a scare like the one he had last night.

When we got to the FBI office, my brother was already there. The three of us sat down and Johnny tried to describe the gunmen, but he still couldn't remember much. I kept asking him, "Did the guys have earrings? Were they tall? Were they skinny? Did they have braided hair, long hair or short hair?" He wasn't much help.

I also didn't agree with his theory that the gunmen were Cuban or Colombian drug dealers. Most of the Cuban and Colombian drug dealers I knew well were already in prison. The others wouldn't have just threatened Johnny—they would have shot him dead right there. Tommy agreed they were a vicious group. I then told Tommy one of the men could have been a drug dealer I knew from the Dominican Republic. Tommy said he would find the guy's mug shot to show to Johnny.

I told Tommy that Gina wanted me to back off with the FBI, just to finish up the trials and move on. Johnny got all excited. "No way. You get every one of those fuckers," he said. I told him I didn't want anything happening to him. "I'll never forgive myself if you get killed," I said.

When we were done, Tommy said I could leave for Alabama. He hadn't been keen on my driving to Baltimore with expired tags in the first place. "I want you to understand my office doesn't condone you driving your vehicle," he said.

Dark Days

On the way home I kept worrying about Johnny. I was thinking about Billy and the trial and all the rotten things that were being said about me on the streets. When I got home, I wrote in my diary: "What a mess this whole thing is. I know people roll every day. The problem with this investigation and the arrests is that there are so many spin-offs and players. This could only happen to me."

I called Tommy to let him know I'd arrived safely. Tommy told me that he had been so worried about me the night Johnny was threatened, he had got out of bed at 2:00 A.M. and had driven to my hotel. He sat in the parking lot until 5:30 A.M.

I realized I hadn't lied to Gina about the FBI watching over me, after all.

Back home, my life returned to the limbo I'd been living for a year. No new identity papers, no steady job, not much of a life. Some days I thought it was just me and my journal.

A month after Johnny almost got killed, I wrote:

"I have been trying to get a volunteer job at a local hospital. I figure maybe I can give something back to the community, since I took so much out of the community. Besides, I am bored and frustrated with my life. I feel like a bum or something. I have been keeping my sanity by writing this journal. I have also been coaching my son's baseball and basketball teams. I almost feel like I am a useless person. I can't meet new friends because I'm not working. I meet some new friends through coaching, but when I tell people I have no employment or I'm retired, they look at me like [I'm] some retard. And now I can't even volunteer my time at a hospital because I have to fill out an application with my social security number and previous employers.

"I'll be honest with you, sometimes I think about going and making a quick score. I also think about all the excitement and good times I used to have, not including the money I had at one time. I feel like a welfare recipient and I wonder how I'm going to support my family once I am cut loose by the government. Sometimes I actually think about calling some friends up north and telling them to come to where I live, because there are some easy scores to be made."

Later that same day I wrote: "I'm having one of those days where it seems like I can't go on any longer. I realize I'm taking my frustrations out on my family. It's not that I'm yelling or screaming at anybody. I have become a silent partner with my wife and a silent father to my children. It's like I'm in a bubble and don't care what is happening outside the bubble. I know it's not fair to my family. So the only solution is to call Bruce in Washington. He always has high spirits and can help me change my attitude around when I'm having one of those days.

I envy Bruce and I think the world of him. The other reason I called Bruce is to tell him that it has been two years this month since I first came to ask him to help me change my life."

The weeks dragged on, with no end in sight. The only thing I had to look forward to was testifying against my old friends at the upcoming murder trials—and wishing they would be over soon. What a thing to look forward to. Even the dates of trials were uncertain. There were long delays with constant postponements and decisions to try the defendants together, then try them at separate trials.

The FBI agents weren't even able to arrest the gunmen who tried to kill Johnny. The guy my brother picked from mug shots had an alibi. His boss said he was at work during the time Johnny was threatened.

The stress had really gotten to me and Gina again. We made a decision to end our marriage. It wasn't a question of who was right or who was wrong. It was just the stress. By late April I called Tommy to tell him we were splitting up. As usual, he was sympathetic. He understood what Gina and the kids were going through, especially since we never got our new IDs with our fake names on them. He said we would each have to go into the witness protection program in separate locations.

I told Tommy I was mentally and emotionally drained. But no matter what happened between me and Gina, I still wanted to testify. And I wanted everything to be over soon. A few days later, though, Gina and I changed our minds. We agreed that we still loved one another and we really didn't want to split up.

I went back to see Father Joe on May 1. I was feeling ashamed of myself and my past life. I was ashamed of some of the things I'd done. I told Father Joe I was confused. "Why should I feel like the guilty party?" I asked. Sometimes I felt like admitting to people in Decatur who

I really was. I wanted to tell them I was ashamed of what I did, but not of who I am. Let people judge me on that, I told him.

That day I wrote in my diary: "Father Joe made a lot of sense to me today. He said, 'Justice has to be carried out.' And he said if I decided to cooperate under no false pretenses, then my heart and soul were in the right place. He also said that when I made the choice to cooperate, I knew it wasn't going to be easy. He said I should give thanks to God every day for my family being safe and surviving through all we have survived."

The Payoff

The same week I met Father Joe, I got a call from the Maryland State Prosecutor's Office. Tommy arranged for them to call me. They were investigating corruption at the Baltimore City Liquor Board and wanted to know about bribes Fat Ricky and I made to liquor inspectors for "protection" from any liquor board citations that might come our way at Joe's Tavern and at Doughboy's.

I spoke with a prosecutor named Mike McDonough, who was investigating Billy Madonna, a bar owner, a former member of the Maryland House of Delegates, a heavy gambler and a man with a lot of political clout in Baltimore. He was especially connected to a powerful state senator named Barbara Hoffman. I read in the *Baltimore Sun* that he had a $54,000 gambling debt in 1997 from Atlantic City casinos. He also had a close friendship and business relationship with Tony Cianferano, the city's chief liquor inspector, who was also under investigation. Even though Billy Madonna was not officially working for the liquor board, he had enough political power to hire and control liquor inspectors.

At that time the Baltimore City Liquor Board was the

last patronage holdout in state politics. To get a job as a liquor inspector, you needed the "sponsorship" of a state senator. And some of those "sponsored" inspectors were known for being corrupt. As a bar owner, you had to grease their palms to keep them off your back. And the inspectors demanded that you purchase thousands of dollars of tickets to political fund-raisers for the state senators who sponsored them.

Consequently, many of the liquor laws were successfully ignored by bar owners. Complaints by neighbors of noise and loud music went uninvestigated. Keeping a lid on underage drinking was a joke. Liquor inspectors gave advance warning to "protected" bar owners so they could flush the teenagers out the back door before inspectors and police came checking IDs. With bribes you could also stay open beyond the 2:00 A.M. closing time. And you wouldn't even get a slap on the wrist if your taxes went unpaid for years. Nobody seemed to care if the legal owner of your bar was just a "front," somebody who never really purchased it and didn't run it. That way you could have convicted felons like me and Billy Isaacs secretly owning bars, even though the law didn't allow it. Frankly, it wasn't much of a secret. Everybody knew felons like Billy Isaacs owned Baltimore's bars. And, of course, those video poker machines we used to make illegal gambling payouts—and to launder drug money—were completely unregulated. Running a bar in Baltimore was a real gravy train. As long as you paid your protection money to the inspectors, there were no rules or regulations.

I told McDonough that Billy Madonna controlled Chief Inspector Cianferano, as well as two liquor inspectors named Donald Harlow and Donald Cassell. Billy Madonna bragged that he had influence over the liquor board and could hire and fire inspectors.

Then I told them about bribing Donald Cassell to protect Joe's Tavern. Fat Ricky was already paying off Cassell to protect Doughboy's, so we decided to get him to protect Joe's, too. I would give money to Fat Ricky for my share of the payoff and Ricky would hand the money to Cassell. I was there for many of the payoffs and saw the money change hands, I told the prosecutor. At first we only paid off Cassell, later Cassell told us that we also could pay Cianferano, who was then the deputy chief liquor inspector and was later promoted to chief inspector. At Joe's we had a doorman who was a neighbor of Cianferano's, so we asked the doorman to arrange a meeting with Tony.

We met Cianferano and Cassell at Kisling's Tavern and Grill on the city's southeast side. I couldn't remember the exact amount of the payoff, but I told McDonough it was about $300 to $400. During lunch I watched Fat Ricky pass the money to Cianferano.

That was in the early 1990s. During the next four years we paid cash to the chief inspector twenty-five to thirty times. The payoffs probably totaled thousands of dollars. On Christmas, Cianferano and Cassell got envelopes each containing several hundred dollars.

The payoffs worked like a charm, I told McDonough. Cianferano and Cassell would always warn us when police were investigating gambling violations; then I would clean out Joe's video poker machines and warn the bartender against making illegal payouts.

One time, I told the prosecutor, there was a stabbing at Joe's. Instead of helping the guy, I tried to throw him out so no one would know the stabbing took place inside the bar. When somebody complained to the liquor board, Fat Ricky and I met with the chief inspector. He advised us to lie to the liquor board and claim we tried to help the guy after he was attacked. He also suggested we drum up some "witnesses" who would testify in support of our made-up story. The woman who was the legal "owner" of Joe's was coached by Cianferano about what to say at the hearing. (Though she was the owner, I never saw her step foot in the bar, not even once, in the years I ran it.)

I also told the prosecutor that liquor inspectors were constantly selling political fund-raiser tickets. Bar owners who wanted to continue being protected were expected to buy at least $1,000 worth of tickets to the senators' fund-raisers. Bar owners who did not buy tickets knew not to expect any favors, I said.

Later, when the Maryland prosecutor's office checked the liquor board files for Joe's Tavern, they found only a $500 fine for catching us one time making illegal gambling payouts. That's a minuscule amount of money, compared to the tens of thousands of dollars we brought into those poker machines each year. They also found complaints for noise, assaults, drugs and handgun violations. And they also discovered that we failed to pay personal property taxes for six years. You're not supposed to get your liquor license renewed unless you pay those taxes. But, of course, we never lost our license. Other than the $500 fine, the liquor board took no disciplinary actions against Joe's Tavern during those years.

An Old Face, A New Friend

A few months later I flew to Baltimore so Tommy could take me to meet McDonough, who wanted to ask me more questions about liquor board corruption. We met Mike, along with a few federal prosecutors, at the U.S. District Courthouse downtown.

When Mike came into the interview room, he had another man with him; he introduced him as Jim Cabezas, the state prosecutor's chief investigator. Mike started asking me some of the same questions he asked me on the phone. The whole time I kept looking at Jim, thinking, *Damn, I know him from somewhere.*

Jim started talking about my old friends as if he knew them, too. He seemed to know everything about The Block, Baltimore's red-light district, where Billy and I hung out in our younger days. I thought, *Holy shit. This guy knows as much as I do about the wiseguys going back years.* He even knew details about their families. *Christ,* I thought, *if one of the wiseguys had a pet frog, I bet Jim Cabezas would know its name.*

After the interview I was told that I would spend the afternoon testifying before a city grand jury about the liquor board payoffs. In the meantime Tommy and Mike McDonough took me to lunch. Jim would join us later at the restaurant.

Mike asked me, "What did you think of Jim?"

I said, "Not to take anything away from any of you guys, but Jim sure knows his shit when it comes to wiseguys and their families." Then I said, "He looks familiar, but I can't place where I've seen him before."

Mike smiled and said, "You should know him, Charlie. He worked undercover as a bartender on The Block." I started to laugh and shake my head back and forth in disbelief. I remembered he was a bartender and a cab-driver back then. Little did I know that his real job was with the Baltimore Police Department. He was an undercover detective, investigating people like me and Billy.

"I knew I recognized him. Why didn't you guys tell me?" I asked.

Tommy smiled. "We wanted to surprise you," he said.

When Jim arrived for lunch, I said, "Jesus Christ, Jim, I knew I'd seen you before, but I couldn't place you." After that, Jim and I were in a world of our own, talking about old times and some of the guys from The Block.

After lunch they escorted me to the city courthouse a

few blocks away. I wasn't afraid of testifying before the grand jury—I was used to that by now. But I was afraid of running into some of the deputy sheriffs who worked there. A few of them were not the most honest guys in the world, especially one by the name of Lew Benson. As I had already told the FBI and state prosecutors, Lew was the professional boxer and a loan shark who almost ran Joe's Tavern with me. As soon as we got into the courthouse, I had to walk right past the sheriff's office. Luckily, I didn't run into Lew or any of the other deputies I knew. I wouldn't be so lucky the next time I was in a Baltimore City courthouse.

Finally we arrived at the grand jury room. I was sworn in and Mike started asking me questions about the liquor board. I noticed that the members of the city grand jury didn't seem very interested in what was going on. I was used to federal grand jurors who acted more eager to learn every little detail about my crimes. But these jurors acted like they didn't want to be there. I even saw a couple of them napping. And only one or two of them asked me a question. After about an hour I was excused. Mike said I did a fine job. Jim and I said our good-byes. Tommy took me back to my hotel, where, as usual, he signed me in under an assumed name.

It would take almost a year to find out the results of my grand jury testimony. In May 1998 Billy Madonna and Tony Cianferano were indicted in a decade-long bribery scheme to avoid enforcing the liquor laws. It would be just one more trial I would have to face down the road.

Ready For A Fight

Finally, in late October 1997, I arrived in Baltimore for Billy's murder trial. As if I weren't stressed out enough,

I got some bad news that really blew my mind. The tape I made of John Derry confessing to the murder and implicating Billy would not be allowed at Billy's trial. Maryland law would only allow it into evidence if Billy himself were on the tape.

I couldn't believe it. I had risked my life to get that tape, thinking it would put Billy in prison for good. Now the jury at his trial couldn't even hear it. I would have to wait for prosecutors to play it at John Derry's trial.

If that weren't bad enough, I also found out that one of Billy's lawyers was Don Daneman, the lawyer who represented me in 1986 when I was convicted of drug charges. I couldn't imagine how ethically he could represent me, then turn around ten years later and cross-examine me on the witness stand. He certainly had an unfair advantage, knowing every blemish on my record from the time he was my lawyer—not to mention anything I may have told him in confidence.

I assumed the prosecutors had gotten the judge to dismiss Daneman as Billy's lawyer, but he was still there when I arrived for the trial. So was another high-powered lawyer named Clarke Ahlers. Billy also hired a jury consultant—like the one O.J. Simpson's lawyers hired in California—to help the defense team choose a jury sympathetic to Billy. And months before the trial, Billy hired a private investigator, supposedly to "interview" witnesses in the case. But I believed the PI was hired to find me so he could pass the word to Billy and his thugs. It didn't surprise me that Billy had spent a bundle of money on his dream team to beat the rap, and it certainly looked like the odds were stacked against me.

When Tommy, Bruce and I arrived at the Baltimore County Courthouse in Towson, the trial had already started with opening statements. During a break we met with the prosecutors Jim Gentry and Pete Johnson.

I asked Jim how things were going. Jim said, "Charlie,

we can't talk about the trial. But I can tell you without
the tape recording this case will be a very weak one in
the eyes of the jury." My testimony against Billy was
pretty much all they had. The jury could either believe
Billy, or they could believe me. Jim told me there was a
pretty good crowd of wiseguys in the courtroom, along
with a newspaper reporter from the *Baltimore Sun.*

Not only do I have to face all the guys, I thought, *but now
a reporter is going to write about me being called a slime bucket.*

The prosecutors told me I wouldn't be testifying until
the next day. In the meantime Bruce took me to lunch
and gave me a pep talk.

"Charlie," he said, "the person who gets up on that
witness stand tomorrow is a different person than the
man you were two and a half years ago. All the guys in
that courtroom will stay the same for the rest of their
miserable lives. They'll always be getting into trouble.
They'll never know when their house is being raided,
they'll never know when they're being taken away from
their families and sent to prison. If they make a score
today, they'll be broke tomorrow."

I told Bruce I wasn't afraid of facing all the guys any
longer. "I'm just embarrassed by the person I used to be."

Later in the day Bruce dropped me off at my hotel so
I could spend another restless night before facing Billy.
I fell asleep around 2:00 and got up at 6:00 A.M. to get
the morning paper.

Luckily, the article on October 30 1997, about the trial
was buried inside the *Sun,* but it still hurt to read it. The
headline read, TESTIMONY THAT MAN ADMITTED TO KILLING IS
EXPECTED.

The story began: "The key prosecution witness in a
long-unsolved Baltimore County murder case is expected to testify today against William R. Isaacs, the first
of three men charged with murdering Mark Schwandt-

ner, whose bloody body was found floating in the Gunpowder Falls in 1978.

"The prosecutors have said that they expect Charles Wilhelm, whom they described as a punk and a paid FBI informant, to tell the jury that Isaacs admitted on June 10, 1978, the day after the slaying, that he had killed Schwandtner."

The article went on to quote Jim Gentry telling the jury that I had come forward because I was "tired of running and wanted to make a clean slate." When Mr. Daneman made his opening statement, he called me a liar and a drug addict who was paid $2,500 a month by the FBI. My former lawyer asked the jury, "How credible is a junkie?" Then he told them I was "slick."

Daneman warned: "You will think he's the best aluminum-siding salesman in Maryland."

By the time Tommy picked me up later that morning, I told him, "I'm ready for a fight today."

Chapter 16

The Trial

At about 10:00 A.M. I entered the courtroom on the third floor. It was packed with familiar faces, but there weren't as many wiseguys as I'd seen during the pretrial hearing the previous February. Many of these people were Hampdenites, not exactly wiseguys, just lowlifes—as Billy called them—from my old neighborhood. Not that everybody in Hampden is a lowlife. There are lots of honest, hardworking people there, but these guys gathered here were Hampden's bottom feeders. Billy never liked them, but now here they were at his murder trial to show their support—maybe hoping to get a little bookmaking, shylocking or drugs deals thrown their way.

But they were just pawns in his chess game—scruffy-looking, paunchy men with gold chains and pinkie rings, looking like life wore them out way too early. I wondered if Billy was losing his power on the streets. Most of the real wiseguys, the bar owners and the dock workers probably told him they weren't coming to his trial because the heat was on them, but that's bullshit. I bet they were hoping he'd get life in prison so they could steal his business on the street.

I sat in the back of the courtroom, waiting to be called

to testify. Luckily, I wasn't alone. I had Tommy, Bruce, Johnny and Johnny's friend Ralph, the guy who once urged me to walk away from my old life. I certainly was nervous, but that's just what happens when you're about to tell a jury that your best friend committed murder.

Right away I could see Billy was on his best behavior in front of the jury. He gave me none of those eye-fucking looks I got at the pretrial hearing when the jury box was empty. The deputy sheriffs had removed his leg irons when they brought him from federal prison, so the jury wouldn't know where he was living. He wore a dark suit and had no expression on his face. The Queen sat across the aisle from me, among the wiseguys and Hampden-ites, all dolled up with a spiked hairdo. She sat with Donna Isaacs, Billy's grown daughter, who looked pretty scared. I looked over at her. She was staring straight at me, as if she wanted to say, "Why did you do this to my father?"

I felt bad for her. I'd known her since she was a baby. Susan, Billy's sister, was also there. Her trial on charges of accessory after the fact of murder—for helping clean out the car—hadn't come up yet.

On my side of the courtroom, up front, sat prosecutors Jim Gentry and Pete Johnson. Ironically, Pete had been a young investigator in the county's state's attor-ney's office who worked on my 1986 drug case. Now I was his star witness. Mark Schwandtner's family sat in the front row, just behind the prosecutors. His father had died, but his mother was there, along with his sisters and brothers. They all looked pretty grim. They were with a few counselors from the state's attorney's victim-witness program.

As I waited to testify, I realized this would be my final match with Billy. It would be a duel of words, not fists. I always imagined our final showdown would be a physi-cally violent match—like the time I wanted to attack him with a hammer when I had lost my mind and had driven from Alabama to Maryland so I could face him at Joe's Tavern. Or the time he came to my bedroom at dawn with wiretap transcripts that showed I was talking to the FBI. Or the time he frisked me for a wire in the men's room of the Rotunda shopping center. I always thought those encounters might end with one of us dead.

But now I realized our final showdown would depend on brain power, not brawn. It would come down to credibility. The winner would be the most honest one, not the meanest one, not the one with the most power or the biggest roll of hundred-dollar bills in his pocket, and not the most intimidating one.

As I said, the odds were against me. Without the tape I made of John Derry implicating Billy, this trial truly depended on my word against his.

To make matters worse, the prosecutors believed Billy's sister had tried to tamper with a witness and get her to change her testimony. The witness was Patricia Hunt, who went by the name Patricia Sellers at the time of the murder when she warned police she was too scared to testify. She had gone on the stand and recanted her statements to police and prosecutors about seeing Billy, John and Ronnie together at the Keswick Inn in Hampden, looking nervous the morning after the murder. I didn't know any of this until after the trial was over, but what follows is what happened before I came into the courtroom.

A Tampered Witness

Agent McNamara took the witness stand and told the jury that in September 1996 two Baltimore County police detectives brought Pat Hunt to his office at the FBI. She told him that Susan, Billy's sister, whose last name was now Thompson, tried

to persuade her to change her testimony, offering her gifts of furniture. Susan had also suggested they go to dinner to discuss the
matter. McNamara tried to set up the dinner meeting between
Pat and Susan. Pat would wear a wire and would be accompanied by an undercover FBI agent, posing as a friend. But Pat
refused to follow through with the FBI's plan and Susan was
never charged with witness tampering.

When it came time for Hunt to testify, she was a very hostile
witness.

> Gentry: Do you remember telling Detective Ramsey and
> myself that "I worked with Susan Rogers at the Keswick
> Inn. . . ."
> Hunt: No, I don't.
> Gentry: If I could finish the question. ". . . on June 9,
> 1978, and we worked five P.M. to two A.M. I think Susan
> [Thompson] was the same hours?" Do you remember
> telling Detective Ramsey that and myself that?
> Hunt: No, I don't.
> Gentry: Ms. Hunt, has someone tried to get you to
> change your testimony?
> Hunt: No, sir.
> Gentry: Has Susan [Thompson] talked to you about
> changing your testimony?
> Hunt: No, sir. You're the one that threatened to put me
> in jail if I didn't get up here and say what you want me
> to say.
> Gentry: So, your testimony is that I threatened you?
> Hunt: You threatened me. You have threatened me
> quite a few times.

A few minutes later, Gentry was still trying to give the jury
some evidence of witness tampering.

> Gentry: Did you tell me that she tried to get you to
> change your testimony?

Hunt: I might have told you that. I don't know what I told you. I drink.

Pat Hunt went on to deny everything she ever told police detectives as far back as 1979. She denied seeing Isaacs, Rogers and Derry at the bar where she worked. She denied telling police that they left in Rogers' blue Malibu the night before the murder, or that she saw them together the next morning. She even denied knowing Charlie Wilhelm back then, even though she told a detective in 1979 that Charlie knew about the murder.

Hunt's denials were reminiscent of the testimony by the little bookmaker Sam "The Breadman" Merlo to a federal grand jury in 1990 about Billy Isaacs tampering with his testimony. Sam developed complete amnesia until federal prosecutors broke him down under relentless questioning. He finally admitted Isaacs tried to shut him up after Isaacs was charged with slapping the bookmaker in the face for not making his juice payments.

Hunt topped off her petulant testimony with a scene in the hallway outside the courtroom, cursing at Gentry at the top of her lungs.

Judgment Day

When it came my turn to testify, I headed up to the witness stand, trying not to look at anybody in the courtroom. A reporter for the *Baltimore Sun* leaned over to Bruce and told him I looked like an FBI agent in my crisp blue suit with my hair neatly trimmed.

The clerk asked me to give my name and address.

"My name is Charles Henry Wilhelm, *W-I-L-H-E-L-M*, and I decline to give my address," I said.

Jim Gentry started asking me questions about how long I'd known Billy and how close we were. I told the jury that Billy was the best man at my wedding and the godfather to my son Justin.

"He was closer than my own brother was. I even gave up my family for Billy, you might as well say. He got mad every time I went around my brother's house, stuff like that, so I stopped going around my brother," I said.

I then went into our illegal activities. That took a while. I explained to the jury how bookmaking and loan-sharking worked and I told them about running Joe's Tavern. Jim asked me how much money I made. "Back in '85, '86, I probably grossed about seven thousand a week selling drugs and stuff."

I tried not to mention where Billy was living. The jury wasn't supposed to know he was in prison. So when Gentry asked me about my role in Joe's Tavern, I just said I had been keeping the business going "for Billy until he came out."

Mr. Daneman almost blew a gasket over that one. "Objection!" he yelled. The lawyers approached the judge's bench so nobody could hear him asking for a mistrial. The judge, Christian M. Kahl, just warned the jury not to speculate "as to the whereabouts of the defendant."

I then went on to tell the jury about the time Billy summoned me to federal prison and he searched me for a wire. The judge wouldn't allow Jim to question me about Billy asking me to kill two guys. In a pretrial motion Billy's lawyers denied he ever asked me to kill Ronnie Jones or Fat Ricky Payne. So Jim Gentry had to dance around the issue. I was only allowed to say that Billy made a request of me that concerned me and that I did not honor the request. The jurors had to fill in the blanks for themselves.

I also testified about my first meeting with Bruce, giving him a hypothetical example of a friend in trouble.

Then we got to the gambling raid on my house in August 1995.

Jim Gentry asked me, "But what is the significance to you? Why did that make a difference to you?"

"When they came in the house and everything, my youngest son," I said.

"How old was he?"

"He was six, and he was sitting there, crying."

"And did that bother you?"

"Yes."

Then I started tearing up. The Hampdenites and wiseguys started snickering from the back of the courtroom and the judge had to warn them to be quiet.

I testified that the police took "numbers stuff, some money," but they didn't find any drugs or arrest me.

Gentry asked me to "tell the jurors what you were thinking about during that time."

"Everything. I was just tired. You know, you can't win. You can't win at it, and I just wanted to get out."

"You wanted to get out of what?"

"Everything."

"And did you then make a decision that you were going to the FBI?"

I told the jury about my first meeting with the Baltimore FBI agents at the hotel near the airport and about later meeting Tommy. I testified that I had no signed agreement with the FBI, the U.S. Attorney's Office or anybody else. And I was never offered immunity by the Baltimore County State's Attorney's Office or any other government agency.

"Did you ever ask for anything when you provided this information about these other things to the FBI? Did you ask for anything?"

"Just protection."

I testified about working for the FBI, buying drugs undercover, wearing a body wire and a concealed tape recorder, and I admitted the FBI paid me for my work.

Finally the questioning came around to what I knew about the murder of Mark Schwandtner.

I walked into Benjamin's Tavern in Hampden, I told the jury.

"There was John Derry, Billy Isaacs and Ronnie Rogers in the back, playing pool and stuff. They were back there giggling. Anyhow, I had walked back there and I went back there and I believe it was Billy [who]come over and said, 'Should I tell him?'"

I told the jury that when they did tell me what was going on, Billy said "'that sick John, that sick motherfucker, we killed a guy last night . . . .' I was asking him what happened and stuff, and he tells me that they took this guy from the Holiday House out to the Gunpowder. . . . It was a river or something and they hit the guy in the head with a bat, and Billy said that John hit the guy so hard that the guy—they threw the guy in the water, and then Billy said he actually had to step on the guy's head to drown the guy."

I told the jury how I instructed them to clean out the Malibu real good and how I helped them throw away bloody clothes in a storm drain at Thirty-third Street and Greenmount Avenue near Memorial Stadium.

I testified that Billy sent me around to John and Ronnie about every six months to warn them with Billy's famous saying, "Nobody talks, everybody walks."

"You didn't have to come up here today and testify, did you?" Gentry asked me.

"No, sir," I answered.

"Are you doing this for money?"

"No, sir."

"Why are you sitting in this chair?"

"I am remorseful. I am sorry. I mean, I was a slime bucket and I just tried to change my life. And even to this day, if I had to do time on this, at least it would be over."

Cross Examined

The easy part of my testimony was over. After lunch I was cross-examined by my former lawyer, Don Daneman, a bearded, graying man familiar in Baltimore courtrooms for decades. The man who used to give me legal advice about how to beat a rap was now going to rip me to shreds over every crime I ever committed. He needed the jury to see me as the most ruthless criminal they'd ever come across. Knocking down my credibility was his main goal. If I didn't sound believable to the jury, it might give them enough reasonable doubt to acquit Billy.

Mr. Daneman started questioning me about money I borrowed from other wiseguys that I didn't repay.

Then he quickly moved on to my family. He brought up the time I threw the cup at Gina and it split her head open in front of our son, back in 1995. I admitted to that. Then he quickly moved on to my cocaine use. He really wanted the jury to see me as a lying junkie. He seemed desperate to want to prove I was snorting cocaine long after I went to the FBI.

"When did you last use cocaine?" he asked.

"The last time I used cocaine was two weeks after I went to the FBI," I said. But that didn't suit Mr. Daneman. He accused me of lying to the FBI and continuing to use cocaine. But it wasn't true, I told him.

Now he was just getting warmed up. I could tell the jury and judge were listening intently. And so was Billy's fan club in the back of the courtroom.

"Now, you certainly wouldn't consider yourself to be a violent person, would you?"

"Yes, at times I can be violent. Yes."

"At what time have you been violent in your past?"

"I guess somebody pushed me to the limit, you know, everybody reaches a point in your life, you could be the nicest guy in your life until somebody pushes you, after a while you fight back."

"You fought back?"

"I tried to."

"You tried to?"

I shook my head up and down.

"Don't you consider yourself more of a ladies' man than bully or fighter?"

"I don't feel that way."

"You don't feel that way?"

"I don't feel that way. No, sir."

"[In] 1978 did you frequent the Holiday House?"

"Yes, sir."

"How old were you?"

"Twenty-three years old, yeah."

"Now, you admitted that you used drugs, right?"

"Yes, sir."

"You were a drug dealer?"

"Yes, sir."

"A thief?"

"Yes, sir."

"Now, let me talk to you about the arsons that you confessed to."

"Are you talking about the arsons me and Mr. Isaacs did or me and Mr. Joe Deems did?" (Joe Deems was a guy from my old neighborhood.)

"And you burned up cars?"

"Yes, sir."

"Were you angry at the owner?"

"No, sir."

"I see. Mr. Isaacs was angry at the owner?"

"No. We got money for doing it."

He then moved on to the 1995 raid on my house, finding a clever line of questioning that defense attorneys used to confuse the jury into thinking I committed more crimes than I had.

During the raid, he asked, the police "found book-making or numbers. How much money?"

"I think around four thousand dollars. I'm not even sure."

"How about rifles?"

"Never found any rifles."

This was just the beginning of the tricks Billy's dream team would play to break down my credibility. By the end of the trial Mr. Daneman and Mr. Ahlers would have the jury thinking that police found drugs—as well as guns—during that raid, which wasn't true. And they'd tell the jury I was charged with crimes after the raid, which also wasn't true. And that I faced twenty years in prison. Also, not true. If only I could have shown the jury the receipt city police gave me after they raided my house, they'd see there were no drugs or guns found. And if only I could bring Spanky Herold to testify, he would have told them I was never charged with any crime after that raid. The police were too busy looking for the leak in their own damn police department to bother with arresting me for gambling.

But the dream team wanted to give the jury many motives for my going to the FBI. They wanted the jury to think I concocted a story about Billy committing murder to save my own skin and stay out of prison.

Let me tell you, these guys were cunning defense lawyers, real cunning. They could have been professional actors, the way they were carrying on. They also told the jury I stole $300,000 from a bookmaker and needed FBI protection from the guy. But I didn't get to tell the whole story. I did steal the money from the bookmaker, but only because Billy told me to. And I didn't need protection from anybody but Billy for that one.

They had another trick up their sleeves to get Billy off, but I didn't know about it until after I finished testifying. This one would be a real winner.

In the meantime Mr. Daneman kept hammering me about my sleazy past.

He even dug up documents that showed I tried to cash in on Melonie's estate after she died, even though we were divorced. He tried to make it look like I wasn't entitled to any of the settlement of a medical malpractice suit against her doctor. But I didn't get a chance to tell the jury that I tried to get the money on behalf of my son Charlie Jr., since I was his legal guardian. And neither I nor my son got a dime out of the suit, even though I bragged to people that I got a million dollars.

"You used [Melonie's] name in vain when you told people that you settled her case for a million dollars?" asked Mr. Daneman.

"Yes, sir, if you want to call it that. Yes, sir."

"You're proud of that?"

"No, I'm not proud of anything I've done, Mr. Daneman."

"Except sitting here today?"

"Know what? Yeah, I'm sort of proud I'm taking the stand. Yes, sir, I am. I am," I said.

He also found out I had put the title of my house in my brother-in-law's name to get a low-interest loan from the city and that I bought hunting rifles for my grown son, even though it was illegal, since I was a convicted felon.

Finally Mr. Daneman got down to what he and Mr. Ahlers would tell the jury was my main motive for ratting—money.

Under his questioning I testified that the FBI paid me $2,500 a month from October or November 1995 until about a month before the trial started in September 1997. Then the FBI paid me a final lump sum of $55,000 for living expenses and to pay debts that included back child support for my son Jason, who was born just after Melonie died.

When Mr. Daneman was just about finished with me, he came back to the subject of drugs. He wanted to leave the jury with the false impression that I continued to snort cocaine long after I went to the FBI.

"And you—you've already testified that as a condition [of working with the FBI], you had to stop using drugs?" asked Mr. Daneman.

"Yes, sir."

"You cured your habit within, what, three weeks?"

"If I used drugs, with common sense, if you went in front of a federal agent using drugs, you would have to be insane. They would have known instantly. As far as the drug thing, that is out," I said.

He was finally finished with me. I stepped down from the witness stand feeling relieved, embarrassed and proud. I was relieved because I finally told the truth and got it off my chest. I was embarrassed for my family and all I'd put them through. And I was proud knowing that with my testimony I knew my life had truly changed for the better. I had stood up to Billy, despite all the intimidation in that courtroom. As I walked down the aisle to the door, I heard one last voice mutter, "You fucking snitch." But I didn't look at anyone. I just held my head up high.

In the hallway I expected more of the usual dirty looks and snide remarks from Billy's peanut gallery waiting outside. Instead, I saw a man who was not one of Billy's gang. Tommy had pointed him out to me before. It was one of Mark Schwandtner's brothers. I walked over to him and said, "I did the best that I could do. I'm sorry if it wasn't good enough." Then he thanked me for finally coming forward after all these years. He really didn't need to thank me. I only wished I'd come forward sooner.

Now it was Tommy's turn to take the hot seat.

Believing Charlie

Agent McNamara began by testifying about his use of informants like Charlie to solve crimes. Then Pete Johnson asked him, "In the time that you have come to know Charles Wilhelm, have you been able to form an opinion as to his truthfulness?"

"I do."

"What is that opinion?"

"I think, by and large, he has been very truthful since he has come to the FBI in 1995 until the present," he said.

"Why do you say that? What is the basis?"

"Of course, someone comes to you in the beginning, you don't trust him. With a man that has a criminal past, we record as many conversations as we could using a body wire, contact other informants, look at the record and see if people have already heard about it, see if the information he is giving is consistent. We found that to be true."

"What else?"

"Well, I suppose just his general demeanor. He came to us saying he wanted to change his life. He certainly has."

He went on to talk generally about the many convictions Charlie helped the FBI with. He also told the jury the FBI seized about $400,000 in the drug cases with Charlie's help.

Clarke Ahlers got up to cross-examine McNamara. The defense attorney was a commanding figure with longish hair swept back off his forehead. He had a temper—both in and out of the courtroom—that he used for dramatic effect. He set out to lay the groundwork to show Charlie was a fraud, insinuating that Charlie's tears on the witness stand were an act, and that his motives for coming clean were less than pure.

"Isn't it true most people come to the FBI about five minutes after the cops knock on the door?" asked Ahlers.

"I don't know if I can say most people. A lot."

"A lot. In other words, you heard the expression they find Jesus. They find God. You know what I mean by that?"

Ahlers then went after McNamara for not charging Charlie

with any crimes after his house was raided and after admitting to the FBI about his criminal past.

"How long was he facing in prison?"

"I have no idea. Certainly, I don't think gambling results in any time at all."

"How about money laundering?"

"I don't know if they had any evidence of money laundering," McNamara said of the city investigation of Charlie.

"How about drug dealing?"

"I don't know if they had any evidence," he said.

Ahlers then turned to the lack of federal charges against Charlie.

"So, he was facing a substantial amount of prison time, more than a decade without parole. If you went to the U.S. attorney and said indict this man . . ."

"I can't give you a figure of how much time he would have spent."

Then Ahlers tried to pin the agent down for not notifying local police about the criminal activities Charlie admitted to the FBI. "Your rules and regulations require you to notify local authorities. Is that correct?"

"I don't know if we notify local authorities when we have somebody cooperating. In fact, when [Charlie] came in, we knew there was a leak in the Baltimore City Police Department and we wouldn't have notified anybody."

After McNamara confirmed that Charlie hadn't been charged with any crimes since coming to the FBI, Ahlers pronounced —with special emphasis for the jury's sake—"Charles Wilhelm has not been charged with so much as a parking ticket!—

"Here is a man that comes in, said, 'I have committed a life-time of crimes,' hundreds and hundreds of crimes, most felonies. I have been arrested two, three times,' is that true?"

"That's true."

"He said, 'I get away with it. I'm such a good con man.'"

"He never said that."

"Never?"

McNamara shook his head from side to side.

"In other words, that he was a con man?" Ahlers restated.

"Yes."

"Please tell the ladies and gentlemen of the jury how you keep yourself from being conned."

Ahlers had McNamara in a bind here. The defense attorney knew the FBI agent was barred from mentioning the tape recording Charlie made of John Derry confessing to murder and implicating Isaacs. That was the biggest piece of evidence the FBI had to prove Charlie wasn't conning them, but Ahlers knew it could never be mentioned in this courtroom.

Ahlers went on to insinuate that Charlie never paid taxes on the money he got from the FBI.

"Just so the men and women of the jury understand, this life-long con man was given over a hundred thousand dollars by the FBI and on the honor system?"

Surprise Witness

The next day Jim Gentry and Pete Johnson came out of the courtroom after a long meeting at the judge's bench. They had shit-eating grins on their faces. "Let's talk in my office," said Jim. We went up to his fifth floor office with Tommy, Bruce and Johnny. "Are you ready for this one?" he asked. "What?" I asked. Jim said the defense was putting a surprise witness on the stand. He was a drug dealer and his name was Earl Fisher. Earl Fisher was a name-dropper, somebody who lived off the names of bigger drug dealers he associated with. Billy and I had known him for almost twenty years. We even gave him a key to our after-hours club so he could open it up when we didn't feel like going up there.

"Earl Fisher is going to testify that Billy didn't kill Mark Schwandtner. You did, Charlie," said Jim. I was shocked, but I knew Earl would say anything to look good in Billy's eyes.

"Not only did you kill Mark, but you told Earl back in 1979 that your brother, John, helped you," said Jim Gentry.

Johnny got all agitated. "There's no way. I never did anything like that," he said. Tommy and the rest of us started cracking up at Johnny's reaction. "Hey, this isn't funny," Johnny protested.

Bruce stopped laughing long enough to say, "Tom, do you want to read him his rights, or do you want me to read them?"

"It gets even better," said Jim. "Earl is going to testify that he doesn't even know Billy Isaacs."

"That's bullshit," I said. "Earl and Billy have known each other for more than ten years. And do you think for one minute that if I had killed someone, I would have told Earl Fisher, out of all the people in the world?"

"I believe you," said Jim. "Remember, we've heard the tape you made of John Derry confessing. There is no doubt in my mind Earl is lying."

After lunch Clarke Ahlers told the jury the defense had a surprise witness.

Before Earl could take the stand, I had to identify him for the jury, so Mr. Ahlers called me back to the stand.

"Mr. Wilhelm, there is a man standing to your left in the well of the courtroom. Do you know who this person is?"

Earl stood there, looking like his sad-sack self, a little man with a craggy face, a mobster wanna-be.

"Yes, it's Earl Fisher." At this point I felt like laughing. Bringing Earl to say that I had killed Mark Schwandtner was so ridiculous, it was funny.

"Mr. Wilhelm, sometime between 1978 and 1980, isn't it true that you told Earl Fisher that you and a man named . . . are you amused?"

"Yes, I am."

"Is it true that you told Earl Fisher that you and a man named John committed murder by taking a man from the Holiday House and killing him in the Gunpowder State Park?"

"That is an absolute total lie," I said.

Jim Gentry got to ask me next about Earl. I told him Earl and I were friends and sold drugs together, but our friendship broke up when I found out he was wearing a wire for the FBI to catch me in a racial case in which a black family's windows were broken. But I was not the one who broke the windows and I was never charged.

"Do you know whether he knows Billy Isaacs?" asked Gentry.

"He has known Billy Isaacs, I would imagine, since '79, '80, somewhere around there." I also told the jury that Billy and I gave Earl the key to the after hours-club.

I had to leave the courtroom for Earl's testimony.

Ahlers first established how Fisher knew Charlie Wilhelm.

"The period of time between 1978 and 1980, did Mr. Wilhelm ever confess a murder to you?"

"[In the] 1970s, the late '70s, we were doing the flow of marijuana through the neighborhood at that time. He wanted to slow up in the drug business because the murder had been committed.

"The murder had been committed at this time. He told me, him and a guy named John had killed somebody and got rid of it in a woody area. We were going to slow up the drugs. I said no. We were making too much money. I want to continue. Nothing else was ever said. We continued into the drug market."

When it was Jim Gentry's turn to cross-examine Fisher, he peppered the witness with questions about Charlie's confession and where he said he'd dumped the body. Fisher didn't have too many details.

"How do you know Billy Isaacs?" asked Gentry.

"I don't really know Billy that good. I never dealt with Billy."

"Do you know him?"

"I know of him."

"Did you know him back then?"

"No, sir."

"How about after hours, you see him up there every once in a while?"

"Yes, sir."

"You just said you didn't know him."

"I don't hang out with him. I don't know you."

"Where was the after-hours club you used to go up to?"

"Chestnut Avenue."

"In Hampden?"

"Yes, sir."

"Well, Billy owned it, you knew that?"

"Billy didn't own nothing. He rented it."

"How did you know he rented it?"

"Because I never seen Billy running it. Charlie ran it."

Gentry then pressed Fisher to tell him why he never told police they got the wrong guy for the murder of Mark Schwandtner.

"I didn't talk to no actual police. I don't care one way [or] the other. I don't get involved in the police . . . I didn't call nobody. I don't care."

Though he didn't talk to the police, Fisher admitted he did talk to a private investigator, hired by Isaacs' defense team.

"When did this private detective for the defense attorney come to you and talk to you about this?" asked Gentry.

"I just said several months ago."

Gentry asked if Isaacs' sister asked Fisher to testify that Charlie committed the murder. Fisher said no.

Billy's Turn

Finally it was Billy's turn to testify. Every wiseguy knows that if you have a bad criminal record, you don't take the witness stand because you will have to admit to your life of crime. In Billy's case that meant two federal convictions of loan-sharking and one of witness tampering. It also meant he would have to tell the jury he was living in federal prison. Though he didn't have to testify, Billy knew it was his chance to convince the jury he was more believable than me. And he knew he had better sound sincere.

Clarke Ahlers called Isaacs' name. Walking the few steps from the defense table to the witness stand, Billy Isaacs was a formidable figure, with his stony expression, his thick neck and immense head popping out of his dark, conservative suit. Alone in a courtroom, Isaacs' presence might have been intimidating, but his entourage of aging gangster types and other ne'er-do-wells actually amused the jurors. For some of them, it would only prove that Isaacs truly was the powerful figure portrayed by Charlie. Isaacs was a man who could fill a courtroom with creepy-looking people just for effect.

After he swore him in, the court clerk asked Isaacs to state his name and address.

"My name is William Raymond Isaacs. I'm currently living in the FCI Cumberland, federal institution."

Ahlers began by asking his client's age—forty-four—and his birthplace—York, Nebraska. After his family moved to Baltimore, his father was a brakeman on the railroad and worked for Western Auto. His father was now dead, but his mother still lived in Baltimore. Isaacs said he never did well in school, had problems learning to read and dropped out in the tenth grade. He worked nights helping his father deliver refrigerators and washing machines. He later worked driving a truck, towing cars and was a doorman at the Holiday House in Northeast Baltimore.

Isaacs denied ever owning or firing a gun or ever using any weapon to hurt another person.

"Mr. Isaacs, I want you to tell the men and women of the jury where you were the night of June 9, the early-morning hours of June 10, 1978."

"I got no idea. I really . . . I don't know because I don't even know if I was working at Holiday House on that time because I had—I quit the Holiday House and worked down at Les Gals on Mount Royal and Charles." (Isaacs pronounced the s in "Les," like "less.")

"I'm showing you what has been previously marked as state's exhibit twenty-five, the photograph of Mark Schwandtner. Have you ever seen this person before?"

"No. No. I don't recall ever seeing him."

"Have you ever met this man before?"

"He doesn't stick out to me, no."

"Did you ever have a disagreement or beef—"

"No."

". . . or fight with this guy?"

"No."

"Did you ever have a motive to kill him?"

"No."

"Never?"

"I don't know the guy."

"You heard testimony that you and others killed this man. Is that correct?"

"That's not so. It's not so."

"Now, there are people sitting in the first pew here who, I believe, are family members of Mark Schwandtner. Could you look and tell them what, if anything, you had to do with the murder of their relative?"

"I had nothing to do with anybody being killed, nothing."

The questioning moved on to how Isaacs met Charlie Wilhelm through Charlie's brother, John, when they were both studying karate.

Isaacs seemed to distance himself from Charlie, never describing him as a close friend. Instead, he described Charlie as "a guy that was always clean, never seen him dirty."

He went on to admit to bookmaking and loan-sharking—and being convicted twice of loan-sharking—though he refuted

Charlie's claims that he sold drugs. He also admitted he was
convicted of witness tampering.

Now it was time for Isaacs' cross-examination. Jim Gentry
was ready for the challenge. The slim, bespectacled assistant
state's attorney had prosecuted many murder trials in this courthouse for more than a decade, but he never had a case with so
little evidence. He set out to depict Isaacs as a vindictive thug,
and he went right for the jugular.

"You just said you didn't know Mark Schwandtner?"

"I don't know him."

"I understand this is twenty years ago. Think back, you knew
of Mark Schwandtner, didn't you?"

"I never knew Mark Schwandtner at all until 1979."

"You told people that you killed him because he was an asshole?"

"I never told anybody anything like that."

"You never hurt anybody if they were an asshole?"

"I never hurt people to begin with."

"You didn't?"

"No."

"Never hurt anybody?"

"No."

Gentry began to ask questions about a particularly vicious
fight Isaacs had with a boxer in Baltimore nearly twenty years
before.

"Never bit anybody's lip off and stepped on it?"

"I didn't bite a lip off and step on it and—yes, sir, I did bite
a lip."

"Stepped on it so [he] couldn't reattach it?"

"That's not so."

"Were you accused of that?"

"Accused of what?"

"Biting somebody's lip?"

"I was accused. I went to trial. I was found not guilty."

"Mr. Isaacs, wouldn't you consider biting a man's lip—"

Before Gentry could finish his question, Isaacs tried to defend his behavior against the boxer.

"Wouldn't you consider him poking eyes, pulling hair and poking eyes out when trying to get away . . . I can explain what happened if you let me."

"I understand you feel justified, that wasn't the question. The question is, whether you ever hurt anybody and you said no."

"He wasn't hurt that bad, I mean."

Isaacs professed to know little about Earl Fisher's claim that Charlie Wilhelm killed Mark Schwandtner. And he said he knew nothing about the FBI's claim that his sister tried to get Pat Hunt to change her testimony.

"Do you have any idea why Patricia Hunt, in 1979, told Detective Wysham and named you, John Derry, Ronnie Rogers and Susan Rogers [Thompson]as suspects?"

"I have no idea. You have to ask her."

Pointing Fingers

Closing arguments began with Gentry's partner, the boyish and portly Pete Johnson. He approached the jury box and began by repeating Isaacs' mantra:

"'Nobody talks, everybody walks.' This is a little saying that has now taken on a little more significance for all us in the last week, is it? And why is that? Because that little saying of Mr. Isaacs' is not just a motto. It is not just a phrase. For him, it is a way of life. It is a creed, if you will."

He went on, hoping to convince the jury to believe Charlie's testimony.

"Mr. Wilhelm was totally candid with you. He wasn't hiding a thing. Was he squirming? Was he fidgety? No. Mr. Wilhelm said this is my life. This is what I have done in the past, and I am not proud of it, but I have turned the corner."

Johnson asked the jurors to believe Charlie's relationship with the FBI was pure and therefore without motive for fingering

Isaacs for murder. He simply wanted to "cleanse his conscience," said the prosecutor.

When Charlie went to the FBI, "he was not a suspect. He was not under investigation for anything. They had absolutely nothing on Charlie Wilhelm. They didn't even know who Charlie Wilhelm was," said Johnson.

He ended his speech with a word of warning about Billy Isaacs.

"This is not a man you want to cross. This is not a man you want to get on the wrong side of. What kind of man would bash someone in the head, help bash someone in the head, drag him out to a remote area of the Gunpowder State Park, help throw him in the river, climb down, and then hold his head underwater and drown him? What kind of man would do that?"

Johnson turned toward Isaacs.

"Have a good look. Not just any kind of man. This man."

When it came time for Clarke Ahlers to address the jury, he quickly reminded them about the lack of any confession by his client on tape.

As often as Isaacs was alleged to have said, "Nobody talks, everybody walks," nobody got it on tape. "If he says it all the time, thousands of times, it is his slogan, get it and play it," said Ahlers.

When he turned to the veracity of Charlie Wilhelm, he described Charlie as a snake "shedding his one skin and living in his new skin" as he "slithered over to the FBI." He called Charlie many names—a con, a manipulator, "the CEO of the underbelly of Baltimore," a man with "chutzpah or testicularity."

He even made fun of Charlie's teary testimony as he described his young son crying during the raid on their house:

"Charlie Wilhelm is an actor. That is his stage. You are his audience, and he cries on cue. That is what manipulators do. That is what cons do, and he is very good at it."

When Ahlers came to the money the FBI paid Charlie, he said, "He made a hundred grand. He made money. I have never seen *this. This guy takes the cake. He turned a lifetime of crime, over-whelming evidence of guilt, into a business opportunity. He manipulated the FBI."*

On the other hand, he called Isaacs: *"A completely innocent man, falsely accused."* Ahlers, of course, made special note of the lack of physical evidence. *"Soil evidence, none. Tire tracks, none. . . . They could do DNA on twenty year-old blood. It wasn't done.*

"So for you to convict, for you to have proof beyond a reason-able doubt, you have decided that you would subject another human being to the penalty of murder on the word of Charles Wilhelm."

Ahlers then began to do what many lawyers do during their closing statements. He stretched the truth beyond exaggeration. He could do this because the jury was warned that closing state-ments are not evidence, but many lawyers hope to confuse jurors into thinking what they say in the end is the truth.

He told the jury that Charlie testified that he helped hide a murder weapon. Not true, though Charlie said he helped throw away bloody clothes.

And this is how Ahlers stretched the truth about the gambling raid on Charlie's house, the raid for which he was never charged with a crime: *"Charlie Wilhelm is going from being an awful man to an improved man, and he goes into the FBI, motivated solely by his conscience. The cops kicking in his door with the search warrant that says, guess what, big boy—guess what, good-time Charlie—we got you on wiretaps going back months. We have you for organized crime. We have you for drug dealing. We have got you for your gambling interest. You are subject to second offender, mandatory minimums, Charlie, twenty years."*

He went on to do something rarely seen in even the most high-profile murder trials in this courthouse. He called the prosecutors liars. He insinuated that the assistant state's attor-neys were less than truthful when they said Charlie Wilhelm received no promise of immunity from prosecution.

"The government comes in here today and they tell you a lie,"

said Ahlers, "that Charlie Wilhelm was motivated by a change of conscience. No, he wasn't. He was motivated by the cops kicking in his door, a lifetime of thefts."

This did not sit well with Jim Gentry, a veteran prosecutor, and—like Ahlers—a former police officer.

As the prosecutor he would be allowed the final word before the jurors headed back to the jury room for deliberation.

"I shouldn't take it personally to be called a liar," he said. "I have listened to a lot of defense attorneys give a lot of closing arguments in a lot of murder cases. . . . I have never, however, been called a liar by the defense attorney, and he said that I lied to you when I told you that there was no agreement, no deal, no promise, no immunity with Charlie Wilhelm. And I will look at you each in your eyes, and I will tell you, there wasn't any deal. There was no promise, there was no immunity. There was no wink, wink, nod, nod. That is offensive.

"This is not about winning and losing. It is about someone dying, a human being, and someone being held accountable for it. . . . "

Billy Isaacs, said Gentry, "did it and he knows he did it." It was Billy Isaacs who "conned a lot of people, manipulated a lot of persons. He has attempted to change the testimony of several witnesses in this case."

Finally he spoke of Charlie Wilhelm. "People can turn a corner. People can change. Forty-one years old, he had had it. He had lived his entire life, most of his adult life, with Billy Isaacs, under the thumb of Billy Isaacs, in an organization orchestrated and run by Billy Isaacs, involved in loan-sharking and everything else you can think of—to a certain extent, afraid of Billy Isaacs. And he knew that he just couldn't walk out of the organization. He couldn't do that. That is not the way it happens."

Finally it was time for the jury to begin deliberations. The judge thanked and dismissed the two alternates and sent the twelve remaining jurors shuffling back to the jury room with their notepads.

As the door shut behind them, they began to speak their minds *finally. It became clear that ten jurors were in favor of conviction, but two held out for acquittal. The two believed Charlie lied for the money the FBI paid him. Maybe he was getting back at Isaacs for something. But all twelve did agree on two things: 1.) Earl Fisher was an unbelievable character who lied when he blamed the murder on Charlie. 2.) Billy Isaacs—through his sister—did influence Pat Hunt's testimony.*

As two jurors later told a Baltimore Sun *reporter, the majority set out to convince the two holdouts that Isaacs was guilty. The foreman believed Isaacs was guilty. No amount of money could make Charlie lie and put his family's safety in jeopardy, he thought. But the majority of jurors were unsuccessful at convincing the others to reach a unanimous verdict. After several hours, the foreman, a U.S. postal carrier, passed out a note to Judge Kahl.*

"We are at a deadlock, so therefore cannot render a decision. What do you want us to do?"

The judge wrote back on the bottom of the note: "Do you believe your inability to agree is permanent and hopeless?"

It was then that Judge Kahl made a fatal mistake that would only prolong Charlie's anxiety. The judge failed to follow the law and show the note to the lawyers—and the defendant. In fact, none of them would learn of it for many months.

But for now, the note seemed unimportant. The jury never wrote back to the judge. Instead, on the second day of deliberation, they finally came to a unanimous agreement.

By then Charlie was safely back in Alabama.

A Little Peace Of Mind

On November 3 the phone rang after lunch. Gina answered it. I heard her shout, "Second-degree murder!" Then I shouted, "Second-degree murder!" She said, "The jury found Billy guilty of second-degree murder."

She handed me the phone. It was Bruce. I was so choked up, I could barely say hello.

"You did it, Charlie," he said. "You got Billy convicted of second-degree murder."

When I hung up, I threw my arms around Gina. I finally saw the light at the end of the tunnel. With Billy's conviction, the worries about my family's safety would ease up tremendously. For the first time I let myself think it might be possible for us to move back to Baltimore. I knew I'd still have to lay low and stay far from my old neighborhood, but I also hoped the wiseguys would no longer bother looking for me. They'd be too busy robbing all the business on the streets that Billy left behind.

Chapter 17

Coming Home

My sense of relief over Billy's conviction didn't last long. A month later I got some shocking news that unraveled my most important accomplishment as an informant. The tape I made of John Derry confessing to murder and implicating Billy was thrown out as evidence in John's trial. The tape was tossed due to the tiniest technicality you can imagine. The news made me panic.

Of course, John's lawyers had been working hard to get that tape thrown out. John had hired two of the best defense attorneys in Baltimore, David Irwin and Joseph Murtha. I could never figure out how a working-class plumber like John Derry could afford lawyers of Irwin and Murtha's caliber. Murtha was the lead lawyer representing Linda Tripp, who was accused of violating Maryland's electronic-surveillance law when she secretly tape-recorded Monica Lewinsky's confessions about her affair with President Bill Clinton. Irwin is a former prosecutor for Baltimore County and the U.S. Attorney's Office.

John's lawyers knew that without that tape, the prosecutors would have to drop the charges against John and he would walk free for bashing in Mark Schwandtner's head. The lawyers discovered that the Baltimore County police had forgotten to do one little thing. They had failed to glue an identification number to the little tape recorder the FBI gave me. Everything else was done to the letter of the law. The FBI and the county police registered the recorder, the FBI supervised me properly and I did everything I was asked to do to make sure I handled the tape legally. But that little ID number—BA1786—was missing from the tape recorder.

Judge Kahl reviewed Maryland law, which requires tape recorders used in criminal trials to be registered with police, with ID numbers attached.

In November 1997, Judge Kahl gave his ruling: "It seems to me it is absolutely fatal to the state's introduction of the tape. It doesn't come in."

Of course, Jim Gentry's office appealed the case to the Maryland Court of Special Appeals, but I would have to wait months for the decision.

In the meantime I sweated it out in Alabama while I waited for Billy to be sentenced in Baltimore. The day came on June 1, 1998.

Finding Justice

At the sentencing hearing Isaacs' lawyer Clarke Ahlers began by seeking a new trial for his client, claiming the prosecutors and the FBI never corroborated Charlie's story.

"The FBI, for reasons known only to the FBI, didn't even subject Charles Wilhelm to the scrutiny that an informant would normally get," said Ahlers.

He also said the judge was wrong when he allowed the prosecutors to tell the jury that Patricia Hunt was the subject of witness tampering because there was no evidence that Isaacs' sister tried to get Hunt to change her testimony.

When it was Jim Gentry's turn, he got to the heart of the jury's verdict.

"The jurors believed Charlie Wilhelm," said the prosecutor. "That is why they convicted William Isaacs. They believed the man on the witness stand, and the defense had every opportunity to impeach Charlie Wilhelm, to cross-examine Charlie Wilhelm about his truthfulness.

"Let's face it. It comes down to Charlie Wilhelm had a conversation with Billy Isaacs, John Derry and Ronnie Rogers at the Keswick Inn after the murder and he said Billy Isaacs told him he did it and John Derry told him he did it.

"That is what he told the jurors. That is what the jurors believed. They believed him. I also think they also believed that Susan Rogers [Thompson] attempted to influence one of the state's witnesses," he said of Patricia Hunt.

Now it was Isaacs' turn to speak, and he had a lot to get off his chest.

His other lawyer, Don Daneman, introduced him: *"I would ask the court to permit him to address you from the trial table. He is emotional, obviously. His family is here. His friends are here and he may be a big man, but, really, he is a very gentle person under his skin."*

Isaacs stood at the table, stone-faced as usual.

"Your Honor, through this whole case I sat back and haven't said a word. Charles Wilhelm got on the stand and lied. I am not upset about this whole deal. I get upset about my kids. I got on the stand to tell them I didn't do it. I don't know how to do it. I don't have the education these people have."

He went on to explain away his 1990 conviction for loan-sharking and witness tampering, saying he got into an argument with Sam Merlo and slapped him. *"It was a push-and-shove thing."*

When he went to federal prison the first time, said Isaacs, he got out of the loan-sharking business. *"I stopped everything."*

Then he repeated his denials from the trial that he killed Mark Schwandtner. *"I don't know Mark Schwandtner and I don't know who killed him. I don't know who killed him. I don't know nothing."*

He did admit that he had got into some fights when he worked as a bouncer, but he told Judge Kahl, "I have never gone and killed anyone."

Of his life of crime, he only had this to say: "I thought it was okay to lend money. The banks do it. I thought it was okay to have a numbers business. The state does it."

He blamed Charlie for committing many of the crimes that Isaacs was accused of committing. And he insisted that Charlie's depiction of organized crime in Baltimore was an illusion. Charlie, he said, stole money from bookmakers and "made a ton of money in illegal activities, drug activities, whatever. . . . Charlie executed this whole thing. There is no organized crime. There is no witness tampering here. It is Charlie's word."

When Isaacs was done, it was Jim Gentry's turn to prove that Charlie had indeed told the truth. And the prosecutor finally had the ammunition he needed. The week before, the Maryland Court of Special Appeals ruled that the John Derry tape could finally be used as evidence in Derry's murder trial. The court said it didn't matter that the little ID number wasn't attached to the recorder, after all.

And although the jury in Billy Isaacs' case had been barred from hearing it, the prosecutor now had a legal window of opportunity to use its contents for the purpose of Isaacs' sentencing.

Gentry stood at the trial table and picked up a transcript of the tape. He began to read Derry's boastful and gruesome account, recited on his doorstep to Charlie on that freezing evening in February 1996:

"'I popped the motherfucker, you know, with a baseball bat. I told Billy to drown the motherfucker, you know. . . . It was just me and Billy. Billy dropped him over there just like a boulder used to drop off a fucking bridge.'"

Then, according to Derry's story, Isaacs asked him if he thought he broke the man's neck. "No, you dumb ass, Billy. You dropped him feet first." Then he told Charlie that Isaacs went down to the water and pushed the body under.

Mark Schwandtner's relatives did not speak at the hearing, but two of his sisters wrote this letter:

"Your Honor, I am the oldest of eight children. Mark was the fifth. Being the oldest, I had responsibilities, such as helping out with homework. Mark had a problem with reading and would get upset at times when he couldn't get through his work. Looking back, I think he may have been dyslexic.

"Mark had gone out of state to school. He would have a friend write his words in letters he sent me. He would speak his mind, and this would get him into trouble at times. But he was also very thoughtful and was not a vengeful person.

"At the time of his death I was married with two children, ages seven and nine. It was very hard to tell them of their uncle's death. The fact of it being murder was even harder.

"I can still see the look on my husband's face after identifying Mark's body. I only want to know why?

"After all these years, I pray that justice will be done for the brutal and senseless murder of my brother. Only then can there be some conclusion for me. I miss him and can only wonder where he would be with his life today."

Another sister wrote, "I remember the day the detectives came to the door to announce what had happened. It hurt to see how it ate away at my parents. I saw them as I never had before. It continues to eat at my mother, aging her . . . The brutal murder of Mark will never stop taking its toll emotionally."

Mark Schwandtner, had he lived, would have been forty-two years old on this day. Finally Billy Isaacs, age forty-five, stood and faced Judge Kahl.

The judge denied the motion for a new trial. Then it was time for sentencing. He had thought about the verdict for a long time, the judge said. "I concluded that I could not, in good conscience, disagree with the verdict of the jury."

Of Charlie Wilhelm's testimony, he said, there were some things that were difficult to believe. But the "key things that he said pertaining to this case, I found credible. . . . "

He went on to say that he not only believed Isaacs was guilty, but that the jury didn't go far enough with its verdict of second-degree murder. If Charlie Wilhelm's testimony was to be believed, he said, then Billy Isaacs actually committed a crime worse than second-degree murder. He committed first-degree murder because the killing was clearly premeditated when he climbed down the embankment and pushed Mark Schwandtner's head under the water.

The judge could not change that verdict, but he could give Isaacs a sentence more appropriate for someone who committed first-degree murder.

Without any theatrics the no-nonsense judge turned to Billy Isaacs.

"The defendant is sentenced to serve thirty years in the Division of Correction, consecutive to the sentence he is now serving in the federal system."

Isaacs showed no reaction. His daughter wept.

Jim Gentry was pleased with the sentence. He had never had another murder trial with so little evidence that had gone unsolved for so long.

Now that the taped confession of John Derry was back in evidence, he could plan for the next trial in the Schwandtner killing.

For Charlie, it moved him one step closer to a normal life—or so he thought.

The Road Ahead

Gina and I were sitting in the kitchen waiting for the news when Bruce called. How much time Billy would spend in prison was so tangled up in the future of my family's safety that we couldn't think of much else that afternoon.

Bruce said, "I thought I would call you before anyone else did. This time I have some good news. Billy was sentenced to thirty years."

I yelled to Gina, "Billy got thirty years!"

She jumped up from the couch and yelled, "Thirty years!" Then she ran into the kitchen and high-fived me, shouting, "Yes, yes, yes!"

"I guess if you can't find a job here," she said, "at least we can go home to Baltimore."

I was thrilled that Billy would spend a long time in prison—though in Maryland prisoners don't always serve their full sentences. Billy might get paroled before half his sentence was up. Still, Gina and I felt much safer knowing he didn't get off easy.

But then I felt the way I did every time one of my wiseguy friends got sentenced. A part of me felt sorry for Billy's daughters. Bruce told me it was okay to feel sorry for Billy's kids, but I shouldn't feel responsible for the outcome of this mess. "It's Billy's fault for killing Mark," he said. "If he hadn't committed the murder, all this would never have happened."

On the Fourth of July weekend I moved my family back to Maryland. We found a town house to rent in the suburbs, far enough away from my old neighborhood to feel safe, but close enough for me to commute into the city for work. We went back to using the name Wilhelm. I knew I'd have to keep my guard up and my antennae out at all times. Tommy wasn't happy at all about my move. He thought I was being careless, but I just couldn't find steady work in Decatur. In Baltimore there are plenty of job opportunities with slumlords if you don't have a résumé, but have carpentry skills.

In my journal I asked myself if I was afraid something might happen to me. "Absolutely yes!!!!" I wrote with all four exclamation points. Still, we were willing to take the chance, as long as we had steady work and could be closer to our family. The FBI took precautions to protect me. My new driver's license did not contain my real address. Instead, it had the address of the Baltimore federal courthouse on Lombard Street.

Gina and I were really sorry to leave Decatur. We'd both grown to like the town. Gina said it was a great place to raise kids, since there wasn't any crime. When we moved there in 1996, we couldn't figure out why strangers kept waving to us. Gina would say, "Do we know them?" Then we realized everybody waves to each other in Decatur, Alabama, so we started waving back. You've got to love a town like that.

My first job back in Baltimore was a dirty one—and I don't mean dirty in the illegal sense. I mean it was physically dirty and grimy. The slumlord who hired me wanted to see how fast I could tear off a garage roof on a city house in one of the toughest neighborhoods in town. I guess he was testing me those first weeks. Though this was the worst job for a guy like me with a bad back, I discovered it helped my post-traumatic stress disorder. The hard work helped keep my mind from spinning back into my past life. The faster and longer I worked, the more I kept those flashbacks from attacking my brain.

You might think I was putting my life on the line with these jobs, since they were only a few miles away from my old neighborhood. But the communities I worked in were mostly black neighborhoods, where my old white wiseguy friends would never be caught dead—or alive. I felt safer there, even though they were Baltimore's highest-crime areas.

One day I was working in a really tough, drug-infested neighborhood called Park Heights in Northwest Baltimore. I was in an alley working on a trapdoor to a basement when I found myself right in the middle of a shoot-out. One of the drug dealers doing the shooting actually told me to stay put while he shot his nine-millimeter pistol. "Stay down, man," he kept yelling to me. I thought, *What if I get killed in the cross fire? What a way to go after all I've been through.*

When it was over, I picked up the spent casings from his gun that landed in the cellar with me. They were still hot when I put them in my pocket. I brought them home to show Gina and we watched the report of the gun battle on the evening news.

You couldn't say I was living the new life I'd imagined. As I said at the beginning of this book, I heard news from Tommy as soon as I returned to Baltimore that there was another contract out on my life. Here I was, wearing a bulletproof vest to work as a carpenter. But I frankly preferred this new life to my old one. In my journal I asked myself what would I have done if I had known that it would take so many years for all the trials to be over with. Would I do it all over again? My answer again was "Absolutely yes!"

It's been a long road, but I wouldn't give up this new life for anything or anybody. I am finally at peace with myself, even though I know people will always look at me and wonder if I really have changed. When I moved home, I had a terrific support system for my new life. I had a wife and a brother who believed one hundred percent that I had done the right thing. I also regained contact with my sister, who had shunned me all the years I was out breaking the law. So many other people have supported me along the way, including Father Joe Culotta down in Alabama and, of course, Bruce Hall.

I still carry in my wallet something Father Joe gave me when I left his Catholic church. It is a good-luck charm I carry with me every day. It's a prayer, written by the Trappist monk Thomas Merton. It's called "Final Prayer: Prayer for Trust and Confidence."

It begins: "My Lord God, I have no idea where I am going. I do not see the road ahead of me. I cannot know for certain where it will end."

And it ends with this: "I will not fear, for You are ever with me, and You will never leave me to face my perils alone."

Keeping it with me is just my way of being one step closer to God. It makes me feel secure. Whenever I have those old nightmares or I just feel down on myself, I pull out the prayer and read it one more time.

Here I was, three years after I first went to the FBI, and my troubles were far from over. I was still waiting to testify against John Derry and the others involved in Mark Schwandtner's killing. Meanwhile, other cases I had discussed with the FBI and Maryland prosecutors were finally heading toward trial.

A Small Town

On an icy day in January 1999, Tommy escorted me to a city courthouse in downtown Baltimore. It had once been a grand old federal courthouse where Vice President Spiro T. Agnew pleaded no contest in 1973 to taking kickbacks from a local contractor. He then became the first United States vice president to resign with a criminal record.

The courthouse had seen better days since Agnew was there. Its old hallways and offices were beyond dingy. I was going to testify in the courtroom of Judge Mabel Hubbard. It was one of the ugliest little courtrooms I have ever been inside, so cramped that the jury box was practically on top of the pews where the public sat. It had been painted maroon for an episode of the TV show *Homicide*, with fake wood-grain paint on the door frames that might have looked good on television, but it just looked like a child's finger painting.

I was there to tell a jury about bribes I paid to liquor

inspectors when I ran Joe's Tavern while Billy was in federal prison.

As I sat on a hard wooden bench in the dim yellow light, I heard an official-sounding voice call from inside the courtroom, "Charles Wilhelm."

My mind went into a panic. I instantly knew that voice. It was the voice of an old friend from my past life. It belonged to Lew Benson—deputy sheriff, professional boxer and loan shark. As I reluctantly walked into that little courtroom, I noticed his gun in its holster by his hip. *Am I ever in trouble,* I thought.

Here I was, about to testify about my paying off liquor inspectors while I was running Joe's. And here was Lew, the man who almost went into business with me at Joe's. *Baltimore is such a small town,* I thought. I walked past Lew to get to the witness stand. He didn't look at me, but I thought I saw him put his hand on his gun. Once I got on the stand, he kept stretching his neck toward me and putting his hand on his gun. My heart was racing a mile a minute and I could hardly concentrate. I had told both the FBI and the Maryland State prosecutors about Lew—but here he was, anyway, guarding the courtroom. I was stunned and confused about how to react.

In my panic I thought maybe this was all a setup to catch Lew. I wondered what I should do if I was asked about the organization. Should I mention Lew's name? Should I interrupt my testimony and tell the judge that the deputy guarding her courtroom was in the wrong chair? Instead of sitting with a loaded gun next to the judge's bench, he should be over at the defense table—in leg chains. I didn't want to blow the FBI's investigation of the Baltimore sheriff's department, so I just kept my thoughts to myself. Since I couldn't catch the attention of Tommy or Mike McDonough, the prosecutor, I just answered the questions as best as I could. But my heart was pounding harder than it had the day I accused Billy Isaacs of murder. After all, Billy didn't have a gun at his trial.

Afterward, I got on the elevator with Tommy. In a panicked voice I started to blurt out what happened.

"Charlie, we can't discuss the trial," he said in his all-business FBI voice.

"I'm not talking about the trial," I said. "I'm talking about Lew Benson."

"Lew Benson?" asked Tommy, sounding surprised. Of course, with his steel-trap mind, he remembered everything I had told him about Lew. "Where was Lew Benson?"

"In the courtroom," I yelled.

"Where in the courtroom?"

I could tell he didn't understand me at first. "Next to the judge," I said. "The guy with the gun."

It finally dawned on him what had happened.

"Oh, Charlie, I'm really sorry. I'm so sorry." He apologized all the way down to the ground floor.

Later I learned that the *Baltimore Sun* reporter covering the trial, Walter Roche, watched in surprise one morning when Lew came into the courtroom. Lew walked right up to Billy Madonna and gave him a big bear hug. Here was the deputy sheriff, paid to keep the courtroom safe during a criminal trial, and he's hugging the defendant!

Apparently, nobody connected with the liquor board investigation realized Lew was the deputy who guarded Judge Hubbard's courtroom and ushered the jury in and out of the jury box every day. It gave me the creeps to think how easily Lew could have whispered to a juror how he believed his friends were innocent.

Lew pleaded guilty about a year later in federal court to giving .38-caliber bullets to a friend he knew was a felon—a man convicted of second-degree murder. He was sentenced to a year in prison and lost his job in the sheriff's office. He had worked there for twenty years.

As part of the FBI investigation of Lew, an informant (not me this time) wore a wire while the two of them ate dinner at the Overlea Diner. The informant had borrowed $1,500 from Lew and was repaying him at an annual interest rate of 300 percent, according to a federal court document.

On the tape Lew boasted to his friend: "I was very close friends with Billy Isaacs for a long time." Lew also bitched about the police and the FBI: "I don't trust the motherfuckers. I'm in law enforcement, been in law enforcement for twenty years, but I don't trust other law enforcement." So much for the likes of Lew Benson keeping the courthouse safe for the citizens of Baltimore.

As for the liquor board trial, Judge Hubbard tossed out the bribery charges against Billy Madonna and Tony Cianferano. The two pleaded guilty to conspiring to thwart the city's liquor laws. Both men got probation, $1,000 fines and were ordered to perform three hundred hours of community service. Of course, Tony Cianferano lost his job with the liquor board. But he got himself a new one—as a mason—with the city's Department of Public Works, a government agency with its own long history of corruption.

Billy Madonna bought a small newsstand in Northeast Baltimore County, where he sold tickets to the Maryland State Lottery.

Two of the jurors interviewed by Walter Roche said they didn't believe my testimony was credible. All I know is that I told the truth and told it as best I could under the circumstances.

Since I had gone to the FBI in 1995, the agents had been trying to find the person in the Baltimore Police Department who was tipping off bookmakers about police raids.

The investigation ground on until 1999 when six members of illegal gambling operations pleaded guilty to gambling charges in federal court. Apparently, none of them would roll on the man the federal government suspected was really the leak. Some of them took big hits for the guy, too. One of them, Augustine "Augie" Tamburello, Frankie Tamburello's brother, got a one-year sentence and was fined $10,000.

Another big bookmaker and bar owner, Vernon Letts, got fifteen months in federal prison and was fined $30,000—despite a written plea to the judge from an influential state senator named Tommy Bromwell to let such a "gentle and compassionate man" go free. The FBI also got to keep the $198,000 they confiscated from Letts' bar in Northeast Baltimore.

In Augie's plea agreement, he admitted he screwed up the city's gambling investigation by getting information from the cops that included search warrants. But he never named names.

The following year, in July 2000, I was just about to celebrate my fifth anniversary of going to the FBI and changing my life. I guess it was a little like a recovering alcoholic celebrating five years of sobriety. Gina and I were both very proud of the new life we had made for ourselves and our children. We finally had found a new set of friends, honest and hardworking people who couldn't imagine I had led the life of a wiseguy. I thought the worst was finally behind me. Boy, was I wrong.

Setback

On July 5 the state's court of special appeals reversed Billy Isaacs' murder conviction from three years before. The reason was another one of those technicalities—like the ID number that wasn't glued to my FBI tape recorder.

This time Judge Kahl had failed to show Billy and his lawyers a little note from the jury saying they were deadlocked. The court's decision didn't mean Billy would automatically walk free. It meant the prosecutors would have to put him on trial all over again—and put me on the witness stand to repeat my testimony.

I thought, *How much more of this can I take?* I couldn't bring myself to tell Gina the news. I didn't know what would happen to me and my family if Billy beat a second trial. If we stayed in Maryland, he would eventually try to get me, I thought. And you could bet he would make sure he had no witnesses. My family couldn't handle another move. I didn't know how we could start all over again in a new town and state. I was damned if I was going to run from him again.

A few weeks later I had this dream: I was in Hampden on Falls Road and Thirty-seventh Street. Billy had been released on bail because of the appeal. Someone shot me three times in the face while Billy watched from a nearby corner. My son Justin was with me. As I lay on the sidewalk, the blood was so thick over my face, I couldn't get up and I couldn't see my little boy. I just heard him crying and screaming, "Daddy, Daddy."

After Billy's conviction was reversed, he was moved from a state prison in Hagerstown to the Baltimore County Detention Center in Towson to wait for a bail hearing and a new trial. His lawyers were doing everything they could to get him free on bail while he waited for his new trial. Naturally, I was scared to death that Billy would get his way.

Déjà Vu All Over Again

In September 2000 the third-floor courtroom of circuit court judge Alexander Wright Jr. was packed with Billy Isaacs' entourage. They had come to be part of an unsightly chorus for this unusual courtroom drama. For anybody else, this scene would have been a simple, low-key bail hearing with few spectators. But nothing is ever low-key for a felon of Billy Isaacs' stature. It began with Jim Gentry arguing that Billy Isaacs "is not the kind of defendant who should be on bail." The prosecutor told the judge that Charlie Wilhelm "is scared if this defendant is to get out. It is this witness that the jurors believed."

But Donald Daneman denied that his client was a danger. He turned to look at the chorus of spectators jammed in the wooden pews behind him. He asked them to stand and show their support for Isaacs, who sat in the chair beside him. More than forty people dutifully rose to their feet, like worshipers about to recite an especially sacred prayer.

"They respect him. . . . They are not afraid of Mr. Isaacs," said his lawyer. He told the judge that at least eight people were willing to put up their homes or businesses to bail out their dear friend. Daneman asked for $250,000 bail for his client.

"My client never threatened Mr. Wilhelm," he said.

When the lawyers were done talking, a poker-faced Judge Wright was ready with his decision. "Bail is denied," he said, and quickly left the bench.

Charlie was relieved to hear that Billy would stay in jail until his second trial. Now he just had Isaacs' retrial to worry about, as well as John Derry's murder trial and the trials of Ronnie Rogers and Susan Thompson. But Jim Gentry wasn't in a hurry to try Isaacs again, so his day in court didn't arrive for another year after his bail hearing.

But when that day came, Charlie was not sitting with his FBI handler in the prosecutor's office, waiting his turn to testify. Instead, he was down in a Northwest Baltimore slum rebuilding a two-story porch, pretending to be an ordinary man working an ordinary job to keep his mind off what was happening ten miles away in the Towson Courthouse.

In the courtroom Isaacs' chorus was nowhere to be seen this time. The jury box was empty, as were most of the wooden pews. His only supporters were his girlfriend, The Queen, wearing dark sunglasses, and a friend she'd brought along. Isaacs wore blue jeans, a denim shirt and leg chains that rested by his tasseled black loafers. He had the pasty-faced complexion of a man who'd been in prison a long time. He looked tired and paunchy, with big bags under his eyes.

Jim Gentry rose to address Judge Robert E. Cadigan. The prosecutor gave the judge a history of the case, then announced that he had reached a plea agreement with Isaacs and his lawyer.

"The defendant will plead guilty to a count of second-degree murder," said Gentry. He explained that Isaacs was making an Alford plea, a type of guilty plea in which the defendant gets to save a little face by claiming he really didn't commit the crime, but knows the prosecutors have enough evidence to convict him anyway. It's similar to the federal no contest plea that Spiro Agnew made when he resigned the U.S. vice presidency.

Gentry and Clarke Ahlers had agreed Isaacs would get a fifteen-year sentence, but the sentence would be backdated to November 4, 1997, the date of his first conviction. It was a good deal for Isaacs. Maybe he didn't want to take another chance on a jury believing Charlie Wilhelm again.

Isaacs took the witness stand briefly to assure the judge he understood the charges against him and the plea he was agreeing to.

Clarke Ahlers asked him, "Are you pleading guilty because you believe there is sufficient evidence against you if you went to trial?"

"Yes," said Isaacs.

Jim Gentry then described the gruesome killing of Mark Schwandtner. He told the judge that the victim's family had okayed the plea agreement. And he noted that Charlie would have testified against Isaacs, if the case had gone to retrial.

"Nobody talked for eighteen years until [Charlie Wilhelm] went to the FBI," said Gentry.

As usual, Isaacs showed no emotion.

When the judge asked him, "Mr. Isaacs, do you have any-thing you want to say?" the defendant simply said, "No, sir."

After the hearing, Isaacs got to stay in the courtroom with his lawyer for a few minutes while a clerk corrected the misspelling of his name on court documents.

The man who had once been one of the most powerful crimi-nals in Baltimore picked up a paper cup of ice water on the defendant's table and took a sip. "This is the first time I've had ice," he said, marveling at the little cup. Then he turned to his lawyer and said, "At least this is done."

Isaacs was taken back to the lockup. Ahlers packed up his files to leave, then handed out a statement, entitled "Defendant's press release."

It read, in part, "In this case, Mr. Isaacs denies that he is guilty of any offense in the 1978 death of Mark Schwandtner, but ac-cepts the state's offer to compromise the case. In fact, had this case proceeded to trial, Mr. Isaacs was prepared to show that no phys-ical evidence or motive connected him to this offense. . . ." The statement went on to accuse the Baltimore County Police Depart-ment of having other suspects in the case that were never cleared. It accused Charlie Wilhelm of being a liar and it attacked the FBI for not keeping proper records on its informant.

"In accepting the State's offer to compromise, Mr. Isaacs is hopeful that this will end his troubles with the law. Mr. Isaacs has been incarcerated for this crime almost four years. Under this plea agreement, Mr. Isaacs will make application for parole and is likely to be paroled in the near future."

The news worried Charlie. He figured Isaacs could get out on parole, easily, in less than ten years. And in Charlie's mind, even ten years was not enough time for his old friend to forget.

Chapter 18

Closure

Almost two years later, Charlie turned to the case against John Derry. The plumber followed Isaacs' lead and pleaded guilty to second-degree murder. Charlie was anxious about Derry's sentencing as soon as he heard the name of the judge who was going to hear the case. Judge John G. Turnbull II had a reputation among the wiseguys as a light sentencer, a judge they liked to get when they were in trouble.

But even worse, Charlie discovered that the judge's daughter, a young lawyer, had recently started working for the law firm of John's defense attorney.

Charlie wondered whether the connection would make the judge go easy on Derry. Charlie wasn't planning to attend the sentencing. Since Derry was pleading guilty, Charlie didn't need to testify. And Charlie didn't want any more trouble seeing anyone from his past life.

There was standing room only that day in Judge Turnbull's glossy new courtroom on the fourth floor of the Towson Courthouse in Baltimore County. Its rich, ribbed cherry-wood paneling and cylindrical wall sconces exuded wealth and comfort. The walls were so finely crafted, you could never notice the hidden trapdoor behind the judge's chair, unless someone pointed it out to you. The secret door was built in case some maniac was devious enough to get a gun past the deputy sheriffs and the metal detectors downstairs. If bullets flew, the judge could simply lean back, swing the door open and tumble right into the jury room.

Being a senior judge, Turnbull was one of the lucky ones to get one of these new courtrooms. Everyone else had the old, drab, beige courtrooms elsewhere in the courthouse, sans the trapdoor.

In the packed courtroom that morning of March 7, 2002, sat Tom McNamara and Steve Clary, who had come to watch this final chapter in a case they had begun working on seven years before.

Jim Gentry came through the double doors and strode down the center aisle with a tape player under his arm and waited for other prosecutors to finish postponing several unrelated cases. Mark Schwandtner's family sat behind the prosecutor's table on the right side of the courtroom. His mother had passed away since Billy Isaacs' murder trial, but there in the second row were two middle-aged brothers and three sisters of the man found floating in the Gunpowder twenty-two years before.

As they waited for the hearing to begin, one of his brothers remarked how far the family had come in those twenty-two years. For a long time after the murder, he confessed, they wanted nothing but revenge. But in recent years they had begun to pray for Billy Isaacs. "We should have been praying for Charlie Wilhelm, instead," he whispered with a smile.

Across the aisle sat John Derry's family with many friends. His blonde wife sat weeping in the front row, with her teenage son from a previous marriage and her mother. Derry had been free on bail now for six years. Today, his judgment day, he did not dress up for the occasion. A big man like Billy Isaacs, he wore baggy, worn blue jeans, a floppy gray sweater with a red T-shirt showing at the neck and work boots. His gray hair needed a cut. He looked pensive.

David Irwin, his lawyer, was known for his aggressive thoroughness. Today he looked tired. He had recently been hired to represent John N. Rusnak, the Allfirst Financial currency trader from Baltimore who lost $691 million in one of the biggest banking-fraud scandals in history. Irwin had spent the previous weeks fending off media questions from scores of reporters from Baltimore to Ireland, while trying to figure out if he could keep Rusnak from doing too much time in federal prison.

When the courtroom cleared of other prosecutors, the floor was Gentry's.

"There had been extensive plea discussions," he told Turnbull. Derry, like Isaacs, would now make an Alford plea to second-degree murder. The prosecutor offered two choices. One was a thirty-year sentence, suspended to all but twelve years. The second offer was a straight fifteen-year sentence. Judge Turnbull was not bound to accept the offer and could easily give him a lighter sentence.

Gentry said he would also drop charges against Ronnie Rogers, who waited in the car during the killing, and his former wife, Susan Thompson, who was charged as an accessory after the fact of murder for helping clean out the car.

Derry got up from his chair and stood next to his lawyer. Judge Turnbull asked his age. Forty-eight, he said. Judge Turnbull then went through a litany of routine questions to make sure Derry understood the kind of guilty plea he was making— that it allowed him not to admit guilt, but to acknowledge that the state had enough evidence to convict him.

Gentry summarized the case.

"The body of Mark Schwandtner was discovered by some fisherman early in the morning of June 10, 1978," he told the judge. The cause of death was drowning, according to the autopsy. He suffered from bruises and blows to the head, said the prosecutor.

If the case had gone to trial, witnesses would have testified that they saw Schwandtner at the Holiday House bar on the night of June 8. Others would place Derry with Billy Isaacs and Ronnie Rogers that night in Hampden at the Keswick Inn and saw them leave in Rogers' blue Malibu and return the next day.

*Then Gentry came to the man who would have been his star
witness against Derry.*

*"Charlie Wilhelm was developed as an FBI informant. Wil-
helm had been a close friend with Isaacs and had a conversation
with Ronnie Rogers and John Derry. They appeared to be
drunk."*

*Gentry went on to read from Charlie's testimony at Isaacs' trial
and details from the autopsy. He then repeated Isaacs' mantra
from the years before Charlie came forward:*

"Nobody talks, everybody walks.'"

*Derry sat quietly, looking down at the trial table, his hands
folded in front of him.*

*Gentry walked up to the judge's bench and put the tape
recorder in front of Turnbull. The prosecutor announced he
would play the tape of Derry admitting to the killing.*

*It had been more than six years since that February evening
in 1996 when Charlie stood on Derry's front step, the little FBI
tape recorder hidden in his coat pocket, and tricked him into
talking about the killing. In all those years the tape had never
been played in a courtroom.*

*Now Gentry wanted the judge to hear about the murder in
Derry's own words. And he especially wanted the judge to listen
to the nuance of his voice.*

*Gentry handed the judge a transcript of the tape. Charlie's voice
came first, stating the time: 8:46 P.M., February. 4, 1996—just
before he got to Derry's house.*

*It was hard to hear the muffled words. But the tone was
clear—and shocking. Here was John Derry, eighteen years after
the murder, telling the story as if he were performing a stand-up
comedy routine. He was laughing as he told Charlie, "I popped
the motherfucker . . . with a baseball bat. I told Billy to drown
the motherfucker. . . You better go down there and make sure he
doesn't wake up."*

*The courtroom was quiet as Gentry turned off the tape
recorder. He reminded the judge, "Derry is the one who beat him
with the baseball bat."*

Now it was Irwin's turn to show the judge his client was a changed man.

"This occurred more than twenty-five years ago." Derry, he said, "is not the same person."

Derry had been married since 1991 and was a good step-father to his wife's son. They had a nine-year-old daughter together. He worked as a plumber.

"I've gotten to know John over the last six years," said his lawyer. "There's a big difference between Billy Isaacs and John Derry. Billy—he's a career criminal with multiple federal and state nonviolent and violent convictions. John Derry deserves a [lighter] sentence. Billy Isaacs has always been the ring leader of any organization he's ever been involved in."

Irwin brought a parade of character witnesses to tell the judge that Derry was a hardworking family man not involved in criminal activity.

"John is one hundred percent family, works all the time, takes care of his wife and child and his stepson," said one friend.

A former employer said he always trusted Derry, even gave him the keys to the business and never had a problem with him.

Another friend said, "John has been our plumber, our friend, our tree surgeon. He's been a good father, good husband."

His mother-in-law got up to speak. John had been kind to her invalid husband after he had a stroke. "It could be two, three in the morning. He comes, picks him up" when he falls out of bed.

Irwin told the judge of Derry's heart problems and his diabetes, for which he needed daily medication. The lawyer also told the judge that Derry had become his personal friend over the years and had even done work for him.

"He is a zero threat. No threat to society. What you need to do is punish him for what he admits is enough evidence to convict him. I would beg, plead and pray to the court for some reduction from the plea agreement."

The lawyer held out more than fifty letters on his client's behalf. He asked the judge, "If you could find mercy in your heart to give him a break."

It was now Gentry's turn and the prosecutor got to the point quickly.

"It's time for John Derry to pay the piper," he said.

He had only two letters to give to the judge. They were from Mark Schwandtner's two sisters.

He read from one letter. The sister described her brother as a "person who never had the opportunity to have a family because somebody decided to end his life."

In 1978, said Gentry, "the decision was made by John Derry to take Mr. Schwandtner down that road.

"Mr. Derry carried with him a baseball bat. He was the one who beat him. At his urging, Billy Isaacs dropped him off the bridge, where he ultimately drowned."

The prosecutor said he understood that Irwin believed his client was a changed man.

"I don't agree with that. In 1996 John Derry is bragging about it. There was a pact to keep silent." And that pact would have been kept forever, "if it had not been for Mr. Wilhelm.

"In 1996 he is not only bragging, but is laughing about it." The tape, he said, "shows a great deal of callousness about it. I think the plea agreement is abundantly fair. I think it's important for him to do time."

Derry got up slowly from his chair.

"I am a changed person. I try to take care of my family," he told the judge. There was no emotion in his voice.

Irwin tapped him on the back, as if prompting him to say something else.

"I'm sorry for the pain everybody had." He paused. As an afterthought he added, "I like helping people." He sat down.

It was time for the sentencing. As Turnbull began to speak, it immediately became clear that Charlie was wrong to predict that this judge would let Derry off easy.

The judge didn't seem moved by Derry's transformation.

"He participated in a brutal murder. . . I'm delighted he's kept a clean life."

The judge made a point of telling Derry that it was hard for murderers in Maryland to get paroled because of the "executive office," meaning that the governor's office was not paroling murderers before their sentences were up.

"He will serve practically every day," said the judge. "The state's been more than reasonable" in its plea bargain.

He then sentenced Derry the thirty years, and suspended all but ten. The sentence would follow with five years of supervised probation. It was not a light sentence for a man with an otherwise clean record. The judge gave the prosecutor almost everything he'd asked for. He only knocked off two years from the plea offer.

Finally, twenty-four years after the murder, the case was over.

Outside the courtroom Schwandtner's family thanked Gentry, Clary and McNamara. One brother said he always wondered about the motive in the murder. Mark had a wad of money with him the night he died. But when the police searched the dead man's pockets, it was gone. Maybe Mark owed Billy a debt. Maybe Billy and John wanted to rob him. The family would probably never be able to answer the "Why?" that their father had asked so long ago.

Then the brothers and sisters asked how Charlie was doing. Was he safe? They were amazed he'd survived without going into the witness protection program.

"Thank him for us."

Epilogue

That August morning in 2002 when I went with Tommy to Quantico, I was sobered by the thought of giving a lecture to a group of FBI agents. I was surprised to learn that I would not be talking to new recruits. These were full-fledged agents who had come from all over the country to be trained in organized crime. I worried they would be suspicious of my claims to being a changed man.

As soon as we arrived, we headed upstairs to the cafeteria. I thought somebody was playing a cruel joke on the agents. The food on the chow line looked just like prison food. There was burned macaroni, greasy hot dogs and something that resembled day-old meat loaf. I chose a Philly cheese steak. Tommy got the so-called meat loaf. After one bite I decided that I'd misjudged the food. Prison food was much better than this. I had never tasted a Philly cheese steak this foul. As we ate lunch, a recruit came over to our table and began talking to Tommy. The man worked as an analyst in the Baltimore field office and was going through training to become an agent. Tommy introduced me only as "Charlie" and as "a 137," the code they use for a cooperating witness or an informant. There were other people sitting nearby, speaking in German and Spanish. Tommy said they were sent here for training by police departments in foreign countries.

After our fine lunch, we headed to the classroom for our presentation. The main building connected to other buildings that I couldn't see from the parking lot. We walked up and down so many flights of stairs, and through so many corridors and hallways, that I felt like we were traveling through a fun-house maze. And I had been wrong when we arrived, thinking the place looked like a ghost town. From the rear of the building I could see squadrons of new recruits running in formation outside. In the hallways people greeted us with hellos. It was a real friendly atmosphere.

When we found the classroom, it was empty. The rows of desks were set up with cards identifying agents from different cities. There must have been place cards for agents from twenty cities, including San Francisco, Los Angeles, Miami, Fort Lauderdale, Denver, New Orleans, Houston and Chicago. In the front of the classroom there was a podium and a blackboard. Tommy gave me copies of the articles in the *Baltimore Sun* written about me in November 2001. As I began to place them on each desk, I started to get more nervous about my presentation. Tommy looked around for a tape recorder. He was going to play the tape I made in 1996 of John Derry admitting to Mark Schwandtner's murder—and implicating Billy.

I sat down and started to think about my notes I had made for the presentation. I worried they weren't good enough and I didn't want to embarrass Tommy with a bad performance. I started to think about the advice Bruce had given me for today. I could always depend on Bruce to steer me in the right direction. He said I should concentrate on three things. First, he said, I should tell them a little about my background and my relationship with Tommy, Steve Clary and the other agents. Then I should talk about the cases and investigations I was in-

volved with. I knew Tommy would help with that one—
he had a mind like an encyclopedia. But only I could
talk about the final subject: closure. In other words, my
transition from bad guy to good guy. That one came
from the heart and only I could explain it.

As Tommy finished setting up the tape recorder, the
agents filed into the room. I was surprised that the men
weren't wearing ties or suits and the women weren't in
dresses. They were all so casually dressed in jeans and
slacks that I felt out of place in my tan suit.

Tommy walked up to the podium and introduced us.
He told them how our relationship developed over the
last seven years. He told them about my unique association with Bruce—a trustworthy childhood friend and
FBI agent who brought me a level of comfort that would
be hard to come by for any other informant. And, of
course, Tommy also told them about Billy. He said Billly
and I were two of Baltimore's top wiseguys and that I was
as loyal as anyone could be to Billy for many years. He
also told them that we were not associated with La Cosa
Nostra and that the Mafia had no foothold in Baltimore.
But he did say that some of our guys with Italian names
did have relatives who were actually soldiers in the Gam-
bino family in New York. Tommy also told the class
about the arrests the FBI made with my cooperation.

Then Tommy looked over to me and looked back toward the class.

"Charlie has made a one-hundred-eighty-degree turn-
around with his life," he said. He told the class that I had
become a hardworking and devoted family man.

I was in total shock. Tommy had never said this to me
in private. With his stiff FBI guard up all the time, I
never really knew what he thought of me. And now he
was finally recognizing me as a changed man. I was so
grateful.

Then Tommy turned on the tape of John Derry's confession to murder. At first it felt like a lifetime ago that I had slipped that little recorder in my heavy coat pocket and drove my old Lincoln to John's house in North Baltimore.

I became very somber listening to John laugh about how he and Billy killed this young guy. I thought about how Billy was absolutely right when he coined his motto, "Nobody talks, everybody walks." And I thought about what a stupid asshole John was. Here he was in prison while his family was doing the most suffering for his mistakes. And I thought, *Maybe he isn't the asshole. Maybe I'm the asshole for making his family suffer.*

As I listened to the tape, I started getting flashbacks about everybody I hurt in the last seven years. I could see Billy sitting in his dark suit in the Towson Courthouse, turning around to smirk at me as I was about to get up to testify against him. Then I suddenly saw us in the old days, laughing and cutting up together. The faces of other wiseguys I put away also came rushing back to me. There I was, double-crossing them with a hidden wire wrapped around my belly or a tape recorder in my pocket. For a few minutes I felt swept away by these flashbacks. I guess I was having another episode due to having post-traumatic stress disorder.

Then all of a sudden, I heard my name being called. Tommy was asking me to come to the podium. I was in such a daze thinking about Billy, John, Frankie and all the other guys, I didn't realize the tape had stopped. I pulled myself together and went up to the podium with my page-and-a-half presentation. As I started to read it aloud, I was pretty nervous, but not as nervous as I'd been facing a courtroom. I knew nobody in this room was going to threaten me or my family. And with the FBI agents, I didn't have to be ashamed of who I used to be.

When I was finished, I asked the class if anyone had a question.

From the second row, a dark-haired male agent from Fort Lauderdale, wearing jeans and tennis shoes, asked the first question: "What made you want to change?"

"I was becoming a piece of shit and I didn't want to kill anyone, let alone some of my own friends," I told him.

A female agent from Las Vegas then asked me, "Why didn't you go to the police instead of the FBI?"

"I couldn't trust the Baltimore police," I told her. "They were corrupt and I would have been dead in three days if I went to them." In other words, a dirty cop would have told the wiseguys that I had turned them in.

"Why did you go to Bruce Hall in Washington, rather than the FBI office in Baltimore?" asked another agent.

"I knew Bruce was the only man I could trust," I answered. "Whether I ended up in prison or not, I knew he would make sure my family was protected. I even told Bruce that I was afraid someone in the Baltimore FBI field office might be dirty and give the information about me to a Baltimore cop. Bruce said he could guarantee that wouldn't happen. He told me the agents in Baltimore would protect my family. But he couldn't guarantee that I wouldn't go to prison.

"Bruce was right about there being no dirty agent in the Baltimore FBI office. The dirty one turned out to be a secretary in the U.S. Attorney's office."

Another agent asked me, "How can we get a CI (criminal informant) to cooperate as fully as you did?"

First, I said, "the CI has to want to get out. You can't force him to get out. Second, you must all show him that you are just like normal people, except you have taken an oath to uphold the law."

I became very blunt with the agents. I said, "Look, you have to understand. FBI agents are stereotyped on television as these stiff-necked bunch of people." I then began to use body language to the class as I walked stiffly

across the floor. I said, "Everybody I know thinks the FBI
is nothing but trouble. Let people know you are not
going to lock everyone up that you interview." By this
time I was right up close to the front row and I was illus-
trating with my hands as if I were holding a pair of
binoculars to my eyes. I said, "Jesus Christ, people are so
paranoid about the FBI that even honest people think
the FBI is hiding in trees investigating them."

I then said, "You have to make your CI feel comfortable, and when you do, he will become truthful and you
will become his best friend.

"You must also find a common denominator with the
CI, whether it's sports or your children or fishing or
something else," I said.

Finally one of the agents asked me what I was going to
do when Billy Isaacs got out of prison. What if he came
looking for me?

"I refuse to keep running from him," I said. "I can tell
you I'm a truly changed man and I have every right in
the world to choose where I live as a free man without
persecution."

"Why should I be ashamed of doing something right
for the first time in my life?"

After our presentation I was so drained of emotion I
almost fell asleep as Tommy drove us back to Baltimore.
I hadn't felt that exhausted from a public appearance
since I testified against Billy.

I never expected my journey to a new life to take this
long or leave this deep an emotional wound. Even now
as I work in the city each day—no longer for a slumlord
at $9 an hour, but for a reputable real estate company at
a decent wage—I feel the consequences of coming clean
almost too heavy to bear. I can never be too safe in a
town where so many people remember who I used to be.

I finally understand what Father Joe Culotta meant

when he said pain comes from righting a wrong. I guess I'll always be a marked man.

But I also know in changing my life, I accomplished more than I'd ever imagined that heart-pounding day in 1995 when I walked into Bruce Hall's office at the J. Edgar Hoover building and spilled my guts.

I go places now that would be unthinkable in my past life: the speech at Quantico. Another one like it that was held at the Baltimore City Police Department with my old rival, Spanky Herold, at my side. The funeral of retired FBI agent Steve Clary, who died of cancer in September 2003. Who would think in a million years that a tough ex-wiseguy like Charlie Wilhelm would cry over the death of an FBI agent? But I did.

There are too many people I care about who depend on my honesty. I can't fail them.

With their help I found a kind of courage I never knew I had in me: the courage to prevent two killings. The courage to bring justice to a family whose murdered son was long forgotten by everybody but them—and me. The courage to stop drug dealers and bookmakers and corrupt Baltimore liquor inspectors. The courage to plug a dangerous leak in the U.S. Justice Department.

The courage to turn my back on my crime family and walk away for good. The courage to walk into a new life and prove to my wife and children that a bad guy really can change.

Where Are They Now?

Good Guys:

FBI special agent Bruce Hall transferred in May 2002 from his job as a forensic mineralogist at the FBI lab at Washington, DC, to work as an agent in the Baltimore regional FBI headquarters.

Special Agent Thomas J. McNamara continues to work at the the Baltimore FBI headquarters.

Special Agent Stephen D. Clary died of cancer in September 2003 after retiring from the FBI.

Special Agent Kevin Bonner continues to work at the Baltimore FBI headquarters.

Jim Cabezas is the chief investigator for the Maryland State Prosecutor.

Carroll "Spanky" Herold retired from the Baltimore City Police Department in June 1999 after thirty years of service. He currently works for the High-Intensity Drug Trafficking Area (HIDTA) as an intelligence analyst.

John Wilhelm is a salesman, specializing in industrial tools.

Gina Wilhelm is an assistant manager at a Maryland supermarket. She and Charlie are still married.

Bad Guys:

Convicted killer Billy Isaacs' sentence in the Maryland State prison system is up in 2011, but he could be released on parole earlier for good behavior.

Drug dealer Frankie Tamburello is scheduled to be released from federal prison in March 2006.

Drug dealer Gussie Alexander was released from federal prison in January 2001. He is believed to be living in Ocean City, Maryland.

Drug dealer Fat Ricky Payne was released from federal prision in June 2000. He is believed to working in a Baltimore bar.

Patricia Wheeler has been seen working as a supermarket clerk since her bribery conviction and firing as a U.S. Justice Department secretary.

Drug dealer Mike Bush is scheduled to be released from federal prison in August 2005

Former Baltimore deputy sheriff Lew Benson was released from federal prison in June 2001. He was last seen working in a bar in a Baltimore suburub.

Acknowledgments

This memoir was written and illustrated with the help of many people who provided us with photographs, legal expertise and their good memories. Some gave us their time by reading chapters, while others provided information and insight that greatly improved our manuscript.

We are especially grateful to our photographer and photo scanner, Bill Barry, for his patience and generosity. John Funari donated his time to take our Alabama photos.

Jim Cabezas reviewed chapters, gave his fine insight into the criminal mind and reunited Charlie with his old nemesis, Spanky Herold. Spanky shared his memories as a vice detective, gave us old surveillance photos of Charlie and reviewed sections of the manuscript for accuracy.

Judge John Prevas and Peter Prevas shared their legal expertise on Maryland's wiretap law and the regulation of video poker machines.

Others who reviewed the manuscript for accuracy include Bruce Hall, Jim Gentry, Pete Johnson and Mike McDonough.

We thank the Schwandtner family for sharing their painful memories with us and letting us use a photograph of their brother Mark.

Our many readers who spent hours reviewing the manuscript include Laura Lippman, Mark Bomster, Sharon Bondroff, Jenna Land Free, Mary Jo Febres, Marina Sarris and Linell Smith. Their advice was crucial and vastly improved our book.

Others who patiently answered questions and solved problems include Wally Roche, Tom McNamara, Bill Toohey, Pete Lally, Dan Richardson, Jean Packard and Sarah Flynn.

We are grateful to our agent, Gail Ross, who introduced us to the world of book publishing, and to our enthusiastic editors, Gary Goldstein and Michaela Hamilton. The splendid copy editing was done by Stephanie Finnegan.

Thanks to the many editors at the *Baltimore Sun* who left their fingerprints on the four-part series about Charlie Wilhelm's life that preceded this book. Special thanks from Joan Jacobson to Jan Winburn for teaching an old newshound the craft of narrative writing.

—CW and JJ

More Nail-Biting Suspense From Your Favorite Thriller Authors